D1535906

# SECURED TRANSACTIONS

## PROBLEMS AND MATERIALS

By

**Paul Barron**
*The Class of 1937 Professor of Law*
*Tulane Law School*

**Mark B. Wessman**
*Professor of Law*
*Tulane Law School*

## AMERICAN CASEBOOK SERIES®

THOMSON
WEST

Mat #40013672

*American Casebook Series* and West Group are trademarks registered in the U.S. Patent and Trademark Office.

COPYRIGHT © 2003 By West, a Thomson business
        610 Opperman Drive
        P.O. Box 64526
        St. Paul, MN 55164–0526
        1–800–328–9352

**ISBN** 0–314–26200–8

 TEXT IS PRINTED ON 10% POST CONSUMER RECYCLED PAPER

*For Arlene who supplied all the vowels*

*P.B.*


*For Julie, Julia, and Kirk*

*M.W.*


\*

# Preface

---

It has been our experience that students approach the course in secured transactions with more apprehension than they do other courses—indeed, far more than the subject matter warrants and far more than is usually generated by the course in sales. We believe that at least two factors are responsible for our students' heightened level of anxiety. First, learning Article 9 of the Uniform Commercial Code requires a student to master a technical vocabulary that is neither familiar nor intuitive. Second, the business context of secured lending and personal property financing is alien territory to most students. All students have bought or sold goods, and studying Article 2 therefore produces only the discomfort caused by a first encounter with statutory materials. Article 9 is quite different. While many students may have experienced the indescribable joy of a secured car loan, only a handful in any given class have any experience with inventory or accounts receivable financing. Fixture financiers seem to be absent altogether. As a result, the difficulty of learning new law is compounded by an unfamiliar transactional context. Students reading traditional casebooks often have as much trouble understanding why the business actors featured in reported cases behave in certain ways as they have understanding the solution Article 9 imposes on the problems the cases present.

We are not certain that any law professor can solve the problems posed by students' lack of familiarity with the business context in which Article 9 operates. It may be that only years of experience as practicing lawyers can do that. However, we would like to find techniques that can begin the process in law school in a way superior to traditional casebooks. To that end, we borrow from those contemporary legal scholars who see value in the use of narrative and simulation as devices for communication and learning. We propose to explore the law of secured transactions from the perspective of a staff attorney at a mythical bank holding company with several financing arms. In the pages that follow, we will introduce Megabank, Inc. and its flagship urban bank, the Bank of New Babylon. Along the way, we will also present a consumer finance subsidiary (Friendly Finance Co.), a commercial finance subsidiary specializing in inventory and accounts receivable financing (NB Commercial Finance Co.), a real estate mortgage loan originator (NB Mortgage Co., Inc.), a subsidiary devoted to credit card operations (NBCard, Inc.), and a (somewhat shaky) small town bank (the Bovine State Bank) acquired by Megabank, Inc. as part of the trend toward consolidation in the banking industry. Naturally, it will also be necessary to introduce some of their competitors. It is our hope, in this process, to provide illustrations of the range of personal property financing transactions, as well as to provide some glimpse into the tasks, pressures, and incentives facing the people involved in them. Expository material that would normally be in notes is provided through the medium of mythical loan officer training and operations manuals.

The reader will note that reports of judicial opinions in appellate cases are entirely absent from this book, although we do occasionally provide case citations in connection with particular problems. The omission of traditional case reports is, in part, a reflection of our hope that narrative may be substituted for them as a means of setting secured transactions in their business context, as well as our intention to shift the focus, at times, from the dispute resolution function of commercial law to its role in planning transactions.

The omission of traditional case reports is also, in part, motivated by the rather awkward state of current personal property lending law. Article 9 of the Uniform Commercial Code supplies the law of secured transactions in all 50 states. Until recently, the 1972 version of Article 9, with a few modest subsequent official modifications and sporadic non-uniform state-specific amendments, was entirely dominant. The case law interpreting the statute for the bulk of the last three decades has thus incorporated the section numbering, the vocabulary, the definitions, and the rules of the 1972 version of Article 9, as modified from time to time. In 1998, the sponsoring organizations for the Uniform Commercial Code officially approved and recommended for adoption an overhauled Article 9, which has been enacted by all of the states. The 1998 version of Article 9 substantially changes the section numbering and definitional sections of the earlier version, and it makes a number of substantive rule changes as well. Because of those changes, our current body of Article 9 case law, though by no means superseded substantively, has become a clumsy teaching vehicle for a course focused on the 1998 version of Article 9.

Most fundamentally, however, our omission of traditional case reports reflects our belief that statutes are mastered best by incremental increases in the ability to work with them, and that such incremental increases are most effectively produced by solving problems before and during class rather than by reading enormous numbers of cases. The citations occasionally accompanying problems are included to satisfy those with more traditional tastes.[1]

The 1998 version of Article 9 became effective on July 1, 2001 in most states and in the rest by January 1, 2002. In addition, the 1998 version of Article 9 provided a one-year transition period during which the earlier version of Article 9 would continue to apply to transactions entered into prior to the effective date of the 1998 version of Article 9. After the one-year transition period, these transactions are subject to the rules in the 1998 version of Article 9. As a result, these materials deal only with the 1998 version of Article 9.[2]

---

**1.** In the hope that we will not break the narrative flow of the book, we introduce the case citations, as well as relevant Code section numbers, in bracketed footnotes.

**2.** For a clear explanation of the transition rules see, Caroline N. Brown, *U.C.C. Revised Article 9: The Transition Rules*, 79 N.C. L. Rev. 993 (2001).

With the foregoing preliminary comments concluded, it is time to meet some of the players in our unfolding story and to provide some introductory background material. To that end, we ask each of our students to assume that he or she is Sidney Carlson, a recent law school graduate. Sidney has just passed the bar examination and is about to commence permanent employment with MEGABANK, Inc.

\*

# Acknowledgements

We gratefully acknowledge the contributions to this book provided by our students over many years. Their use of successive versions of these materials in class, and their comments on many of the problems, have been enormously helpful. The students are too numerous to list individually, but they have our thanks. As always, we must also thank Senior Program Coordinator Camella M. Dimitri, who has assisted us on this project from the beginning and has put up with both of us longer than should be required of any human being.

PB
MBW

\*

# Summary of Contents

|  | Page |
|---|---|
| PREFACE | v |
| ACKNOWLEDGMENTS | ix |
| TABLE OF CASES | xix |
| TABLE OF STATUTES | xxiii |

**Chapter 1. Introduction** — 1

I. The Distinction Between Secured and Unsecured Credit — 4

II. The Distinction Between Consensual and Non–Consensual Security Interests — 8

III. The Development of Consensual Security Interests in Personal Property in the United States — 13

IV. Bankruptcy and Secured Transactions — 17

V. Some Basic Article 9 Concepts — 20

**Chapter 2. The Scope of Article 9** — 28

I. The Inclusive Provisions — 28

II. The Inapplicability Provisions — 39

III. The Applicability of Other Law — 40

**Chapter 3. Creating the Security Interest** — 43

I. Overview — 43

II. Attachment by Possession — 44

III. The Security Agreement Alternative — 47

IV. Creating a Security Interest in Proceeds — 64

**Chapter 4. Perfecting the Security Interest** — 68

I. Introduction — 68

II. Automatic Perfection — 72

III. Perfection by Possession or Control — 74

IV. Perfection by Filing — 79

V. Perfection as to Proceeds — 87

VI. Perfection of Property Subject to a Certificate of Title — 89

**Chapter 5. Priorities** — 93

I. Introduction — 93

II. Priority Disputes Between Two or More Secured Creditors — 94

III. Priority Disputes Between Secured Creditors and Lien Creditors — 114

IV. Priority Disputes Between Secured Creditors and Buyers — 121

Page

V. Priority Disputes Between Secured Creditors and Real Estate
   Interests (Fixtures) ........................................................ 130
VI. Special Problems that Arise When the Debtor Files in Bank-
    ruptcy ..................................................................... 135

**Chapter 6.  Multi–Jurisdictional Transactions** ................ **140**
   I. Introduction to Multi–Jurisdictional Transactions .............. 140
  II. Perfection in Multi–Jurisdictional Transactions ............... 141
 III. Priorities in Multi–Jurisdictional Transactions ............... 148
  IV. Perfection and Priorities When a Foreign Jurisdiction Is In-
      volved ................................................................. 149

**Chapter 7.  Default, Remedies, and Debtor Protections** ...... **151**
   I. Meaning of Default and Limitations on the Exercise of Reme-
      dies ..................................................................... 151
  II. Alternative Remedies ............................................... 157
 III. Debtor's Right of Redemption ................................... 169
  IV. Remedies for Creditor Misbehavior ............................. 170

INDEX ............................................................................ 175

# Table of Contents

**Page**

PREFACE ............................................................................ v
ACKNOWLEDGMENTS ........................................................... ix
TABLE OF CASES ................................................................ xix
TABLE OF STATUTES ........................................................... xxiii

**Chapter 1. Introduction** ................................................. 1
 I. The Distinction Between Secured and Unsecured Credit .......... 4
 II. The Distinction Between Consensual and Non–Consensual Security Interests ............................................................. 8
  A. Judicial Liens ....................................................... 8
  B. Common Law or Statutory Liens ................................. 9
  *Problem 1–1* ........................................................ 11
 III. The Development of Consensual Security Interests in Personal Property in the United States ......................................... 13
  A. Limitation to Personal Property ................................. 13
  B. Pre–Code Security Devices ....................................... 13
  C. The Advent of Article 9 of the Code ............................ 15
 IV. Bankruptcy and Secured Transactions ............................ 17
  A. Overview ............................................................ 17
  B. Bankruptcy Functionaries ........................................ 19
 V. Some Basic Article 9 Concepts ..................................... 20
  A. An Overview of the Structure of Article 9 ..................... 20
  B. Article 9 Definitions .............................................. 21
  C. A Brief Survey of Three Critical Article 9 Concepts .......... 22
  D. Consumer Transactions ........................................... 26

**Chapter 2. The Scope of Article 9** ................................. 28
 I. The Inclusive Provisions ............................................. 28
  A. The General Provision ............................................. 28
  B. "By Contract" ...................................................... 29
  *Problem 2–1* ........................................................ 30
  C. "Personal Property or Fixtures" ................................. 31
  D. "A Transaction, Regardless of Its Form, That Creates a Security Interest" ................................................... 31
   1. In General ........................................................ 31
   *Problem 2–2* ...................................................... 32
   2. Leases ............................................................ 32

**Page**

I. The Inclusive Provisions—Continued
       *Problem 2–3* ......................................................... 34
       *Problem 2–4* ......................................................... 35
  E. Sales of Accounts, Chattel Paper, Payment Intangibles, or
     Promissory Notes ................................................. 36
  F. Consignments ........................................................ 37
II. The Inapplicability Provisions .................................... 39
  A. Partial Exclusions ................................................ 39
  B. Full Exclusions .................................................... 39
  C. Mixed Transactions ............................................... 40
III. The Applicability of Other Law ................................. 40
       *Problem 2–5* ......................................................... 40
       *Problem 2–6* ......................................................... 41
       *Problem 2–7* ......................................................... 42

**Chapter 3.  Creating the Security Interest** ................... **43**
  I. Overview ............................................................... 43
  II. Attachment by Possession ....................................... 44
       *Problem 3–1* ......................................................... 45
       *Problem 3–2* ......................................................... 45
  III. The Security Agreement Alternative ....................... 47
    A. Overview ........................................................... 47
       *Problem 3–3* ..................................................... 48
       *Problem 3–4* ..................................................... 49
    B. Collateral Description ......................................... 51
       *Problem 3–5* ..................................................... 52
       *Problem 3–6* ..................................................... 52
       *Problem 3–7* ..................................................... 53
       *Problem 3–8* ..................................................... 54
    C. Authentication .................................................... 55
       *Problem 3–9* ..................................................... 55
       *Problem 3–10* ................................................... 56
    D. Future Advances and After–Acquired Property ........ 57
       *Problem 3–11* ................................................... 57
    E. Rights in the Collateral ..................................... 58
       *Problem 3–12* ................................................... 58
       *Problem 3–13* ................................................... 58
    F. Value ................................................................. 61
       *Problem 3–14* ................................................... 61
       *Problem 3–15* ................................................... 63
  IV. Creating a Security Interest in Proceeds .................. 64
       *Problem 3–16* ................................................... 64
       *Problem 3–17* ................................................... 65
       *Problem 3–18* ................................................... 66
       *Problem 3–19* ................................................... 66

**Chapter 4.  Perfecting the Security Interest** ............... **68**
  I. Introduction .......................................................... 68
    A. Overview of the Methods of Perfection ................. 68
    B. Purchase Money Security Interests ...................... 70
       *Problem 4–1* ..................................................... 70

Page

I. Introduction—Continued
    *Problem 4–2* ........................................................................ 71
    *Problem 4–3* ........................................................................ 72
II. Automatic Perfection ........................................................... 72
  *Problem 4–4* ........................................................................ 73
  *Problem 4–5* ........................................................................ 74
III. Perfection by Possession or Control ..................................... 74
  *Problem 4–6* ........................................................................ 75
  *Problem 4–7* ........................................................................ 75
  *Problem 4–8* ........................................................................ 76
  *Problem 4–9* ........................................................................ 76
  *Problem 4–10* ...................................................................... 77
  *Problem 4–11* ...................................................................... 78
IV. Perfection by Filing .............................................................. 79
  A. Debtor's Name .............................................................. 80
    *Problem 4–12* .................................................................. 80
    *Problem 4–13* .................................................................. 82
    *Problem 4–14* .................................................................. 83
  B. Description of Collateral ................................................ 83
    *Problem 4–15* .................................................................. 83
    *Problem 4–16* .................................................................. 84
  C. Place of Filing ................................................................. 85
    *Problem 4–17* .................................................................. 85
  D. Lapse ............................................................................... 86
    *Problem 4–18* .................................................................. 86
V. Perfection as to Proceeds ..................................................... 87
  *Problem 4–19* ...................................................................... 88
  *Problem 4–20* ...................................................................... 89
VI. Perfection of Property Subject to a Certificate of Title ......... 89
  *Problem 4–21* ...................................................................... 91

**Chapter 5.   Priorities** ............................................................ **93**
I. Introduction ......................................................................... 93
II. Priority Disputes Between Two or More Secured Creditors ..... 94
  A. The Standard Rule ........................................................ 94
    *Problem 5–1* .................................................................... 95
    *Problem 5–2* .................................................................... 97
    *Problem 5–3* .................................................................... 97
    *Problem 5–4* .................................................................... 98
    *Problem 5–5* .................................................................... 99
    *Problem 5–6* .................................................................... 100
  B. Purchase Money Security Interest Superpriority ............. 101
    *Problem 5–7* .................................................................... 101
    *Problem 5–8* .................................................................... 103
    *Problem 5–9* .................................................................... 103
    *Problem 5–10* .................................................................. 104
    *Problem 5–11* .................................................................. 105
  C. Priority as to Proceeds ................................................... 106
    *Problem 5–12* .................................................................. 106
    *Problem 5–13* .................................................................. 107
    *Problem 5–14* .................................................................. 109

Page

II. Priority Disputes Between Two or More Secured Creditors— Continued
    *Problem 5–15* ............................................................. 110
    *Problem 5–16* ............................................................. 110
  D. Accessions and Commingled Goods ............................. 111
    *Problem 5–17* ............................................................. 111
    *Problem 5–18* ............................................................. 113
    *Problem 5–19* ............................................................. 113
III. Priority Disputes Between Secured Creditors and Lien Creditors ................................................................................ 114
  A. In General ..................................................................... 114
    *Problem 5–20* ............................................................. 114
    *Problem 5–21* ............................................................. 114
    *Problem 5–22* ............................................................. 115
    *Problem 5–23* ............................................................. 116
    *Problem 5–24* ............................................................. 117
    *Problem 5–25* ............................................................. 117
  B. Federal Tax Liens ......................................................... 118
IV. Priority Disputes Between Secured Creditors and Buyers ......... 121
  A. Introduction ................................................................. 121
  B. Unperfected Secured Creditor Versus a Buyer .............. 122
    *Problem 5–26* ............................................................. 122
  C. Perfected Secured Creditor Versus a Buyer .................. 123
    *Problem 5–27* ............................................................. 123
    *Problem 5–28* ............................................................. 124
    1. Farm Products Exception and the Food Security Act of 1985 ..................................................................... 125
    *Problem 5–29* ............................................................. 127
    *Problem 5–30* ............................................................. 127
    *Problem 5–31* ............................................................. 128
    *Problem 5–32* ............................................................. 129
V. Priority Disputes Between Secured Creditors and Real Estate Interests (Fixtures) ........................................................... 130
    *Problem 5–33* ............................................................. 131
    *Problem 5–34* ............................................................. 133
    *Problem 5–35* ............................................................. 134
    *Problem 5–36* ............................................................. 134
VI. Special Problems that Arise When the Debtor Files in Bankruptcy .............................................................................. 135
    *Problem 5–37* ............................................................. 137
    *Problem 5–38* ............................................................. 138
    *Problem 5–39* ............................................................. 138
    *Problem 5–40* ............................................................. 139

**Chapter 6. Multi–Jurisdictional Transactions** ...................... **140**
  I. Introduction to Multi–Jurisdictional Transactions ............... 140
  II. Perfection in Multi–Jurisdictional Transactions .................. 141
    A. Place of Initial Perfection .......................................... 141
    *Problem 6–1* ............................................................. 141
    *Problem 6–2* ............................................................. 141
    B. Location Changes Affecting Perfection ....................... 142
    *Problem 6–3* ............................................................. 142

Page

II. Perfection in Multi–Jurisdictional Transactions—Continued
    *Problem 6–4* ------------------------------------------------------- 143
    *Problem 6–5* ------------------------------------------------------- 144
  C. Certificate of Title Issues------------------------------------ 145
    *Problem 6–6* ------------------------------------------------------- 145
III. Priorities in Multi–Jurisdictional Transactions ------------------ 148
    *Problem 6–7*------------------------------------------------------- 148
IV. Perfection and Priorities When a Foreign Jurisdiction is In-
    volved ------------------------------------------------------------ 149
    *Problem 6–8*------------------------------------------------------- 149
    *Problem 6–9*------------------------------------------------------- 149

**Chapter 7. Default, Remedies, and Debtor Protections** ------ **151**
  I. Meaning of Default and Limitations on the Exercise of Reme-
    dies -------------------------------------------------------------- 151
    *Problem 7–1*------------------------------------------------------- 152
    *Problem 7–2*------------------------------------------------------- 153
    *Problem 7–3*------------------------------------------------------- 154
    *Problem 7–4*------------------------------------------------------- 154
    *Problem 7–5*------------------------------------------------------- 155
  II. Alternative Remedies ------------------------------------------ 157
    A. Collection Rights of Secured Parties------------------------ 157
    B. Obtaining Possession of the Collateral-------------------- 159
      *Problem 7–6* -------------------------------------------------- 159
      *Problem 7–7* -------------------------------------------------- 161
    C. Alternative Ways of Obtaining Possession------------------ 161
    D. Sale of Collateral------------------------------------------ 162
      *Problem 7–8* -------------------------------------------------- 162
      1. Contents and Recipients of Notification ------------- 164
      *Problem 7–9* -------------------------------------------------- 165
      *Problem 7–10*------------------------------------------------- 166
      2. Distribution of the Proceeds and Protections for the
      Transferees of the Collateral------------------------- 166
      *Problem 7–11*------------------------------------------------- 166
    E. Retention of Collateral in Satisfaction of Debt ------------ 167
      *Problem 7–12*------------------------------------------------- 167
      *Problem 7–13*------------------------------------------------- 168
      1. Procedures for Strict Foreclosure----------------------- 169
III. Debtor's Right of Redemption ------------------------------- 169
    *Problem 7–14*----------------------------------------------------- 169
IV. Remedies for Creditor Misbehavior ------------------------------ 170
    A. Introduction ------------------------------------------------ 170
      *Problem 7–15*------------------------------------------------- 172

EPILOG------------------------------------------------------------- 173
INDEX ------------------------------------------------------------- 175

\*

# Table of Cases

References are to pages. Cases cited in principal cases and within other quoted materials are not included.

Battista v. Savings Bank of Baltimore, 67 Md.App. 257, 507 A.2d 203 (Md.App. 1986), 154

Benschoter v. First Nat. Bank of Lawrence, 218 Kan. 144, 542 P.2d 1042 (Kan.1975), 160, 161

Berry, In re, 189 B.R. 82 (Bkrtcy.D.S.C. 1995), 42

Biglari Import Export, Inc., In re, 130 B.R. 43 (Bkrtcy.W.D.Tex.1991), 78

Bing v. General Motors Acceptance Corp., 237 F.Supp. 911 (E.D.S.C.1965), 161

Bloomquist v. First Nat. Bank of Elk River, 378 N.W.2d 81 (Minn.App.1985), 159

Bluegrass Ford–Mercury, Inc., In re, 942 F.2d 381 (6th Cir.1991), 84

Calderon v. United Furniture Co., 505 F.2d 950 (5th Cir.1974), 160

Census Federal Credit Union v. Wann, 403 N.E.2d 348 (Ind.App. 1 Dist.1980), 159

Chrysler Credit Corp. v. Koontz, 277 Ill. App.3d 1078, 214 Ill.Dec. 726, 661 N.E.2d 1171 (Ill.App. 5 Dist.1996), 160

Clark Pipe & Supply Co., Matter of, 893 F.2d 693 (5th Cir.1990), 154

Clovis Nat. Bank v. Thomas, 77 N.M. 554, 425 P.2d 726 (N.M.1967), 126

Cox v. Galigher Motor Sales Co., 158 W.Va. 685, 213 S.E.2d 475 (W.Va.1975), 160

Crocker Nat. Bank (Credit Alliance) v. Clark Equipment Credit Corp., 724 F.2d 696 (8th Cir.1984), 111

Davenport v. Chrysler Credit Corp., 818 S.W.2d 23 (Tenn.Ct.App.1991), 173

Dearman v. Williams, 235 Miss. 360, 109 So.2d 316 (Miss.1959), 159

Deavers v. Standridge, 144 Ga.App. 673, 242 S.E.2d 331 (Ga.App.1978), 160

District of Columbia v. Thomas Funding Corp., 593 A.2d 1030 (D.C.1991), 81

Downing, In re, 286 B.R. 900 (Bkrtcy. W.D.Mo.2002), 164

Duffield v. First Interstate Bank of Denver, N.A., 13 F.3d 1403 (10th Cir.1993), 157, 172

Filtercorp, Inc., In re, 163 F.3d 570 (9th Cir.1998), 58

First and Farmers Bank of Somerset v. Henderson, 763 S.W.2d 137 (Ky.App. 1988), 160

First Maryland Leasecorp. v. M/V Golden Egret, 764 F.2d 749 (11th Cir.1985), 62

Fish, In re, 128 B.R. 468 (Bkrtcy.N.D.Okla. 1991), 45

Five Points Bank v. Scoular–Bishop Grain Co., 217 Neb. 677, 350 N.W.2d 549 (Neb. 1984), 126

Fuentes v. Shevin, 407 U.S. 67, 92 S.Ct. 1983, 32 L.Ed.2d 556 (1972), 162

Gaynor v. Union Trust Co., 216 Conn. 458, 582 A.2d 190 (Conn.1990), 154

General Elec. Credit Corp. v. Timbrook, 170 W.Va. 143, 291 S.E.2d 383 (W.Va.1982), 160

Girard v. Anderson, 219 Iowa 142, 257 N.W. 400 (Iowa 1934), 160

Gregory v. First Nat. Bank of Or., 241 Or. 397, 406 P.2d 156 (Or.1965), 159

Gulf Oil Corp. v. Smithey, 426 S.W.2d 262 (Tex.Civ.App.-Dallas 1968), 160

Henderson v. Security Nat. Bank, 72 Cal. App.3d 764, 140 Cal.Rptr. 388 (Cal.App. 1 Dist.1977), 159, 160

Hester v. Bandy, 627 So.2d 833 (Miss.1993), 160

Howell v. Ford Motor Credit Co., 1975 WL 22851 (Okla.App.1975), 159

Hudak v. Central Bank of The South, 529 So.2d 936 (Ala.1988), 154

**In re (see name of party)**
ITT Diversified Credit Corp. v. First City Capital Corp., 737 S.W.2d 803 (Tex. 1987), 106

Ivy Properties, Inc., In re, 109 B.R. 10 (Bkrtcy.D.Mass.1989), 42

James Talcott, Inc. v. Franklin Nat. Bank, 292 Minn. 277, 194 N.W.2d 775 (Minn. 1972), 98
J.I. Case Co. v. Borg–Warner Acceptance Corp., 669 S.W.2d 543 (Ky.App.1983), 111

Kessel v. Western Sav. Credit Union, 463 N.W.2d 629 (N.D.1990), 154
Kham & Nate's Shoes No. 2, Inc. v. First Bank of Whiting, 908 F.2d 1351 (7th Cir.1990), 154, 172
King v. General Motors Acceptance Corp., 140 F.Supp. 259 (M.D.N.C.1956), 159
KMC Co. v. Irving Trust Co., 757 F.2d 752 (6th Cir.1985), 154, 172
Kroeger v. Ogsden, 429 P.2d 781 (Okla. 1967), 159

Lane v. John Deere Co., 767 S.W.2d 138 (Tenn.1989), 154
Laurel Coal Co. v. Walter E. Heller & Co., 539 F.Supp. 1006 (W.D.Pa.1982), 160
L.C. Williams Oil Co. v. NAFCO Capital Corp., 130 N.C.App. 286, 502 S.E.2d 415 (N.C.App.1998), 35
Leasing One Corp. v. Caterpillar Financial Services Corp., 776 N.E.2d 408 (Ind.App. 2002), 35
Lehigh Press, Inc. v. National Bank of Georgia, 193 Ga.App. 888, 389 S.E.2d 376 (Ga.App.1989), 85
Luthy v. Philip Werlein Co., 163 La. 752, 112 So. 709 (La.1927), 161

Manhattan Credit Co. v. Brewer, 232 Ark. 976, 341 S.W.2d 765 (Ark.1961), 160
Martin v. Dorn Equipment Co., 250 Mont. 422, 821 P.2d 1025 (Mont.1991), 160
Martin Specialty Vehicles, Inc., In re, 87 B.R. 752 (Bkrtcy.D.Mass.1988), 154
**Matter of (see name of party)**
MBank El Paso v. Sanchez, 836 S.W.2d 151 (Tex.1992), 160
Mitchell v. W. T. Grant Co., 416 U.S. 600, 94 S.Ct. 1895, 40 L.Ed.2d 406 (1974), 162
MJK Clearing, Inc., In re, 286 B.R. 109 (Bkrtcy.D.Minn.2002), 65
Moe v. John Deere Co., 516 N.W.2d 332 (S.D.1994), 154
Morris v. First Nat. Bank & Trust Co. of Ravenna, 21 Ohio St.2d 25, 254 N.E.2d 683 (Ohio 1970), 160

Nevada Nat. Bank v. Huff, 94 Nev. 506, 582 P.2d 364 (Nev.1978), 154
North Georgia Finishing, Inc. v. Di–Chem, Inc., 419 U.S. 601, 95 S.Ct. 719, 42 L.Ed.2d 751 (1975), 162

Oaklawn Bank v. Baldwin, 289 Ark. 79, 709 S.W.2d 91 (Ark.1986), 159

Owensboro Canning Co., In re, 46 B.R. 607 (Bkrtcy.W.D.Ky.1985), 50

Pickle Logging, Inc., In re, 286 B.R. 181 (Bkrtcy.M.D.Ga.2002), 52
Pierce v. Leasing Intern., Inc., 142 Ga.App. 371, 235 S.E.2d 752 (Ga.App.1977), 159
Pioneer Finance & Thrift Corp. v. Adams, 426 S.W.2d 317 (Tex.Civ.App.-Eastland 1968), 159
Pleasant v. Warrick, 590 So.2d 214 (Ala. 1991), 160
Pristas v. Landaus of Plymouth, Inc., 742 F.2d 797 (3rd Cir.1984), 104

Raffa v. Dania Bank, 321 So.2d 83 (Fla.App. 4 Dist.1975), 159
Rea v. Universal CIT Credit Corp., 257 N.C. 639, 127 S.E.2d 225 (N.C.1962), 159
Reid v. Key Bank of Southern Maine, Inc., 821 F.2d 9 (1st Cir.1987), 154
Riley State Bank of Riley v. Spillman, 242 Kan. 696, 750 P.2d 1024 (Kan.1988), 154

Schmode's, Inc. v. Wilkinson, 219 Neb. 209, 361 N.W.2d 557 (Neb.1985), 168
Security Pacific Housing Services, Inc. v. Cape Mobile Home Mart, Inc., No. CV191–866CC (Franklin County, Mo.1995), 154
Sniadach v. Family Finance Corp., 395 U.S. 337, 89 S.Ct. 1820, 23 L.Ed.2d 349 (1969), 162
Southtrust Bank of Alabama v. Borg–Warner Acceptance Corp., 760 F.2d 1240 (11th Cir.1985), 104
Stone Machinery Co. v. Kessler, 1 Wash. App. 750, 463 P.2d 651 (Wash.App. Div. 3 1970), 160
Systran Financial Services Corp. v. Giant Cement Holding, Inc., 252 F.Supp.2d 500 (N.D.Ohio 2003), 158

Tepper Industries, In re, 74 B.R. 713 (9th Cir.BAP (Cal.) 1987), 54
Thompson v. Ford Motor Credit Co., 550 F.2d 256 (5th Cir.1977), 160
Thompson v. Ford Motor Credit Co., 324 F.Supp. 108 (D.S.C.1971), 159
Thorp Commercial Corp. v. Northgate Industries, Inc., 654 F.2d 1245 (8th Cir. 1981), 84

Universal C.I.T. Credit Corp. v. Farmers Bank of Portageville, 358 F.Supp. 317 (E.D.Mo.1973), 108

Van Brunt v. BancTexas Quorum, N.A., 804 S.W.2d 117 (Tex.App.-Dallas 1989), 163
Viscount Furniture Corp., In re, 133 B.R. 360 (Bkrtcy.N.D.Miss.1991), 47

Wade v. Ford Motor Credit Co., 455 F.Supp. 147 (E.D.Mo.1978), 154

Walker v. Walthall, 121 Ariz. 121, 588 P.2d 863 (Ariz.App. Div. 1 1978), 160

Westinghouse Credit Corp. v. Shelton, 645 F.2d 869 (10th Cir.1981), 154

*

# Table of Statutes

## UNITED STATES

### UNITED STATES CODE ANNOTATED

#### 11 U.S.C.A.—Bankruptcy

| Sec. | This Work Page |
|------|------|
| 101(54) | 137 |
| 301 | 114 |
| 362 | 77 |
| 362 | 114 |
| 362(a)(4) | 115 |
| 362(b)(3) | 115 |
| 503(b)(4) | 47 |
| 541(a)(1) | 45 |
| 542(a) | 45 |
| 544(a) | 25 |
| 544(a) | 73 |
| 544(a) | 77 |
| 544(a) | 114 |
| 544(a) | 135 |
| 546(b) | 115 |
| 547 | 77 |
| 547(b) | 114 |
| 547(b) | 137 |
| 547(b) | 138 |
| 547(b) | 139 |
| 547(c)(2) | 138 |
| 547(c)(3) | 139 |
| 547(c)(4) | 139 |
| 547(c)(5) | 139 |
| 547(e) | 137 |
| 547(e) | 139 |
| 547(e)(3) | 139 |
| 1112(a) | 47 |

#### 26 U.S.C.A.—Internal Revenue Code

| Sec. | This Work Page |
|------|------|
| 6321—6323 | 11 |
| 6323(b)(2)(A) | 119 |
| 6323(b)(3) | 119 |
| 6323(b)(5) | 119 |
| 6323(d)(1) | 120 |

### REVISED UNIFORM COMMERCIAL CODE

| Sec. | This Work Page |
|------|------|
| Art. 1 | 16 |

## REVISED UNIFORM COMMERCIAL CODE

| Sec. | This Work Page |
|------|------|
| Art. 1 | 172 |
| 1–103(a)(3) | 17 |
| 1–103(b) | 17 |
| 1–103(b) | 154 |
| 1–201—1–205 | 17 |
| 1–201(b)(3) | 50 |
| 1–201(b)(9) | 121 |
| 1–201(b)(9) | 123 |
| 1–201(b)(9) | 124 |
| 1–201(b)(9) | 125 |
| 1–201(b)(20) | 172 |
| 1–201(b)(25) | 56 |
| 1–201(b)(25) | 142 |
| 1–201(b)(25) | 145 |
| 1–201(b)(27) | 56 |
| 1–201(b)(27) | 142 |
| 1–201(b)(27) | 145 |
| 1–201(b)(29) | 60 |
| 1–201(b)(29) | 61 |
| 1–201(b)(29) | 121 |
| 1–201(b)(29) | 144 |
| 1–201(b)(30) | 60 |
| 1–201(b)(30) | 61 |
| 1–201(b)(30) | 121 |
| 1–201(b)(30) | 144 |
| 1–201(b)(35) | 30 |
| 1–201(b)(35) | 31 |
| 1–201(b)(35) | 48 |
| 1–201(b)(35) | 60 |
| 1–201(b)(37) | 48 |
| 1–202 | 123 |
| 1–202 | 129 |
| 1–203 | 33 |
| 1–203 | 35 |
| 1–203 | 58 |
| 1–203 | 98 |
| 1–204 | 62 |
| 1–301 | 149 |
| 1–302 | 157 |
| 1–303 | 58 |
| 1–303 | 154 |
| 1–303 | 157 |
| 1–304 | 154 |
| 1–304 | 157 |
| 1–304 | 172 |
| 1–309 | 153 |
| 1–309 | 154 |

## UNIFORM COMMERCIAL CODE

| Sec. | This Work Page |
|---|---|
| 1–102(2)(c) | 17 |
| 1–102(3) | 157 |
| 1–103 | 17 |
| 1–103 | 154 |
| 1–103 | 166 |
| 1–103 | 170 |
| 1–103 | 171 |
| 1–105 | 149 |
| 1–201 | 17 |
| 1–201 | 21 |
| 1–201(3) | 50 |
| 1–201(9) | 121 |
| 1–201(9) | 123 |
| 1–201(9) | 124 |
| 1–201(9) | 125 |
| 1–201(19) | 172 |
| 1–201(24) | 65 |
| 1–201(24) | 76 |
| 1–201(25)(c) | 123 |
| 1–201(27) | 129 |
| 1–201(28) | 56 |
| 1–201(28) | 84 |
| 1–201(28) | 142 |
| 1–201(28) | 145 |
| 1–201(30) | 56 |
| 1–201(32) | 60 |
| 1–201(32) | 61 |
| 1–201(32) | 121 |
| 1–201(32) | 144 |
| 1–201(33) | 60 |
| 1–201(33) | 61 |
| 1–201(33) | 121 |
| 1–201(33) | 144 |
| 1–201(37) | 30 |
| 1–201(37) | 31 |
| 1–201(37) | 33 |
| 1–201(37) | 35 |
| 1–201(37) | 48 |
| 1–201(37) | 58 |
| 1–201(37) | 60 |
| 1–201(37) | 98 |
| 1–201(39) | 48 |
| 1–201(44) | 62 |
| 1–201(44) | 63 |
| 1–201, Comment 28 | 84 |
| 1–203 | 154 |
| 1–203 | 157 |
| 1–203 | 172 |
| 1–205 | 58 |
| 1–205 | 126 |
| 1–205 | 154 |
| 1–205 | 157 |
| 1–205(4) | 126 |
| 1–208 | 153 |
| 1–208 | 154 |
| 1–208, Comment | 153 |
| 2–319 | 60 |
| 2–326(2) | 39 |
| 2–326, Comment 1 | 39 |
| 2–401 | 30 |
| 2–401 | 60 |
| 2–403 | 60 |

## UNIFORM COMMERCIAL CODE

| Sec. | This Work Page |
|---|---|
| 2–403(1)(b) | 61 |
| 2–501 | 60 |
| 2–702 | 11 |
| 2–702(2) | 60 |
| 2–702(3) | 60 |
| Art. 2B | 16 |
| 4–104(a)(5) | 76 |
| 6–104 | 11 |
| 8–106 | 76 |
| 8–301 | 76 |
| Art. 9 | 10 |
| Art. 9 | 17 |
| Art. 9 | 20 |
| Art. 9 | 24 |
| Art. 9 | 25 |
| Art. 9 | 29 |
| Art. 9 | 31 |
| Art. 9 | 32 |
| Art. 9 | 33 |
| Art. 9 | 37 |
| Art. 9 | 38 |
| Art. 9 | 40 |
| Art. 9 | 64 |
| Art. 9, Pt. 6 | 151 |
| 9–102 | 17 |
| 9–102 | 107 |
| 9–102(2) | 32 |
| 9–102(34) | 41 |
| 9–102(44) | 41 |
| 9–102(a) | 44 |
| 9–102(a)(2) | 36 |
| 9–102(a)(2) | 42 |
| 9–102(a)(2) | 55 |
| 9–102(a)(2) | 65 |
| 9–102(a)(2) | 74 |
| 9–102(a)(2) | 89 |
| 9–102(a)(2)(A)—(a)(2)(D) | 39 |
| 9–102(a)(3) | 158 |
| 9–102(a)(5) | 10 |
| 9–102(a)(5) | 29 |
| 9–102(a)(6) | 86 |
| 9–102(a)(6) | 142 |
| 9–102(a)(7) | 48 |
| 9–102(a)(7) | 56 |
| 9–102(a)(9) | 64 |
| 9–102(a)(9) | 65 |
| 9–102(a)(9) | 89 |
| 9–102(a)(11) | 36 |
| 9–102(a)(12) | 65 |
| 9–102(a)(12) | 89 |
| 9–102(a)(12)(A) | 87 |
| 9–102(a)(13) | 57 |
| 9–102(a)(18) | 83 |
| 9–102(a)(19) | 38 |
| 9–102(a)(20) | 105 |
| 9–102(a)(21) | 38 |
| 9–102(a)(23) | 53 |
| 9–102(a)(23) | 65 |
| 9–102(a)(23) | 73 |
| 9–102(a)(26) | 26 |
| 9–102(a)(28) | 56 |
| 9–102(a)(28) | 144 |

## UNIFORM COMMERCIAL CODE

| Sec. | This Work Page |
|------|------|
| 9–102(a)(28)(A) | 143 |
| 9–102(a)(29) | 47 |
| 9–102(a)(33) | 53 |
| 9–102(a)(33) | 55 |
| 9–102(a)(33) | 65 |
| 9–102(a)(33) | 73 |
| 9–102(a)(33) | 89 |
| 9–102(a)(34) | 55 |
| 9–102(a)(34) | 66 |
| 9–102(a)(34) | 125 |
| 9–102(a)(42) | 36 |
| 9–102(a)(42) | 55 |
| 9–102(a)(42) | 73 |
| 9–102(a)(43) | 153 |
| 9–102(a)(43) | 154 |
| 9–102(a)(43) | 157 |
| 9–102(a)(44) | 73 |
| 9–102(a)(46) | 74 |
| 9–102(a)(47) | 46 |
| 9–102(a)(47) | 89 |
| 9–102(a)(48) | 55 |
| 9–102(a)(48) | 66 |
| 9–102(a)(48) | 125 |
| 9–102(a)(52) | 25 |
| 9–102(a)(52) | 62 |
| 9–102(a)(52) | 114 |
| 9–102(a)(58) | 64 |
| 9–102(a)(58) | 65 |
| 9–102(a)(58) | 89 |
| 9–102(a)(59) | 56 |
| 9–102(a)(59) | 63 |
| 9–102(a)(61) | 36 |
| 9–102(a)(64) | 65 |
| 9–102(a)(64) | 89 |
| 9–102(a)(64) | 167 |
| 9–102(a)(64)(A) | 64 |
| 9–102(a)(64)(B) | 87 |
| 9–102(a)(65) | 36 |
| 9–102(a)(65) | 46 |
| 9–102(a)(69) | 48 |
| 9–102(a)(70) | 81 |
| 9–102(a)(70) | 141 |
| 9–102(a)(70) | 142 |
| 9–102(a)(70) | 145 |
| 9–102(a)(70) | 149 |
| 9–102(a)(73) | 48 |
| 9–102(a)(74) | 83 |
| 9–102(a)(75) | 73 |
| 9–102(a)(76) | 149 |
| 9–102(a)(77) | 65 |
| 9–102(a), Comment 4.a. | 53 |
| 9–102, Comment 2.a. | 63 |
| 9–102, Comment 4.a. | 55 |
| 9–102, Comment 4.a. | 66 |
| 9–102, Comment 4.a. | 73 |
| 9–102, Comment 5.d. | 73 |
| 9–102, Comment 9(b) | 56 |
| 9–102, Comment 11 | 81 |
| 9–102, Comment 13.c. | 65 |
| 9–102, Comment 14 | 38 |
| 9–103 | 71 |
| 9–103 | 103 |

## UNIFORM COMMERCIAL CODE

| Sec. | This Work Page |
|------|------|
| 9–103 | 104 |
| 9–103 | 108 |
| 9–103 | 115 |
| 9–103(a)(1) | 72 |
| 9–103(d) | 38 |
| 9–103(d) | 105 |
| 9–103, Comment 3 | 71 |
| 9–103, Comment 3 | 72 |
| 9–103, Comments | 103 |
| 9–104 | 76 |
| 9–104 | 111 |
| 9–104(a) | 47 |
| 9–104(b) | 76 |
| 9–104, Comment 3 | 76 |
| 9–104—9–107 | 44 |
| 9–108 | 52 |
| 9–108 | 54 |
| 9–108(a) | 66 |
| 9–108(b) | 85 |
| 9–108(b)(3) | 54 |
| 9–108(c) | 85 |
| 9–108(e) | 51 |
| 9–108(e) | 97 |
| 9–108(e)(1) | 57 |
| 9–108(e)(2) | 53 |
| 9–108, Comment 5 | 53 |
| 9–109 | 76 |
| 9–109 | 115 |
| 9–109(a) | 29 |
| 9–109(a)(1) | 32 |
| 9–109(a)(5) | 30 |
| 9–109(a)(5) | 60 |
| 9–109(b) | 42 |
| 9–109(c)(13) | 76 |
| 9–109(d) | 41 |
| 9–109(d) | 42 |
| 9–109(d)(2) | 40 |
| 9–109(d)(11) | 42 |
| 9–109, Comment 2 | 32 |
| 9–109, Comment 4 | 37 |
| 9–109, Comment 6 | 38 |
| 9–109, Comment 7 | 42 |
| 9–110 | 30 |
| 9–110 | 60 |
| 9–110 | 115 |
| 9–201(a) | 24 |
| 9–201(a) | 46 |
| 9–202 | 32 |
| 9–203 | 23 |
| 9–203 | 24 |
| 9–203 | 46 |
| 9–203 | 48 |
| 9–203 | 58 |
| 9–203 | 62 |
| 9–203 | 63 |
| 9–203 | 66 |
| 9–203 | 100 |
| 9–203 | 143 |
| 9–203(b) | 84 |
| 9–203(b)(1) | 43 |
| 9–203(b)(2) | 43 |
| 9–203(b)(3)(A) | 52 |

## UNIFORM COMMERCIAL CODE

| Sec. | This Work Page |
|---|---|
| 9–203(b)(3)(A) | 56 |
| 9–203(b)(3)(B) | 45 |
| 9–203(b)(3)(D) | 47 |
| 9–203(b), Comment 6 | 43 |
| 9–203(d) | 83 |
| 9–203(d) | 84 |
| 9–203(d) | 100 |
| 9–203(e) | 83 |
| 9–203(e) | 84 |
| 9–203(f) | 65 |
| 9–203(f) | 89 |
| 9–203(f) | 167 |
| 9–203(g) | 42 |
| 9–203, Comment 3 | 32 |
| 9–203, Comment 4 | 46 |
| 9–203, Comment 5 | 54 |
| 9–204 | 58 |
| 9–204 | 100 |
| 9–204(a) | 66 |
| 9–204(b)(1) | 57 |
| 9–204(b)(1) | 97 |
| 9–204(b)(2) | 57 |
| 9–204, Comment 7 | 58 |
| 9–207 | 78 |
| 9–207(a) | 79 |
| 9–210 | 85 |
| 9–301 | 141 |
| 9–301 | 142 |
| 9–301 | 143 |
| 9–301 | 149 |
| 9–301(3) | 148 |
| 9–301, Comment 5 | 142 |
| 9–301, Comment 5.c. | 142 |
| 9–303 | 146 |
| 9–303 | 147 |
| 9–303, Comment 2 | 148 |
| 9–303, Comment 3 | 148 |
| 9–307 | 141 |
| 9–307 | 142 |
| 9–307 | 145 |
| 9–307 | 149 |
| 9–307(a) | 21 |
| 9–307(b) | 148 |
| 9–307(c) | 150 |
| 9–309—9–314 | 75 |
| 9–309(1) | 73 |
| 9–309(1) | 89 |
| 9–309(1) | 124 |
| 9–309(1) | 146 |
| 9–309(2) | 73 |
| 9–309(5) | 74 |
| 9–309, Comment 4 | 73 |
| 9–310 | 146 |
| 9–310(a) | 89 |
| 9–310(b)(2) | 73 |
| 9–310(b)(3) | 92 |
| 9–310(c) | 71 |
| 9–311 | 92 |
| 9–311 | 146 |
| 9–311, Comment 7 | 92 |
| 9–312 | 89 |
| 9–312(a) | 76 |

## UNIFORM COMMERCIAL CODE

| Sec. | This Work Page |
|---|---|
| 9–312(e)—(h) | 72 |
| 9–313 | 46 |
| 9–313 | 76 |
| 9–313(a) | 76 |
| 9–313(b) | 77 |
| 9–313(b) | 92 |
| 9–313(b) | 147 |
| 9–313(d) | 77 |
| 9–313, Comment 3 | 76 |
| 9–313, Comment 4 | 76 |
| 9–314 | 76 |
| 9–314 | 89 |
| 9–315 | 65 |
| 9–315 | 89 |
| 9–315 | 107 |
| 9–315 | 108 |
| 9–315 | 110 |
| 9–315 | 124 |
| 9–315 | 143 |
| 9–315(1) | 64 |
| 9–315(a)(1) | 84 |
| 9–315(a)(1) | 87 |
| 9–315(a)(1) | 125 |
| 9–315(a)(1) | 128 |
| 9–315(a)(1) | 144 |
| 9–315(a)(2) | 64 |
| 9–315(a)(2) | 67 |
| 9–315(a)(2) | 87 |
| 9–315(a)(2) | 167 |
| 9–315(d) | 89 |
| 9–315, Comment 2 | 98 |
| 9–315, Comment 2 | 128 |
| 9–315, Comment 3 | 65 |
| 9–316 | 146 |
| 9–316 | 147 |
| 9–316(a) | 143 |
| 9–316(a) | 144 |
| 9–316(a) | 145 |
| 9–316(a) | 150 |
| 9–316(b) | 144 |
| 9–316(b) | 145 |
| 9–316(d) | 77 |
| 9–316(d) | 92 |
| 9–316(e) | 77 |
| 9–316, Comment 2 | 143 |
| 9–316, Comment 2 | 145 |
| 9–317 | 77 |
| 9–317 | 135 |
| 9–317(a) | 117 |
| 9–317(a) | 144 |
| 9–317(a)(2) | 73 |
| 9–317(a)(2) | 114 |
| 9–317(a)(2)(A) | 25 |
| 9–317(a)(2)(B) | 62 |
| 9–317(b) | 123 |
| 9–317(b) | 144 |
| 9–317(b) | 147 |
| 9–317(e) | 113 |
| 9–317(e) | 115 |
| 9–317(e) | 123 |
| 9–319(a) | 38 |
| 9–319(a) | 105 |

**UNIFORM COMMERCIAL CODE**

| Sec. | This Work Page |
|---|---|
| 9–319(b) | 38 |
| 9–320 | 124 |
| 9–320(a) | 125 |
| 9–320(a) | 127 |
| 9–320(b) | 124 |
| 9–320(b) | 127 |
| 9–322 | 96 |
| 9–322 | 98 |
| 9–322 | 99 |
| 9–322 | 100 |
| 9–322 | 107 |
| 9–322 | 108 |
| 9–322 | 110 |
| 9–322 | 113 |
| 9–322 | 114 |
| 9–322 | 124 |
| 9–322 | 129 |
| 9–322 | 135 |
| 9–322(a) | 144 |
| 9–322(a)(1) | 26 |
| 9–322(a)(1) | 103 |
| 9–322(a)(2) | 25 |
| 9–322(a)(3) | 24 |
| 9–322, Comment 2 | 96 |
| 9–322, Comment 4 | 96 |
| 9–322, Comment 5 | 96 |
| 9–323 | 96 |
| 9–323 | 98 |
| 9–323 | 100 |
| 9–323 | 116 |
| 9–323(a) | 99 |
| 9–323(b) | 116 |
| 9–323(d) | 129 |
| 9–323(e) | 129 |
| 9–323, Comment 3 | 96 |
| 9–323, Comment 3 | 98 |
| 9–323, Comments | 99 |
| 9–324 | 111 |
| 9–324 | 124 |
| 9–324(a) | 103 |
| 9–324(a) | 108 |
| 9–324(a) | 113 |
| 9–324(a) | 150 |
| 9–324(b) | 104 |
| 9–324(b) | 105 |
| 9–324(b) | 110 |
| 9–324(b) | 114 |
| 9–324(g) | 103 |
| 9–324, Comment 3 | 103 |
| 9–325 | 100 |
| 9–325 | 124 |
| 9–325 | 143 |
| 9–325 | 144 |
| 9–326 | 83 |
| 9–326 | 84 |
| 9–326 | 100 |
| 9–326 | 143 |
| 9–327 | 108 |
| 9–327 | 110 |
| 9–327 | 111 |
| 9–330 | 110 |
| 9–330 | 111 |

**UNIFORM COMMERCIAL CODE**

| Sec. | This Work Page |
|---|---|
| 9–330, Comments | 110 |
| 9–330, Comments | 111 |
| 9–331 | 89 |
| 9–331 | 110 |
| 9–332 | 89 |
| 9–332 | 110 |
| 9–332 | 128 |
| 9–333 | 40 |
| 9–333 | 117 |
| 9–333 | 148 |
| 9–333(a) | 29 |
| 9–333(b) | 29 |
| 9–334 | 132 |
| 9–334 | 133 |
| 9–334 | 134 |
| 9–334 | 135 |
| 9–335 | 113 |
| 9–335(d) | 113 |
| 9–335, Comment 7 | 113 |
| 9–336 | 114 |
| 9–336, Comments | 114 |
| 9–337 | 147 |
| 9–338 | 82 |
| 9–339 | 106 |
| 9–340 | 108 |
| 9–340 | 109 |
| 9–340 | 111 |
| 9–501 | 141 |
| 9–501 | 142 |
| 9–501(a) | 86 |
| 9–501(a)(2) | 89 |
| 9–501, Comment 3 | 142 |
| 9–502 | 81 |
| 9–502 | 82 |
| 9–502(a)(3) | 85 |
| 9–502(b) | 86 |
| 9–502(b) | 142 |
| 9–502(d) | 49 |
| 9–502, Comment 2 | 49 |
| 9–502, Comment 2 | 84 |
| 9–502, Comment 2 | 85 |
| 9–502, Comment 5 | 142 |
| 9–503 | 81 |
| 9–503(a) | 83 |
| 9–503(a)(1) | 81 |
| 9–503(c) | 81 |
| 9–503, Comment 2 | 81 |
| 9–504(2) | 85 |
| 9–505 | 98 |
| 9–506 | 81 |
| 9–506 | 83 |
| 9–507 | 83 |
| 9–507 | 100 |
| 9–507 | 143 |
| 9–507(a) | 84 |
| 9–507(a) | 144 |
| 9–507, Comment 3 | 84 |
| 9–507, Comment 3 | 144 |
| 9–508 | 100 |
| 9–508(b) | 83 |
| 9–508(b) | 84 |
| 9–508, Comment 2 | 83 |

## UNIFORM COMMERCIAL CODE

| Sec. | This Work Page |
|---|---|
| 9–508, Comment 2 | 84 |
| 9–508, Comment 3 | 83 |
| 9–508, Comment 3 | 84 |
| 9–508, Comment 4 | 143 |
| 9–508, Comments | 100 |
| 9–509 | 86 |
| 9–509(a) | 83 |
| 9–509(a) | 84 |
| 9–509(b) | 87 |
| 9–509(d)(2) | 84 |
| 9–509(d)(2) | 99 |
| 9–510(a) | 84 |
| 9–510(c) | 87 |
| 9–510, Comment 2 | 84 |
| 9–512(a) | 87 |
| 9–513 | 99 |
| 9–513(c) | 84 |
| 9–514 | 115 |
| 9–515 | 87 |
| 9–515 | 145 |
| 9–515(c) | 118 |
| 9–515, Comment 3 | 118 |
| 9–516(a) | 81 |
| 9–516(a) | 82 |
| 9–516(a) | 83 |
| 9–516(b) | 81 |
| 9–516(b)(5)(C)(ii) | 82 |
| 9–516(b)(7) | 87 |
| 9–516(d) | 81 |
| 9–516(d) | 82 |
| 9–516, Comment 3 | 81 |
| 9–516, Comment 3 | 82 |
| 9–517 | 81 |
| 9–520(a) | 81 |
| 9–520(a) | 87 |
| 9–521(a) | 83 |
| 9–601(a)(1) | 151 |
| 9–601(e) | 151 |
| 9–601, Comment 4 | 77 |
| 9–602(6) | 161 |
| 9–603(b) | 161 |
| 9–607(a)(1) | 57 |
| 9–609 | 77 |
| 9–609 | 161 |
| 9–609(a)(2) | 161 |
| 9–609(c) | 161 |
| 9–609, Comment 3 | 160 |
| 9–610 | 167 |
| 9–610(a) | 163 |

## UNIFORM COMMERCIAL CODE

| Sec. | This Work Page |
|---|---|
| 9–610(b) | 164 |
| 9–610, Comment 2 | 165 |
| 9–610, Comment 3 | 165 |
| 9–610, Comment 3 | 168 |
| 9–610, Comment 5 | 166 |
| 9–610, Comment 5 | 167 |
| 9–610, Comment 11 | 167 |
| 9–611 | 163 |
| 9–611 | 165 |
| 9–611(c)(2) | 165 |
| 9–611(e) | 165 |
| 9–612 | 163 |
| 9–613(1)(E) | 164 |
| 9–613(2) | 164 |
| 9–613(3) | 164 |
| 9–613, Comment 2 | 164 |
| 9–614(1)(C) | 170 |
| 9–615 | 167 |
| 9–615(a)(1) | 170 |
| 9–617 | 167 |
| 9–617, Comment 2 | 167 |
| 9–620 | 167 |
| 9–620(b) | 168 |
| 9–620(e) | 167 |
| 9–620(f) | 167 |
| 9–620, Comment 5 | 168 |
| 9–623 | 170 |
| 9–624(b) | 167 |
| 9–625 | 85 |
| 9–625 | 173 |
| 9–625(b) | 84 |
| 9–625(b) | 99 |
| 9–625(b) | 167 |
| 9–625(b) | 168 |
| 9–625(c)(4) | 84 |
| 9–625(e) | 99 |
| 9–626 | 168 |
| 9–626 | 173 |

## ABA MODEL RULES OF PROFESSIONAL CONDUCT

| Rule | This Work Page |
|---|---|
| 3.4(a) | 161 |
| 4.2 | 56 |
| 8.4(d) | 161 |

# SECURED TRANSACTIONS
## PROBLEMS AND MATERIALS

\*

# Chapter 1

# INTRODUCTION

---

*Three days after receipt of the good news that you passed the bar examination, the following letter arrived at your apartment.*

---

MEGABANK, INC.
BANK OF NEW BABYLON BUILDING
THIRTY–SECOND FLOOR
100 MAIN STREET
NEW BABYLON, GILMORIA 01487

*Office of Associate General Counsel*

Sidney Carlson, Esquire
2500 Melville Place #6
New Babylon, Gilmoria 01482

Dear Sidney:

Thank you for your voice mail message regarding your passing the Gilmoria bar examination. Congratulations on your achievement! We had every confidence you would, but it's always nice to have one's judgment confirmed. In any event, this fulfills the last condition precedent to your employment with Megabank, and we therefore anticipate that you will commence work as an attorney in my office on the first of next month, pursuant to the terms and conditions outlined in my offer letter to you. You will report directly to me. (As you know, I report to Vice President and General Counsel I. N. Houseman, who in turn reports directly to our President and CEO, Peter Pompous. I expect that you won't have much contact with Mr. Houseman unless you do something truly awful.)

I am attaching a few excerpts from the Loan Officer Training and Operations Manual of our major banking subsidiary, the Bank of New Babylon. Unless the bar exam has completely fried your brain, I suspect most of the stuff on secured lending will seem quite elementary to you.

Read it anyway. I want you to have some idea of how much legal knowledge the business types you will be dealing with can be presumed to have.

As we have previously discussed, it is our understanding that, during your initial year of employment, you will work with all of our major divisions and subsidiaries in order to familiarize yourself with their basic operations and legal requirements. Just to refresh your memory, you will, from time to time, provide research and advice to the following entities:

1. The largest entity is the Bank of New Babylon (BNB), which is my primary responsibility. BNB is the region's largest bank, with headquarters in our new office tower in downtown New Babylon and branches throughout metropolitan New Babylon and Gilmoria, as well as a few in surrounding states. We do most of the big deals, including major real estate acquisition and development loans and operating financing for large corporations. We also provide operating financing for a variety of smaller businesses, although that is really the specialty of NB Commercial Finance Co., Megabank's commercial finance subsidiary. BNB also provides the usual range of retail consumer banking services, although I doubt you will have much to do with that end of the business.

2. NB Mortgage Co., Inc. (NB Mortgage) is a key subsidiary as well. It is the primary responsibility of Assistant General Counsel John Morgan. Megabank formed this corporation a few years ago to handle residential real estate mortgages. The company makes loans to finance home purchases and takes back purchase money mortgages. Occasionally, it finances the acquisition or improvement of non-residential real estate. It retains a servicing portfolio consisting of approximately half of the home mortgage loans it originates and makes collections on those loans. The other half is sold in the secondary mortgage market. The company has a couple of offices in the suburbs of New Babylon, where most of the residential building and buying is going on at the moment.

3. NB Commercial Finance Co. (NB Commercial) is the third entity. Its legal matters are overseen by Assistant General Counsel Roy Comstock. You will probably find this to be an interesting company. It started out as an independent company, Nationwide Commercial Finance Co., and was not even affiliated with a retail bank for most of its existence. Megabank bought the company 15 years ago, during the mergers and acquisitions boom. It operates in all 50 states and has regional offices in 12. It does nothing but make loans secured by the inventory and/or accounts receivable of businesses of various kinds and sizes, including manufacturers, wholesalers and retailers. In that branch of the business, it is the third largest player in the country. The folks at NB Commercial are specialists, and they have a reputation for playing hardball. Fifteen years after the acquisition, they still have their own way of doing things.

4. Friendly Finance Company (Friendly) is one of our smaller operations. Assistant General Counsel Dan Conseco has responsibility

for this entity. Friendly also started out as an independent company, but its operations are on a much smaller scale than those of NB Commercial (it operates only within the State of Gilmoria). Megabank acquired Friendly about 10 years ago. Friendly is basically a consumer lending operation, and its maximum loan to any one customer is $50,000. It makes a few unsecured loans to particularly creditworthy customers, but most of its loans are secured by whatever the customer wants to buy with the loan funds (which can be anything from an air conditioner to a dump truck). Friendly will also make occasional purchases of retail installment contracts from a variety of retail stores.

5. NB Bankcard, Inc. (NB Bankcard) also falls within my area of responsibility. Megabank formed this company about 10 years ago. It is incorporated and located in South Dakota, where the regulatory and tax environment is more favorable than Gilmoria. NB Bankcard issues credit cards to customers nationwide, and these customers proceed to use them to acquire the debt burden of which we are all so fond. Since NB Bankcard pays off the merchants, the customers are actually debtors of NB Bankcard. The debt is all unsecured, but the fees charged to the merchants generate nice cash flow, and the interest rates on the consumer debt can be phenomenal.

6. The Bovine State Bank (BSB) is the final subsidiary of Megabank. Unfortunately, it is also within my area of responsibility. This assignment is the one that might turn your hair gray. BSB is located in the hinterlands of Gilmoria (specifically, in the town of Desolation). Five years ago, when BSB was on the brink of collapse, the FDIC encouraged us to buy it and try to revitalize its operations. Megabank did so (in return for some favorable regulatory treatment from FDIC), and some of us have regretted it ever since. We have tried to clean house, but BSB is still a little too casual in its approach to the banking business. I hope you like the country, as you will undoubtedly be spending time with these people.

I will provide you with more specific information on your initial assignments when you arrive. We at Megabank look forward to working with you, and I am particularly pleased that you decided to join us.

Sincerely yours,

*Jane Robinson*
Jane Robinson
Associate General Counsel

Megabank, Inc.

Attachments

*Anxious about whether you will be able to meet your boss's expectations, you begin to read the excerpts from the Loan Officer Training and Operations Manual that she included with her letter.*

## BANK OF NEW BABYLON
## LOAN OFFICER TRAINING AND
## OPERATIONS MANUAL

## CHAPTER 1: INTRODUCTION

Congratulations. If this book has been provided to you, it means you have been hired by the Bank of New Babylon as a loan officer or promoted to that position. The purpose of this book is to acquaint you with the Bank's operating procedures and give you the information you need to do your job. We begin with some basic distinctions and information.

### I. The Distinction Between Secured and Unsecured Credit

Initially, it is important that you understand the difference between two fundamental types of credit arrangements, usually referred to as **secured credit** and **unsecured credit**. While a creditor with a secured claim (sometimes called a **secured creditor**) does not have absolute assurance that the debtor will pay the claim, the secured creditor's position is nonetheless far better than that of a creditor who holds only an unsecured claim (often called an **unsecured creditor** or a **general creditor**). This becomes obvious when basic features of the two types of credit arrangements are compared.

The simplest form of unsecured credit is backed solely by the debtor's contractual promise to repay a loan of money or an extension of credit. The creditor with an unsecured claim relies on the belief that the debtor's income stream or assets will be sufficient to pay the debt when it becomes due. Unsecured credit is quite common. It is found in the consumer setting in purchases of small items, the use of credit cards, and loans from family and friends. Business debtors commonly incur unsecured debt for trade purchases of goods or services or in the form of loans.

Secured credit, on the other hand, is backed not only by the debtor's simple contractual promise to pay, but also by a "second contract" in which the debtor commits specific assets to the transaction to ensure repayment. Under the "second contract," the debtor, in effect, grants the secured creditor an interest in specific assets of the debtor that allows the secured creditor to proceed directly against those assets if the debtor defaults on the promise to pay or other aspects of the underlying loan contract. Secured credit is commonly extended in the consumer setting for large loans, including loans for the purchase of a car or a home. Larger loans and continuing credit arrangements are often secured in the business setting as well.

If the debtor fails to repay unsecured credit, the creditor with an unsecured claim must follow a three-step process to effect collection. First, the creditor must obtain a judgment for the amount owed by bringing a lawsuit on the loan contract or other credit arrangement. Second, the creditor must get the sheriff to identify and seize appropriate assets of the debtor. Finally, the sheriff must hold a sale of the property and apply the proceeds first to the cost of the seizure and sale and then to payment of the debt. Obviously, this is both a time-consuming and expensive process for the unsecured creditor. While out of pocket expenses may be reimbursed, time lost in court appearances, or in attending a seizure and a sale, is rarely compensated.

More importantly, there is no assurance that the debtor will have the necessary assets to pay the debt, let alone the out of pocket expenses, even if this collection process is carried out in a relatively expeditious manner. A consumer debtor may have lost his or her job or health, and the income stream upon which the unsecured creditor relied may have ceased. A business debtor may have sold off all of its equipment, inventory and other property, dissipated all its cash, and closed its doors. An unscrupulous debtor of either type may have secreted his or her assets so that the sheriff cannot find any assets to seize and sell.

**Exemption statutes** may further diminish the assets available for seizure by a creditor with an unsecured claim. Each state has a statute that exempts certain specific categories of assets from seizure by unsecured creditors. Exemption statutes are designed to allow the debtor to retain the ability to earn a living, to permit the debtor and the debtor's family to avoid becoming charges of the state, and perhaps even to enable the debtor to regain the capacity to repay outstanding debts over time.

For the most part, exemption statutes protect assets that would be considered the necessities of life, such as furniture, clothing, and tools necessary to continue a trade. In many states there is also an exemption for all or a portion of a debtor's home. This exemption is generally referred to as the "homestead exemption." Most exemption statutes describe exempt property by type, and many add a value limitation. For example, a statute might exempt a family heirloom regardless of its value but only exempt a motor vehicle up to a value of $1,500. The coverage of particular state exemption statutes varies widely and, therefore, statutory schemes may protect little of debtor's assets against seizure in one state and protect a great deal of an identical debtor's assets in another. The following is the exemption statute for the state of Gilmoria:

### § 2232. *General exemptions from seizure*

*A. The following property of a debtor is exempt from seizure under any writ or process whatsoever:*

*(1) That property necessary to the exercise of a trade, calling, or profession by which the debtor earns a livelihood, which shall be limited to the following:*

*(a) Tools.*

*(b) Instruments.*

*(c) Books.*

*(d) One pickup truck with a gross weight of less than three tons, or one motor vehicle used for personal transportation; and*

*(e) One utility trailer.*

*(2)(a) The clothing, bedding, linen, chinaware, non-sterling silverware, glassware, living room, bedroom, and dining room furniture, cooking stove, heating and cooling equipment, one noncommercial sewing machine, equipment for required therapy, kitchen utensils, pressing irons, washers, dryers, refriger-*

*ators, deep freezers, electric or otherwise, used by debtor or a member of debtor's family.*

    *(b) The family portraits.*

    *(c) Debtor's arms and military accoutrements.*

    *(d) The musical instruments played or practiced on by debtor or a member of debtor's family.*

    *(e) The poultry, fowl, and one cow kept by debtor for the use of debtor's family.*

    *(f) All dogs, cats, and other household pets.*

    *(3) Any wedding or engagement rings worn by either debtor or debtor's spouse up to a value of five thousand dollars for each ring.*

*B. Section A shall not apply to any writ or process issued to enforce a consensual security interest in personal property or purchase money mortgage of real property.*

In the past, a creditor contemplating an extension of unsecured credit might have responded to the obstacle imposed by an exemption statute by seeking a contractual waiver of the protection of the statute at the time a debt was incurred. To combat this and similar practices, the Federal Trade Commission issued "Credit Practice Rules." One of these rules prohibits a lender from obtaining a waiver of exemption rights from a consumer. See Federal Trade Commission Credit Practice Rules, 16 C.F.R. Section 444.2(a)(2). (Copies of the Credit Practice Rules are available in the Legal Department.[1]) Exemption statutes thus continue to pose a practical obstacle to the collection rights of an unsecured consumer creditor.

The situation is substantially different when a debtor fails to repay a secured claim. The creditor with a secured claim is not confined to the mechanisms for enforcement of simple contractual promises to pay that were just described. A secured creditor may directly exercise rights under the "second contract" of security to which the debtor has agreed. Under the latter "contract," the secured creditor is entitled to appropriate and liquidate the specific assets securing repayment of the debt (generally referred to as the "**collateral**").

Indeed, under some forms of secured credit arrangements, the secured creditor may have possession of the collateral from the outset of the credit transaction. If the secured creditor is not already in possession of the collateral, the creditor may, under certain circumstances, obtain possession of the collateral without the involvement of the sheriff. However, even if the sheriff must be used to obtain possession of the collateral, the process is somewhat easier, since expedited legal procedures are often available. Moreover, the precise property to be seized is already identified by the "second contract" of security. This avoids the problem of liability for seizure of too much property or exempt property, which is sometimes imposed when a sheriff seizes property to satisfy a judgment obtained on a simple unsecured debt. Furthermore, a sheriff's sale is not always necessary for the liquidation of collateral for a secured debt. The collateral, even if seized by the sheriff, may be turned over to the creditor. Under certain circumstances, the secured creditor may simply retain the collateral in satisfaction of the debt. Alternatively, the secured creditor may sell the collateral, and

---

    **1.** [The FTC Credit Practice Rules are included in your statutory supplement.]

there is greater flexibility in the requirements for sales by secured creditors than for sheriffs' sales. Finally, in most cases, exemption statutes do not prevent the satisfaction of a secured creditor's claim by sale of the collateral.

Obviously, this more streamlined process normally saves a creditor with a secured claim substantial time and expense. But that is not the sole, or even the major, advantage of a secured claim. While the greatest danger for the creditor with an unsecured claim is that the debtor will have no assets at the time the creditor attempts to collect the debt, the greatest advantage of the creditor with a secured claim is the substantial assurance that the collateral will be available when the creditor seeks payment.[2] This assurance results from the fact that the creditor's claim to the collateral remains, in most cases, even if the debtor transfers it to someone else. In addition, when there is a transfer of the collateral the creditor with a secured claim automatically obtains a right to substituted assets of the debtor whether or not the transfer eliminates the creditor's claim to the collateral in the hands of the transferee.

It should be noted that secured credit is not a safe harbor from all risks. For example, the debtor may still secrete his or her assets so that there is no collateral to be found when the creditor attempts to collect. Further, the collateral committed to secure the debt may have decreased in value over time to the extent that the proceeds received on its sale fail to cover the costs of seizure, the costs of sale, and the outstanding debt. Nevertheless, the risk to a creditor with a secured claim is significantly smaller than the risk to a creditor with an unsecured claim.

Given the advantages that secured credit offers over unsecured credit, most of the Bank's loans are secured. Indeed, you might wonder why the Bank, or any other creditor, would ever lend money on an unsecured basis. Generally, one major reason is cost. Creating the contract of security, generally called obtaining a **security interest**, can be somewhat complicated and time consuming. Therefore, if a transaction is small, or if the time between the extension of credit and payment is short, the Bank might choose to forgo security to keep the cost of the transaction lower. In such a case, the Bank might compensate for the greater risk by charging a higher interest rate. Other creditors—notably the "trade creditors" who supply goods or services to a business—might extend credit on an unsecured basis because the market in which they operate is so competitive that their customers can demand it.

One final concept should be emphasized. A creditor can have both a secured claim and an unsecured claim arising out of the same extension of credit. A creditor with a secured claim is one who has entered into a contract to obtain a direct claim to collateral. However, a debt actually is secured only to the extent of the **unencumbered value** of the collateral. For example, a creditor who lends a debtor $10,000 and takes a security interest in collateral worth $8,000 is a creditor with a secured claim of $8,000 and an unsecured claim of $2,000. Effectively, the creditor has both types of claims.

This same situation could also arise even if the collateral is worth $10,000 at the time the loan is made. First, some other creditor might have a prior claim to the collateral to secure a debt of $2,000 leaving only $8,000 worth of unencumbered collateral. The creditor's secured debt would then be equal to the unencumbered

---

**2.** Secured credit also helps to protect against risky investments by the debtor. See Robert E. Scott, *The Truth About Se-* *cured Financing*, 82 Cornell L. Rev. 1436, 1447–1454 (1997).

portion ($8,000) and the remaining $2,000 claim would be unsecured. Second, as noted above, the value of the collateral could drop over time. As a result, if the collateral is worth only $8,000 at the time the creditor attempts to collect, the creditor would, again, have a secured claim of $8,000 and an unsecured claim of $2,000.

Even though the same creditor can have both a secured claim and an unsecured claim arising out of the same transaction, it is normal to refer to a creditor with a valid security interest as a **secured creditor** and a creditor without a valid security interest as an **unsecured creditor**. However, always keep in mind that a secured creditor may ultimately find some portion of his or her claim unsecured. In part, your job as a loan officer will be to take steps to avoid such a possibility.

## II. The Distinction Between Consensual and Non–Consensual Security Interests

As discussed above, the secured creditor is generally said to have obtained a ''security interest'' in the debtor's assets. The type of security interest referred to so far is a **consensual security interest**. This simply means that the debtor agrees by *contract* to give the secured creditor the security interest in the collateral. You might think of the creation of a consensual security interest as a transaction in which the debtor, in return for a loan or extension of credit, conveys to the secured creditor part of the group of rights that collectively constitute ownership of the collateral. Through a voluntary contract, the secured creditor receives the right to appropriate and sell the collateral if the debt is not paid or the debtor otherwise defaults.

It is possible, in some circumstances, for a creditor to obtain what is essentially the equivalent of a security interest by operation of law, without any agreement by the debtor. The creation of a non-consensual security interest can occur in a number of ways. While the focus of this Manual is generally on consensual security interests, it is important to have some understanding of non-consensual security interests. The reason it is important is that you may occasionally find the Bank, as the holder of a consensual security interest, in a priority conflict with the holders of one or more non-consensual security interests.

Non-consensual security interests are generally referred to as ''**liens**,'' and a creditor holding such a lien is referred to as a ''**lien creditor**.'' Non-consensual liens can be divided into two broad categories. The first category consists of **judicial liens** that arise during or upon completion of a legal action to establish or satisfy a debt. The debt may arise from a loan transaction, a sales transaction, or from a variety of other legal claims, including a tort action. The second category includes **common law** or **statutory liens** that arise automatically when a debt is created or a contracting party defaults in some fashion.

### A. Judicial Liens

There can be a substantial delay—sometimes years—between the time an unsecured creditor files suit on a loan contract and the time the unsecured creditor obtains a judgment confirming the debt. During this time the assets of the debtor, upon which the unsecured creditor is relying, may be dissipated. This can occur through gradual financial deterioration, or the debtor may take some intentional action to remove the assets from the creditor's reach in anticipation of the unsecured creditor obtaining a judgment. To protect against this dissipation or removal of the debtor's assets, state law permits an unsecured creditor, under certain (increasingly rare) circumstances, to obtain a pre-judgment **attachment lien** by applying to a court and asserting the reasons why the attachment lien is justified.

Traditionally some states had a general attachment lien provision that could be invoked whenever the unsecured creditor felt that the debtor's assets might be dissipated, regardless of the reason.[3] Most states still permit the judicial creation of a pre-judgment attachment lien if an unsecured creditor can present specific evidence that the debtor is about to conceal assets or place them beyond the reach of creditors. Finally, many states permit the judicial creation of an attachment lien if the debtor's assets are located in the jurisdiction in which the action is brought but the debtor is a citizen of another jurisdiction. Presumably, this type of lien, known as a **foreign attachment**, is based on an assumption that the debtor's local assets could easily be moved to another jurisdiction, making seizure more difficult.

The second type of lien arising out of the judicial process to establish or satisfy a debt is the **judgment lien**. This lien arises at the time a judgment against the debtor is appropriately recorded. The judgment lien exists in all jurisdictions, but in most states the judgment attaches only to the real property of the debtor located in the county in which the judgment is recorded. In a few states, the judgment lien attaches to the personal property of the debtor located in the county as well.

The final lien that arises out of the judicial process to establish or satisfy a debt is the **execution lien** or **lien by levy**. When an unsecured creditor with a final judgment wishes to seize the debtor's property so that it can be sold to satisfy the underlying debt, the unsecured creditor must obtain a document from the clerk of the court in which the judgment was obtained. The document must show that a valid judgment exists and set out the property to be seized. This document, generally known as a "**writ of execution**," is delivered to the sheriff of the county in which the property to be seized is located. The sheriff then proceeds to take control of the property, a process generally referred to as "**levy**." Taking control normally will consist of actual physical removal of the property.[4] However, depending on the nature of the property, it may also consist of posting a notice, disabling the property, or taking an inventory. In most jurisdictions, a lien arises in favor of the unsecured judgment creditor at the time of the actual levy by the sheriff. In a few states, the lien relates back to the time the writ of execution is delivered to the sheriff, so long as levy actually occurs.

## B.  Common Law or Statutory Liens

The second general category of non-consensual security interests or liens consists of **common law** or **statutory liens**. They are referred to as common law or statutory liens because, in the vast majority of cases, the current statutory liens are

---

**3.** In the last three decades, a number of these general prejudgment seizure statutes were attacked by debtors' attorneys as violations of the Constitution of the United States. Accordingly, the Legal Department should always be consulted before resorting to such a procedure.

**4.** Of course, most debtors have assets that are not tangible and so cannot be physically seized. Examples of such intangible assets include obligations of third parties to the debtor, such as the obligation of the debtor's employer to pay the debtor's wages or the obligation of the debtor's bank arising out of the debtor's bank deposits. The functional equivalent of a levy on such assets on behalf of a judgment creditor is normally possible, and the writ by which it is accomplished is usually called a writ of garnishment.

legislative versions of liens created at common law. Usually, the statutory version was enacted to permit actual sale of the property to which the lien attached (which was often not possible at common law), or to insert some consumer protection provisions for debtors that did not exist at common law. In a number of jurisdictions, courts have held that the enactment of a statutory version of the common law lien does not necessarily do away with the common law version, i.e., that both versions of the lien continue to exist in tandem.

Generally, these liens (which will be referred to simply as "statutory liens" for the sake of brevity) were created to protect certain types of unsecured creditors who might otherwise have difficulty collecting a debt. One typical type of statutory lien arises in favor of a person who supplies services to another. In contrast to the seller of goods, the supplier of services is not able to create a consensual security interest in what the seller is supplying, and the seller, therefore, arguably deserves the special protection of a lien arising by operation of law.

The most common form of this type of statutory lien is called a **mechanics' lien**.[5] Initially, this lien arose in favor of an individual who built or repaired a structure for another and had not yet been paid for these services. Because the individual's effort resulted in enhancement of the value of the structure that could not be easily recaptured, a lien on the property itself, for the value of the services performed, was automatically conferred on the individual. Eventually, the same lien was extended to a person who supplied materials that were incorporated into the structure, again on the theory that it would be difficult to reclaim such materials. This lien is often called a **materialman's lien**.

The same concept is now applied to the repair of other large items, particularly motor vehicles, with the development of the **garageman's lien**. However, the garageman's lien differs from the mechanic's or materialman's lien in that, normally, it only lasts as long as the garageman has possession of the vehicle. Similarly, in many jurisdictions, a landlord is given a lien on the tenant's furniture for unpaid rent and an attorney is given a lien on the client's papers for unpaid fees, but only so long as the landlord or the attorney maintains possession of the furniture or the papers, respectively. One could find perhaps hundreds of different possessory statutory liens in a survey of the states. Finally, in recent years, **agricultural liens** have assumed increasing importance in priority contests with consensual security interests. Agricultural liens are nonconsensual liens on the products produced by a farmer in favor of a person who either (i) furnishes goods or services to a debtor in connection with the debtor's farming operation or (ii) leases land to a debtor in connection with a farming operation.[6]

Four other rights of this type deserve specific mention because they frequently conflict with the rights of consensual secured creditors. Under certain circumstances, Article 2 of the Uniform Commercial Code (hereafter referred to as the "U.C.C". or the "Code"), which governs sales of goods, creates a right in goods in favor of the seller

---

**5.** For a good overview of mechanics' lien law see, Ethan Glass, *Old Statutes Never Die ... Nor Do They Fade Away: A Proposal For Modernizing Mechanics' Lien Law By Federal Action*, 27 Ohio N.U. L. Rev. 67. 67–78 (2000).

**6.** Indeed, the 1998 version of Article 9 of the Uniform Commercial Code emphasizes the importance of agricultural liens by subjecting them to many of the same requirements that are imposed on consensual security interests. See Section 9–102(a)(5).

when the seller discovers that the buyer of the goods is insolvent.[7] Likewise, Article 6 of the Code, which regulates bulk sales of inventory, creates a right, under certain circumstances, in the inventory transferred in a bulk sale. However, this right arises in favor of the creditors of the transferor, rather than the transferor himself or herself.[8] The third right is that of **set off**. As the name denotes, the right of set off arises when Party A owes a debt to Party B and Party B owes a return debt to Party A. You will undoubtedly have occasion to exercise this right, as it most commonly arises between a bank and one of its depositors. Suppose a customer establishes a deposit account with our Bank and later borrows a sum of money from the Bank. The customer owes a debt to the Bank equal to the sum borrowed, and the Bank owes a debt to the customer equal to the balance of the deposit account. Under the right of set off, if the customer fails to pay the loan when due, the Bank has the right, under common law, under contract, or under state statute, to reduce or set off its debt on the deposit account against the amount of the loan.

The fourth right deserving special mention is the **Federal Tax Lien**. By federal statute, a lien arises on all of a taxpayer's property upon the failure of the taxpayer to pay federal tax after assessment. Since federal law creates this lien, its provisions take precedence over state legislation like the U.C.C.[9] Similarly, states and political subdivisions of states generally have a statutory lien on all or certain assets of state taxpayers who fail to pay state or local tax assessments. The most common lien of this kind arises when a landowner fails to pay real estate taxes.

––––––

*At this point, recognizing that the manual material is hardly the most scintillating thing you have ever read, you put it aside for the day. Your thoughts turn to recreation, and you decided to pick up a pizza with "the works" and rent a video. The selection at the video rental outlet is limited, and your best option turns out to be a well-worn copy of the movie, "Brave Heart." One pizza, two beers, half a movie, and forty-five minutes later, you are asleep on your couch having the following dream:*

### Problem 1–1

#### The Dream

You find yourself in medieval Scotland, firmly in power as the head of all the Scottish clans. (You also look a lot like Mel Gibson, which is only a good thing if you are male). One day, four of your subjects—McBride, McShane, McTeague, and McLaughlin—come to you and ask you to resolve a dispute over a dozen sheep. It seems that nine of the sheep originally belonged to McShane. Six months ago, McShane was approached by another man, McDonald, who asked to buy the sheep. They agreed on a price of four gold pieces per sheep. McDonald had only half that amount on hand. McDonald, in fact, needed to shear and sell the wool from the sheep to raise

---

**7.** See Section 2–702.

**8.** See Section 6–104.

**9.** The Federal Tax Lien statute is included in your statutory supplement. See 26

U.S.C. §§ 6321–6323. Federal Tax Liens are discussed in more detail in Chapter 5, Section III B of this Manual.

the rest of the money. Accordingly, he and McShane agreed that McDonald would take the sheep to his farm and graze them until shearing season, at which time he would shear and sell the wool and pay McShane the balance of the purchase price. McShane insists, however, that McDonald specifically agreed that, until all was paid, "they were all still my sheep."

McDonald took the sheep to his own (somewhat barren) land and put them out to pasture. In a few weeks, three of the original sheep had lambs, bringing the total size of the herd to twelve. A few days later, McDonald's wealthy cousin McLaughlin visited the farm. McDonald asked McLaughlin for a loan of twenty-four gold pieces to enable him to buy additional food for the sheep. When McLaughlin balked initially, McDonald showed him his herd of sheep, and said, "Dinna ye worry, laddie. I can always sell yon sheep to pay you back." McLaughlin then made the loan.

Unfortunately, McDonald did not use McLaughlin's gold to buy animal feed. Instead, he spent it on whiskey and riotous living. The sheep survived, but they grew thin as time wore on and were soon worth no more than two gold pieces each. Ultimately, a farmer from the next glen, McBride, agreed to buy all twelve sheep at that price. McBride paid the purchase price and went home, intending to return with his sheep dogs the following day and drive the sheep home. That evening, however, McDonald took what was left of McLaughlin's and McBride's money, hopped in his wagon and fled to England, where he is still in hiding. In his haste and carelessness, he drove his wagon into McTeague's brother, who was returning home by the same road. McTeague's brother suffered serious injuries, but McDonald did not even slow down.

When McBride arrived at McDonald's farm the next day for the purpose of retrieving his sheep, he was met by McShane, McLaughlin, and McTeague. McShane had never been paid and claimed that the sheep were still his. McLaughlin claimed the sheep were necessary to satisfy his debt. McTeague claimed a right to sell the sheep to pay for his brother's treatment. McBride insisted he had just bought the sheep. Rather than settling their differences with sword and lance, the parties to the dispute have brought it to you. There is no law in Scotland. Or rather, your word is law in Scotland. To whom will you give the sheep? How will you explain the reasons for your decision?

––––––

*Upon awakening around midnight, you resolve never to consume an entire pizza with "the works" again, and you retire for the evening. Over coffee the following morning, you continue reading the manual excerpts attached to the letter from your new boss. Perhaps because reviewing for and taking the bar examination produced the "purge valve" memory so characteristic of practicing lawyers, the information contained in the operations manual does not seem as familiar as your boss anticipated. Today you read the following material:*

––––––

## BANK OF NEW BABYLON
## LOAN OFFICER TRAINING AND
## OPERATIONS MANUAL

## CHAPTER 1: INTRODUCTION

### III. The Development of Consensual Security Interests in Personal Property in the United States

#### A. Limitation to Personal Property

Property of a person has traditionally been divided into two broad categories: real property and personal property, or as the civil law systems more descriptively label them, immovables and movables. This Manual focuses on security interests in personal property, although it also includes some treatment of items of personal property that become permanently attached to real property (commonly known as "fixtures"). This focus on personal property financing should not be interpreted as a suggestion that security interests in real property are economically unimportant. On the contrary, real property is a major source of collateral to secure loans in this country, and real estate financing is an important part of the business of the Bank and its affiliates. However, separate treatment of real property and personal property financing reflects the fact that, historically, the law relating to real property security has been more localized than the law relating to security interests in personal property. This probably is a result of the greater mobility of personal property and the fact that transactions involving the sale and purchase of personal property, the setting in which many early financing and security devices arose, were more likely to be interstate transactions than the sale and purchase of real property. Hence, there was a greater drive for uniformity in laws relating to security interests in personal property than in laws relating to similar interests in real property, which remain to this day somewhat idiosyncratic by state. This desire for uniformity in the laws relating to security interests in personal property was part of the reason for the adoption of the U.C.C., which contains an article (specifically, Article 9) devoted to security interests in personal property.

#### B. Pre–Code Security Devices

At the outset, you need some basic knowledge of the security devices that preceded the U.C.C., both because such knowledge sheds some light on the U.C.C. itself and because the pre-Code devices are still occasionally used. While personal property is useful as a broad category, it includes many different types of assets, ranging from tangible property (like a ring), through intangible property represented by a document (like a debt represented by a note), to intangible property not represented by a document (like accounts receivable).[10] Not surprisingly, the earliest types of

---

**10.** While both a note and an account are, at bottom, intangible rights to payment, they differ in the degree to which they are embodied by a tangible document. A note so completely represents the underlying right to payment that proper endorsement and physical delivery of the note actu-ally transfers ownership of the underlying debt. An account is one step further toward intangibility, for, although there may be a written record of an account, physical delivery of that written record does not transfer ownership of the account.

security devices involved tangible property. New devices were developed, first at common law and then by statute, as debtors and creditors sought to use as collateral all of the different types of assets the debtor had available.

The earliest security device was the **pledge**. As the name implies, the creditor took possession of the collateral until the loan the creditor had extended was repaid. In its earliest form, the pledge only gave the creditor the right to hold the property. Later the creditor acquired a right to sell the collateral and use the proceeds to pay the debt. The disadvantage of the pledge was that it could only be used if the debtor had no need to retain possession of the collateral during the repayment period. If the collateral was a piece of equipment necessary to the production of goods that, in turn, were to be sold to pay off the loan, the pledge was an unworkable security device.

To meet the need for a non-possessory security device, creditors developed the **chattel mortgage**. (The term "chattel" refers to an item of personal property.) The chattel mortgage was based on the concept of the real estate mortgage, which is also a non-possessory security device. When first used, the chattel mortgage ran afoul of long-standing statutes known as **fraudulent conveyance statutes**. As interpreted at the time, fraudulent conveyance statutes prohibited the retention of collateral by a debtor on the theory that it would tend to mislead subsequent third parties who dealt with the debtor into believing that the debtor had more assets than the debtor really had. Upon the basis of such erroneous belief, the third parties might enter into transactions with the debtor (e.g., sales or loans) that they would have avoided if accurately apprised of the debtor's true asset pool. This potential for misleading creditors through the separation of ownership rights and possession is often referred to as the problem of **ostensible ownership**. To overcome the initial resistance to chattel mortgages, state legislatures passed special statutes that validated the chattel mortgage as a security device. The usual solution to the problem of ostensible ownership created by the chattel mortgage was to require some type of public recordation of the chattel mortgage as a condition of its effectiveness against third parties.

While the chattel mortgage was a substantial breakthrough, it became clear that specialized security devices were needed to cover certain types of transactions or certain types of collateral. The first of the special devices that emerged was designed to facilitate the extension of credit in the sale of goods. The device, known as the **conditional sale**, consisted essentially of a contract clause providing that ownership of the goods sold did not pass until the full purchase price was paid. A variation on this approach was the **bailment lease**, which restricted the buyer to a leasehold interest in the goods until the purchase price was paid and the "true" sale took place.

While the conditional sale and bailment lease were well suited to individual sales of large items of equipment, or even to individual sales of consumer goods, they did not provide a way to use business inventory as collateral, since inventory was (and is) normally a constantly changing mass. Three different devices arose to meet the need for a more flexible inventory security device. The first was the **trust receipt,** an adaptation of the law of trusts. The seller of inventory would technically sell it to the lender financing the sale, who would, in turn, "entrust" the inventory to the real debtor. The debtor would sign a trust receipt in favor of the lender and take possession of the inventory.

As an alternative, a practice called **field warehousing** was available. Under a field warehousing arrangement, inventory sold to the debtor and financed by the debtor's lender was delivered to an area that was located on the debtor's premises but separated from the general selling area. The lender would hire an individual to control the separate area. At least in theory, the debtor could not get the inventory out of the field warehouse until a resale had been arranged and the debtor was able to repay a proportionate part of the credit extended by the lender.

When the debtor already owned inventory and wanted to use it as collateral for a new loan, a device known as a **factor's lien** could be used. The debtor subject to a factor's lien was normally a manufacturer of goods. A broker or a commission merchant, who was in the business of distributing the manufacturer's products, would advance funds to the manufacturer and take possession of some of the manufacturer's goods for the purpose of sale to third parties. The advances were secured by a pledge by the manufacturer to the broker or commission merchant of the inventory held for resale. Most states had factor's lien statutes expressly validating this arrangement as a form of security interest. The factor's lien ultimately evolved so that the lien attached not only to the goods in question but also to the accounts receivable generated by their resale.

The final special commercial need was for devices that would allow a debtor to use accounts receivable as direct collateral for loans. Historically, this was initially accomplished by assignment of the accounts receivable to the lender at the time of the loan, notification of the assignment to the parties that owed the accounts (the "account debtors") and direct payment by the account debtors to the lender. In the 1930s, creditors sought an alternative method that would allow the use of the accounts as collateral without notification to the account debtors. Ultimately, state legislatures passed specific statutes to permit such arrangements.

As can be seen from the brief overview set out above, pre-Code history was marked by the parallel evolution of a variety of different security devices. This resulted in three major problems. First, if a particular type of asset did not fall into one of the established categories for which there was a security device, there was no general way to create a security interest in it. Second, within each state, the various devices had different requirements, leading to substantial confusion as to what was required to ensure an effective security interest. If a secured creditor "guessed wrong" and mischaracterized the transaction in the eyes of a subsequent reviewing court, the secured creditor's security interest might ultimately prove ineffective. Third, while there were some attempts to promote uniformity, security devices in one state differed from security devices for the same type of collateral in another state. These differences created enormous confusion in interstate transactions. It was in this context that the idea for the U.C.C. was born.

## C.   The Advent of Article 9 of the Code

There were some early attempts to promote uniformity from state to state in the enactment of statutes authorizing specific security devices. To the extent uniformity was achieved, it was largely due to the efforts of the National Conference of Commissioners on Uniform State Laws (NCCUSL), established in 1896. The NCCUSL commissioned the drafting of a number of uniform laws, which were then submitted to each state legislature for adoption. Its first project, the Uniform Negotiable Instruments

Law, drafted in 1896, was ultimately adopted in every state. The NCCUSL experienced similar success with the Uniform Warehouse Receipts Act. However, a number of other uniform laws, including the Uniform Conditional Sales Act, were adopted by substantially less than all the states.

By the 1930s, even the uniform laws that had been generally adopted had become outmoded due to the enormous increase in commercial activity within and between the states. In 1940, William A. Schnader, a Philadelphia lawyer and President of the NCCUSL, suggested that a comprehensive commercial code be developed for adoption by all the states. Mr. Schnader enlisted the aid of Professor Karl N. Llewellyn, then at Columbia Law School, to work on the project, which was approved by the NCCUSL. Progress was initially somewhat slow because of the Second World War. In 1944, the effort received a significant boost when the American Law Institute (ALI), a prestigious organization of practicing lawyers, judges, and academics concerned with organizing and clearly articulating the law, agreed to co-sponsor the project. Professor Llewellyn was named the "Chief Reporter" and an editorial board was formed. The Code was to be divided into a number of Articles, each dealing with a given substantive area of commercial law. Principal drafters of each article were also appointed. The individuals chosen to draft the Article on security interests in personal property were Allison Dunham and Grant Gilmore.

The first Official Draft of the Code was promulgated in 1952 and adopted by Pennsylvania in 1953. New York began to study the Code in 1953, and, in 1955, its State Law Revision Commission concluded that the concept of a uniform code was a promising one, but that extensive revisions were required before New York should adopt the Code. Because New York was then the commercial center of the United States, New York's adoption of the Code was considered crucial to its success. Therefore, the sponsoring organizations made substantial revisions, and a new Official Draft was promulgated in 1957. Minor additional changes were made in 1958 and 1962. It was the last of these official versions that New York adopted in 1962, assuring the Code's success. By 1968, the U.C.C. had been adopted by 49 states, the District of Columbia and the Virgin Islands. The only state at that time not to adopt all of the articles of the Code was Louisiana.

As initially drafted, the U.C.C. had nine substantive Articles. In recent years, two new Articles, Article 2A (covering leases of personal property) and Article 4A (covering fund transfers), have been added.[11] Article 1 contains general provisions applicable to each of the other Articles.[12] Articles 2 through 9 cover specific areas of commercial law. Secured Transactions, which is the subject matter covered by this Manual, is Article 9.

**11.** Efforts to supplement the U.C.C. with another new article, Article 2B on information licensing, proved unsuccessful. While drafting of the new article was completed, it received the support of only one of the sponsoring organizations, the NCCUSL. In the absence of ALI support, proposed Article 2B was not added to the Official Text of the Code. It survives as proposed uniform legislation sponsored by NCCUSL alone and is now known as the Uniform Computer Information Transactions Act.

**12.** NCCUSL and the ALI promulgated a revised version of Article 1 in 2001. As of June 2003, the revised version has been adopted in Minnesota, Texas, Virginia, and the Virgin Islands and has been introduced in the California, Connecticut, Hawaii, Illinois, Massachusetts, North Dakota, and Oklahoma legislatures. Since it is likely that there will be wide adoption of the revised Article 1, parallel citations are provided in these materials. The revised version will be cited as "Rev. Section 1-___."

One of the other major innovations of the Code was the establishment of a Permanent Editorial Board (PEB) to ensure that the text and interpretation of the Code would evolve in a uniform fashion. Over the years, the PEB has proposed a number of additions and amendments to the Official Text. There have also been complete revisions of various articles. One of the most extensive and successful was the general revision of Article 9 in 1998.[13]

You should be aware that the Code in general and Article 9 in particular have never been either comprehensive or completely uniform among the states. For example, as noted earlier, Article 9 does not cover the creation of mortgages on real property. Indeed, no Code article is devoted to that subject, and real estate law is still largely local. Even when the Code purports to cover a particular transaction, it may not contain provisions dealing with every issue that may arise. The Code, in fact, presupposes the common law of contracts as a background, and Section 1–103[14] provides that "unless displaced by the particular provisions of this Act, the principles of law and equity . . . shall supplement its provisions."

Further, because the Code is state law, non-uniform changes in the Official Text have been introduced at the time of adoption by various state legislatures. In addition, the courts of different states have not always interpreted the same Code language consistently.

Notwithstanding these potential (and perhaps inevitable) impediments to uniformity, promotion of uniformity in state law was and is one of the Code's principal goals.[15] As part of the effort to avoid non-uniform judicial interpretation, the drafters and sponsors of the Code have supplied a number of interpretive aids that promote uniformity. Article 1 includes a set of definitional sections applicable to all the Code articles,[16] and Article 9, in particular, has its own extensive set of definitions for critical terms.[17] In addition, the drafters of the Code and its successive revisions have included a set of **Official Comments** to the Code. Courts have generally given the official comments great deference. Finally, in recent years, the PEB has issued new commentaries on specific Code sections, usually in response to recurring problems of interpretation. Both the Official Comments and the PEB commentaries can be extremely helpful and should be consulted when considering particular sections of Article 9. However, one must always remember that only the language of the relevant code section itself has actually been enacted by the state legislature.

## IV. Bankruptcy and Secured Transactions

### A. Overview

In the course of your employment with the Bank, you will encounter customers of varying degrees of financial strength and responsibility. Part of your job is to ensure that our borrowers avoid incurring a debt burden that disables them from repaying the

**13.** The Drafting Committee had suggested July 1, 2001 as the proposed effective date for the revised Article 9 in each of the states. Most states met this guideline with the balance providing effective dates between July 1, 2001 and January 1, 2002. All references in these materials are to the 1998 version of Article 9 unless indicated otherwise.

**14.** Rev. Section 1–103(b).

**15.** See Section 1–102(2)(c) and Rev. Section 1–103(a)(3).

**16.** See Section 1–201 and Rev. Sections 1–201–1–205.

**17.** See Section 9–102.

Bank's loan, or at least to ensure that the Bank is repaid before such a slide into financial distress becomes too advanced. Of course, because of mistakes or occasional instances of customer deception or misconduct, some of our borrowers find themselves saddled with a level of debt they simply cannot service. One of the options for such an overburdened debtor is to seek protection under the federal bankruptcy law known as the **Bankruptcy Code**.[18] The Bankruptcy Code interacts with state law on secured transactions in two ways. First, in the context of resolution of a bankruptcy proceeding, an interpretation of Article 9 may be required. Hence, some of the cases interpreting Article 9 will be bankruptcy cases using bankruptcy vocabulary and concepts. Second, as federal law, the Bankruptcy Code provisions preempt Article 9 of the Code to the extent the two statutes are inconsistent. As a result, the rights of a secured creditor as set forth under the U.C.C. may be altered if the debtor enters bankruptcy.[19]

The Bankruptcy Code offers a debtor two alternative responses to his or her financial difficulties. The first, **liquidation**, is the approach that most people think of when bankruptcy is mentioned. In bankruptcy liquidation, all of the debtor's assets, other than those exempt from seizure, are taken over by the bankruptcy court. The court liquidates them, pays secured creditors to the extent of the value of their security, pays the administrative expenses of the bankruptcy proceeding, and then pays unsecured creditors a pro rata share of whatever is left (usually little or nothing). The individual debtor, but not a corporate debtor,[20] is then, with some limited exceptions, discharged from further obligation on those debts. This has the effect of protecting the debtor's future earnings from pre-bankruptcy creditors.

The second approach is **reorganization** or **rehabilitation**. Under this approach, the debtor's assets are not liquidated. Rather, the debtor's creditors are held at bay while the debtor attempts to devise a plan that will, over time, repay the unsecured creditors more than they would have received if liquidation had occurred. If the plan is successful, the debtor emerges from the reorganization having satisfied existing debts (though, perhaps, at some reduced rate) and with all or a portion of its assets intact. In effect, the debtor is "buying back" his or her assets from the creditors (for whose benefit the assets would otherwise be liquidated) through payments under the plan out of the debtor's future earnings. Depending on the type of debtor and the particular type of reorganization proceeding, the debtor is discharged from any further liability for the unpaid portions of the original debts either upon court approval of the plan or once the plan is completed.

The Bankruptcy Code is divided into eight chapters: 1, 3, 5, 7, 9, 11, 12, and 13. Chapters 1, 3 and 5 of the Bankruptcy Code contain general provisions applicable to both liquidation and reorganization proceedings. Chapter 7 contains the provisions specifically applicable to liquidation proceedings whether they involve an individual or a business. Chapter 11 covers rehabilitation of business entities and Chapter 13 covers rehabilitation of individuals. As a result, most people refer to a liquidation proceeding as a "Chapter 7" and a reorganization proceeding as a "Chapter 11" or "13"

---

**18.** [The Bankruptcy Code is reprinted in your statutory supplement.]

**19.** Some of these effects are discussed in Chapter 5, Section VI of this Manual.

**20.** This corporate debtor simply goes out of existence.

depending on the type of debtor involved. Chapter 9 covers municipal bankruptcy and Chapter 12 regulates the bankruptcy of family farmers.

## B.   Bankruptcy Functionaries

The Bankruptcy Code authorizes the appointment of a particularly significant court officer known as the "**trustee**." The appointment of a trustee is routine in a liquidation case and a reorganization case involving an individual. In a business reorganization case, the debtor initially assumes the role of the trustee (in which role the debtor is referred to as the "**debtor in possession**"), although there are circumstances even in reorganization cases in which a trustee independent of the debtor may be appointed. The trustee oversees the affairs of the debtor and technically assumes possession of all of the debtor's assets. In a liquidation case, the trustee also attempts to enlarge the size of the asset pool ultimately available for distribution to unsecured creditors. To accomplish this goal, the trustee is given certain powers to avoid some asset transfers made by the debtor prior to filing in bankruptcy. The transfers can include gifts or sales of assets by the debtor, but the concept of a "transfer" under the Bankruptcy Code also includes the transfer of a security interest in property by the debtor to a secured creditor.

While the trustee has a number of "avoiding powers," one in particular deserves mention at this point. Under Section 544(a) of the Bankruptcy Code, the trustee is automatically given the status of a hypothetical creditor holding an execution lien created by levy on all of the debtor's personal property as of the date of the filing in bankruptcy. In Article 9 vernacular, the trustee becomes a "lien creditor" as of the filing date. As will be discussed in detail later, under certain defined circumstances, a lien creditor may have a claim to the collateral that is superior to that of the holder of a consensual Article 9 security interest. The trustee in bankruptcy is perhaps the most common, and the most effective, beneficiary of that special priority.

Two other bankruptcy officials also deserve brief mention. The first is the **bankruptcy judge**. Specialized federal bankruptcy courts, presided over by a bankruptcy judges, handle most bankruptcy matters. Bankruptcy judges are federal appointees but do not have the lifetime tenure given federal district court or circuit court judges. The other official is the **U.S. Trustee** who carries out administrative duties during the bankruptcy process, including the appointment of trustees in the appropriate types of cases.

––––––––

*It is you first day at work and you are feeling a little out of sorts. Lisa Sanchez, the Manager of Human Resources for the Bank of New Babylon, had been helpful. You filled out all of the remaining paperwork, got a tour of the Legal Department, and you are now ensconced in your office. You are pleased that there is a window and the computer appears to be new. The major problem is that you do not know what to do now. On the one hand you do not want to call attention to yourself, and on the other, you figure that if you do not find some work to do, they might figure out that they really do not need you. It occurs to you, however, that you never finished reading the attachments to Jane Robinson's letter, and so you take up the following:*

**BANK OF NEW BABYLON
LOAN OFFICER TRAINING AND
OPERATIONS MANUAL**

## CHAPTER 1: INTRODUCTION

## V. Some Basic Article 9 Concepts

### A. An Overview of the Structure of Article 9

While your job as a loan officer does not require a level of Article 9 expertise equivalent to a member of the Legal Department, you cannot do your job successfully without a basic understanding of Article 9 concepts and rules. For your purposes, there are five basic questions which Article 9 addresses:

1. What transactions does Article 9 cover? This question of scope is addressed principally in Sections 9–109 and 9–110.

2. If Article 9 covers a transaction, how does one structure the transaction so that it creates a security interest in the desired collateral that will be enforceable against the debtor? In Article 9 jargon, the process of creating such a security interest is known as **attachment** of the security interest. The requirements for attachment are addressed in Subpart 1 of Part 2 of Article 9, of which the most important provision is Section 9–203.

3. Assuming a secured party's[21] security interest has attached to collateral, (a) is it necessary for the secured party to take additional steps to give notice of the security interest to third parties? And (b) if so, what steps are required? In Article 9 jargon, answers to these questions provide the requirements for **perfection** of the security interest. Those requirements are found primarily in Subpart 2 of Part 3 and Part 5 of Article 9.

4. Once a secured party has a security interest in particular collateral, is the secured party's claim superior or subordinate to those of other parties who assert claims to the same collateral? (In Article 9 jargon, one who answered this question would be determining the secured party's **priority**.) Article 9 addresses questions of priority primarily in Subparts 3 and 4 of Part 3.

5. If the debtor defaults on the loan obligation, what remedies does the secured party have against the debtor? Conversely, what protections, if any does Article 9 afford the defaulting debtor? The answers to these questions are found in Part 6 of Article 9.

Most of these questions are discussed in detail later in this Manual. However, at the outset, there are three aspects of Article 9 that require introductory discussion because familiarity with them will be helpful in orienting you as you consider Article 9 further.

---

**21.** Article 9 uses the term "secured party" rather than "secured creditor," but the use of the latter term is at least as common in both banking and legal circles. The terms "secured party" and "secured creditor" are used interchangeably in this Manual.

## B. Article 9 Definitions

In many cases, Article 9 has its own specialized vocabulary and, in other cases, words that have a common general meaning have a peculiar meaning in Article 9. Section 9–102 contains 80 definitions that apply to all of Article 9, and there are, in addition, a number of other Code sections containing their own section-specific definitions.[22] In addition Article 1 of the Code, in Section 1–201, contains general definitions that are applicable to all of the articles of the Code, including Article 9. An understanding of these definitions, and the ability to resort to them when necessary, is indispensable in working with Article 9 and the transactions within its scope.

One of the best examples of the Article 9 scheme of definitions can be found in the words used to describe various types of collateral. These terms will prove critical later in analyzing questions of attachment, perfection and priority, and it is important that you begin developing a facility with them immediately. To that end, the Bank has devised a pair of exercises as part of your training. Immediately below you will find two scenarios. The first is a particularly poignant homespun illustration that originally appeared in the Operations Manual of our recent rural acquisition, the Bovine State Bank. The second is derived from the Bank of New Babylon's experience with a small furniture business for which the Bank provided financing. Consider the following two scenarios and determine what term in the Article 9 vocabulary is appropriate for each type of collateral:

### Scenario 1

Suppose a Manufacturer produces both liquid hand soap and special patented dispensers to hold it. The Manufacturer sells both soap and dispensers to a Retailer, who resells the soap and dispensers as well as other products. A number of people buy the soap and dispensers from Retailer. One is Building Owner, who installs the dispensers and soap in restrooms in one of his commercial office buildings. Another is Dairy Farmer, who puts the dispensers in his barn and uses the soap to clean his cows' udders. Still another is Ordinary Joe, who puts the soap and dispenser in the sink in his home tool shed, where he cleans the fish he catches on weekends.

Suppose further that the Bank loans money to all these people and wants to take a security interest in everything each of them has, including the soap and dispensers. The soap and dispensers are movable and so qualify as goods under Section 9–102(a)(44) in the hands of any of these people. But what type of goods they are varies depending upon which of these individuals we are considering. Make a list of the borrowers and specify the Article 9 term that would be used to describe the soap and dispensers as collateral for a loan to each borrower.

### Scenario 2

Furniture Store sells various pieces of furniture to customers on credit. Thereafter, Furniture Store decides that it wants to obtain a loan from the Bank and use as collateral the debts owed to Furniture Store by the various buyers.

---

**22.**   See e.g. Section 9–307(a).

How would you classify this collection of debts, assuming they are in the following forms:

a. Furniture Store does not have any of the buyers sign any documents. It simply bills the buyers each month for a portion of the debt.

b. Furniture Store has each buyer sign a "promissory note" for each buyer's debt. Each note spells out the agreed interest rate and when the payments must be made.

c. Furniture Store has each buyer sign a "retail sales agreement." The retail sales agreement contains language that recites the debt, the agreed interest rate, and the payment terms. It also has language creating a security interest in the piece of furniture purchased on credit.

Specify the term Article 9 uses to describe the collateral in each of these three cases.

The answers to the questions posed in both scenarios can be found by reading the following sections of Article 9:

§ 9–102(a)(2)      § 9–102(a)(11)      § 9–102(a)(23)      § 9–102(a)(33)

§ 9–102(a)(34)      § 9–102(a)(47)      § 9–102(a)(48)      § 9–102(a)(65)

Once you have completed the exercise in writing, ask your supervisor for the answer sheet and compare it with your answers. In the event of discrepancies between the answer sheet and your answers, review the Code sections listed above again and try to ascertain the reason for your mistakes. If you are unable to do so, schedule a meeting with your supervisor and ask for an explanation.

## C. A Brief Survey of Three Critical Article 9 Concepts

Most of the borrowers for whom you will act as a loan officer will probably meet their obligations in a timely fashion. A few will not. In some instances, customers who default on their obligations will be indebted to lenders or creditors in addition to the Bank. When that happens, if there is not sufficient value in the collateral to satisfy all such claims, there will be a conflict between two or more persons or entities (including the Bank) over the order in which the claimants can appropriate the debtor's property and liquidate it to satisfy their respective claims. That order is referred to in Article 9 as the relative **priority** of the claimants.

The relative priority of two such claimants may not be important if the value of the property at issue is sufficient to satisfy both claims. However, you will soon learn that defaults tend to occur in situations in which this is not the case. Thus, if Secured Party A is prior to Secured Party B with respect to particular collateral, and the value of the collateral is less than the sum of the secured claims, Secured Party A will satisfy his or her claim in full out of the proceeds of the sale of the collateral before Secured Party B receives anything. Secured Party B may be entitled to the remaining proceeds (if any), but his or her claim will turn out to be at least partially unsecured and, in all likelihood, uncollectible. It is therefore your job to ensure that the Bank has the highest possible priority. A brief review at this point, of some of the most common determinants of Article 9 priorities will help you understand what is at stake and how to obtain priority for the Bank's security interest.

In general, under Article 9, the priority of a particular claimant turns on whether a security interest has "attached" to the collateral, whether that attached security interest has been "perfected," and the timing of the events and actions resulting in attachment and perfection in relation to the time at which the interests of rival claimants arose.

Some of the easiest priority disputes are those in which a purported secured party fails to fulfill the requirements for "attachment." As noted earlier, **Attachment** is the term used in Article 9 to indicate that the creditor's security interest has become enforceable against a particular debtor and the collateral the debtor has committed to secure a loan or extension of credit. A creditor who fails to follow the Article 9 requirements for attachment[23] will be treated as an unsecured creditor with no claim to the collateral. Unless such a creditor follows the rather time-consuming process necessary to become a judicial lien creditor or execution lien creditor, his or her claim to the "collateral" is not even superior to the debtor's. *A fortiori*, it will be subordinate to a true secured party whose interest **is** superior to the debtor's.

Other priority disputes depend on the concept of perfection, or, more precisely, on the fact and timing of perfection. **Perfection**, as the term is used in Article 9, refers to the additional steps, if any, a secured party must take to strengthen his or her rights so they are superior to potential claimants other than the debtor. These rival claimants may include unpaid sellers of the collateral, judgment creditors, rival secured creditors, or buyers of the collateral. The most common form of perfection is the filing of a notice of a security interest in specific public records. This notice is referred to in Article 9 as a **financing statement**. In many cases, a secured party also has the option of perfecting his or her security interest by **taking possession** of the collateral or **having control** of the collateral, since possession or control also normally has the effect of giving at least constructive notice to third parties that the secured party has a claim to the debtor's property. In a very limited number of circumstances, a security interest is perfected without taking any steps beyond attachment. This is known as **automatic perfection**.

A secured party that has perfected his or her security interest by one of these methods is known as a **perfected secured party**, and the security interest is known as a **perfected security interest**. A secured party who has failed to perfect is, not surprisingly, referred to as an **unperfected secured party** and the security interest is known as an **unperfected security interest**. To encourage secured parties to give this constructive notice by filing a financing statement or taking possession or control of the collateral, Article 9 generally gives a perfected secured party priority over an unperfected secured party as well as a variety of other rival claimants.

The combined significance of these concepts of attachment and perfection is that, for purposes of Article 9, a creditor's status normally falls into one of three categories. The first, and lowest, is that of an unsecured creditor. The second is that of an unperfected secured party, and the third, and highest, is that of a perfected secured party. In general, priority is initially dependent on which status the creditor

---

**23.** In general, attachment occurs when value has been given (usually through a loan or other extension of credit); when the debtor has rights in the collateral or, at least, the power to transfer rights to it; and either the debtor has signed a proper security agreement or the secured party has taken possession of the collateral or the secured party has "control" over the collateral. See Section 9–203. All of these requirements will be discussed in more detail in Chapter 3 of this Manual.

holds. The higher the status a creditor has, the higher the priority and the higher the claim to the collateral. Within the class of unsecured creditors, claims are treated proportionally in bankruptcy cases and according to a "race of diligence" in effecting a levy outside the bankruptcy context. In the unlikely event there are multiple unperfected secured parties, they rank in order of attachment. Unperfected secured parties are generally subordinate to perfected secured parties (as well as a variety of other potential claimants, including lien creditors). Within a class of multiple perfected secured parties, generally priority is based on when the steps necessary to achieve that status are taken.[24]

Examples of the some of the priority rules under Article 9 should be helpful at this point.

1. Debtor borrows money from BNB and agrees to give BNB a security interest in a piece of machinery as security for the loan. Because of an error by BNB (e.g., the failure to have the Debtor sign a security agreement), the requirements under Article 9 for attachment of a security interest are not met. BNB also fails to take the steps necessary to perfect the security interest. Debtor thereafter borrows money from Second Bank and agrees to give Second Bank a security interest in the same piece of machinery. Second Bank meets the requirements under Article 9 for its security interest to attach but takes no steps to perfect its security interest. Debtor fails to pay either BNB or Second Bank. Under Article 9, BNB is an unsecured party while Second Bank has an unperfected security interest in the machinery. BNB has no direct claim to the collateral at all, as it has not taken the steps an unsecured creditor must take to become a nonconsensual lien creditor and its attempt to create a consensual security interest has failed.[25] Second Bank, however, can have the machinery sold to satisfy its debt, since even attachment gives Second Bank rights superior to the Debtor in default.[26] In practice, this form of dispute is quite rare.

2. Assume the same facts as in Example 1, except that BNB properly meets the requirements under Article 9 for attachment of its security interest. This would be a true priority dispute among secured creditors, in that both BNB and Second Bank have unperfected security interests in the same machinery. Assuming that the value of the machinery is not sufficient to pay the full debt of both claimants, the Article 9 priority rule between two or more unperfected secured parties is that the first party to achieve attachment of its security interest has priority.[27] Hence, BNB has the initial right to liquidate the machinery to pay off its debt. Note that Second Bank would be entitled to the remaining balance of the collateral value to pay its claim and would have an

**24.** You should take this statement only as a crude generalization. There are many nuances to the timing issue as well as outright exceptions to the general "first in time" rule. These complications will be discussed in detail later in this Manual.

**25.** This, in actuality, is not an Article 9 priority issue since there is only one party that can claim an interest in the machinery.

**26.** This result follows from Section 9–203 and the general rule of Section 9–201(a)

that a security interest is enforceable against the Debtor and rival claimants unless the Code provides otherwise. In this (admittedly rare) case, nothing in the Code "provides otherwise." More commonly, however, the Code does "provide otherwise" with respect to unperfected security interests, as the remaining examples will show.

**27.** This priority rule can be found in Section 9–322(a)(3).

unsecured claim against Debtor for the balance of the debt not paid from the proceeds of the machinery. As a practical matter, it is quite unlikely that a dispute between secured parties would proceed to litigation with neither party perfected.

3.  Debtor borrows money from BNB and agrees to give BNB a security interest in a piece of machinery as security for the loan. BNB properly meets all of the requirements under Article 9 for attachment of its security interest. BNB either does not take the steps necessary to perfect the security interest or errs in its attempt to take them. Debtor thereafter borrows money from Second Bank and agrees to give Second Bank a security interest in the same piece of machinery. Second Bank meets the requirements under Article 9 for its security interest to attach and, the same day, takes the required steps under Article 9 to perfect its security interest. Debtor fails to pay either BNB or Second Bank. BNB has an unperfected security interest and Second Bank has a perfected security interest. Since Second Bank has higher status it would have priority over BNB even though BNB's security interest was the first to attach.[28] Hence, Second Bank has the initial right to appropriate the value of the machinery to pay off its debt. Note that BNB would be entitled to the balance of the collateral value to pay its claim and would have an unsecured claim against Debtor for any balance of its debt not retired by appropriation of the residual collateral value.

4.  Assume the same facts as in Example 3, but add the fact that, after Second Bank's security interest attached and was perfected, Tort Claimant obtained a judgment against Debtor. Tort Claimant then had the sheriff levy on (seize) the machinery, thereby giving Tort Claimant a judicial lien on the machinery and further giving Tort Claimant the status of a "lien creditor" under Article 9.[29] Under Article 9, lien creditors have priority over unperfected secured parties, but are subordinate to perfected secured parties.[30] Hence, Second Bank, as a perfected secured party, has the initial right to appropriate the value of the machinery to pay off its debt. Tort Claimant has the second priority claim to the machinery to pay off his or her debt. BNB, as an unperfected secured party and thus subordinate to a lien creditor, would have the third priority claim.[31]

---

**28.** This priority rule can be found at Section 9–322(a)(2).

**29.** The definition of a lien creditor can be found at Section 9–102(a)(52).

**30.** This priority rule can be found at Section 9–317(a)(2)(A).

**31.** The Article 9 rule that subordinates an unperfected secured creditor to a lien creditor acquires special significance if the Debtor files for protection under the federal Bankruptcy Code. As noted earlier in this Manual, Section 544(a) of the Bankruptcy Code gives the Trustee in Bankruptcy the powers of a perfect hypothetical lien creditor as of the commencement of the bankruptcy case. Thus, in example 4, even if there had been no Tort Claimant and no actual levy by a sheriff, if the Debtor filed in bankruptcy before BNB had taken the steps necessary for perfection, the Trustee in the Debtor's case would take priority over BNB. Since the Trustee in Bankruptcy, with some exceptions, is subordinate to perfected secured creditors, the order of priority example 4 would put Second Bank in the first position, the Trustee in the second position, and BNB last, effectively reduced to an unsecured creditor. As the Trustee collects on behalf of all unsecured creditors, BNB would share with pro rata with them in whatever remained for the Trustee after Second Bank's claim was paid out of the collateral proceeds.

5. Assume the same facts as in Example 3, except that on the same day BNB's security interest attached, BNB took the steps necessary to perfect its security interest. In this example, both BNB and Second Bank are perfected secured parties. Under Article 9, if there is a priority dispute between two perfected secured parties, the secured party that first took the steps necessary for perfection (i.e. filed a financing statement, or took possession or control of the collateral[32]) has first claim to the value of the machinery.[33] Hence, BNB has the initial right to sell the machinery to pay off its debt. Note that Second Bank would be entitled to the balance of the collateral value to pay its claim and would have an unsecured claim against Debtor for the balance of the debt not retired by the sale of the machinery.

The unfavorable outcomes of Examples 1, 3 and 4 should make it obvious why a critical part of your duties is to ensure that the Bank obtains a security interest, that the security interest properly attaches, and that it is properly perfected. The Legal Department is available to help with any questions you might have regarding these issues.

## D.  Consumer Transactions

The majority of the lending that you will approve and supervise will involve business borrowers. However, because BNB provides a range of retail banking services, you will encounter **consumer transactions**[34] on occasion. Consumer transactions can complicate your job as a loan officer in at least two ways. First, Article 9 contains a number of provisions that apply specifically to consumer transactions and that are protective in nature. The basis for these provisions is an assumption that consumers are generally less sophisticated borrowers and lack detailed knowledge of lending practices and the technical requirements of Article 9. As a result, if you are involved in a consumer transaction, you must be aware that special rules may apply and make sure you follow them carefully.[35]

Second, you will occasionally find an Article 9 provision that states a rule and then expressly confines it to transactions other than consumer transactions. The effect, where no separate rule is expressly provided for consumer transactions, is to leave it entirely unclear what the rule would be in a consumer transaction. Section 9–626 is a particularly good example of this somewhat puzzling approach to statutory draftsmanship. This approach resulted from a compromise reached between consumer advocates and lender advocates involved in the drafting process at the time of the 1998 revision of Article 9. The consumer advocates had proposed a number of additional protective provisions for consumer transactions that the lender advocates found

---

**32.** If either security interest is entitled to automatic perfection, the attachment of the security interest in question is equivalent to taking the necessary steps for perfection.

**33.** This priority rule can be found at Section 9–322(a)(1). Note the language "in time of filing or perfection." The significance of the words "of filing" will be discussed in detail later in this Manual.

**34.** Article 9 defines a consumer transaction in Section 9–102(a)(26) as a "trans-

action in which (i) an individual incurs an obligation primarily for personal, family, household purposes, (ii) a security interest secures the obligation, and (iii) the collateral is held or acquired primarily for personal, family, or household purposes."

**35.** For a list of these provisions, see Edward J. Heiser, Jr., *Operations and Compliance Under the New provisions of revised Article 9*, 34 UCCL.J. 115, 120–123 (2001).

unacceptable. An impasse between the two groups might have derailed the revision process, but they managed to reach a compromise. The compromise was to include certain rules in the 1998 revision that consumer advocates felt were not protective enough if applied to consumers, but to exempt consumer transactions from those rules and leave the rules to be applied in consumer transactions to the courts, which have historically been sympathetic to consumers.[36] When you encounter such provisions, you should consult with the Legal Department, as legal research will be required to determine what rule will apply in a consumer transaction.

**36.** For a more complete discussion of what occurred see, Marion W. Benfield, Jr., *Consumer Provisions on Revised Article 9*, 74 Chi–Kent L. Rev. 1255, 1255–1259 (1999).

# Chapter 2

# THE SCOPE OF ARTICLE 9

---

*At this point you notice, for the first time, a folder on the side of your desk. You open it and find the following memorandum on top a group of papers.*

## MEGABANK, INC.
## INTEROFFICE MEMORANDUM

TO:       S. Carlson
FROM:    J. Robinson *JR*
RE:       Various Matters

Sidney: Sorry I could not be here for your first day. Family matters will keep me away from the office for a few days. I hope you have had a chance to settle in. I have included in this folder a few items that I would like you to deal with before I get back and we can meet. I do not think they will pose much of a problem, but if you absolutely need to talk to me, you can get me through my assistant, Jerry Golden, who I assume you met this morning. Jerry's extension is in the Bank's phone directory.

The second page in the folder is an additional excerpt from the Loan Officer Training and operations Manual:

## BANK OF NEW BABYLON
## LOAN OFFICER TRAINING AND
## OPERATIONS MANUAL

### CHAPTER 2: GENERAL COVERAGE OF ARTICLE 9

## I.  The Inclusive Provisions

### A.  The General Provision

Any well-drafted commercial statute must somehow provide rules for distinguishing those transactions to which it applies from those to which it does not. The key provision for this purpose in Article 9 is the rather lengthy Section 9–109. Section 9–109(a)(1) begins with the apparently simple statement that Article 9 applies to "a transaction, regardless of its form, that creates a security interest in personal property or fixtures by contract. . . ." As soon as one examines the constituent phrases of the sentence, however, the appearance of simplicity disappears.

## B. "By Contract"

The inclusion of the phrase, "by contract," should be no surprise. The domain of Article 9 consists primarily of **consensual** transactions, even if Article 9 sometimes states priority rules for resolution of disputes between consensual Article 9 security interests and nonconsensual interests created outside Article 9 (e.g., the interests of lien creditors).

Immediately, however, Section 9–109 identifies some express exceptions to the general rule that Article 9 transactions are consensual. Section 9–109(a)(2), for example, extends Article 9 to agricultural liens. While agricultural liens are related to consensual transactions between farmers and their suppliers or lessors, the liens are creatures of statute and arise by operation of law.[1] Agricultural liens were brought within the scope of Article 9 by the 1998 revision of the statute, largely because of the economic importance of liens on farm products in a number of states.[2]

Some additional nonconsensual interests are brought within the scope of Article 9 by Sections 9–109(a)(5) and (6). Generally, those subsections bring security interests that arise under other articles of the Uniform Commercial Code within Article 9, at least to some extent. Many, though not all, of those "imported" security interests arise by operation of law, even if they are related to consensual transactions. For example, under Section 2–711(3), a buyer of goods who justifiably rejects them (e.g., for non-conformity to the sale contract) has a security interest in the rejected goods in his possession that secures payments he or she has made to the seller. While the underlying sale transaction was undoubtedly consensual, the security interest that arises upon rightful rejection arises by operation of law. Nevertheless, Section 9–109(a)(5) subjects it to Article 9, although Section 9–110 provides for a special set of perfection and priority rules.[3]

Thus, it is no longer true that a nonconsensual interest cannot be an Article 9 interest. However, the consensual security interest is still the paradigm case for Article 9, and nonconsensual Article 9 interests are the exception rather than the rule.

---

**1.** The term "agricultural lien" is defined in Section 9–102(a)(5).

**2.** For a discussion of the background of agricultural liens see, Donald W. Baker, *Some Thoughts on Agricultural Liens Under the New U.C.C. Article 9*, 51 Ala. L. Rev. 1417, 1421–1425 (2000).

**3.** A final, and more limited exception to the consensual nature of Article 9 interests, which is not included in Section 9–109(a), relates to certain non-consensual "possesso-ry liens" created by state or federal law. These liens are defined in Section 9–333(a). While most Article 9 requirements do not apply to such possessory liens, Article 9 does contain a priority rule for contests between an Article 9 security interest and a non-consensual possessory lien in the same asset. This rule is found in § 9–333(b). This type of lien is discussed in more detail later in this Manual.

## Problem 2–1

*Just as you finish this, your phone rings. Gingerly, you pick it up.*

S.C.: Hello, this is Carlson.

D.C.: Hi. This is Dan Conseco, the Assistant General Counsel in charge of Friendly Finance. I hope you are settling in O.K. I am sorry to bother you on your first day, but we are a little short-handed here and I need someone to look into a small matter for me. Do you have the time?

S.C.: [You already know that there is no right answer to that question.] Sure. What can I do for you?

D.C.: About a year ago, we at Friendly Finance made a $5,000 loan to Fred Zapp, a local electrical contractor. Fred, at the time, had a large generator that looked pretty new, and we took a security interest in it to secure the loan. Fred made his payments for a while, but the construction business around here has been slow and Fred is in default now. We notified him of our intention to foreclose and asked him to surrender the generator to us for sale. The next day, I got a call from the credit manager for a company called Terminal Generators who said that it has first claim to the generator. It seems Zapp had bought the generator on credit from Terminal about two months before our loan to Zapp. The credit manager faxed me a document entitled "Title Retention Contract." The document states that Zapp is buying the generator from Terminal over a two-year time period, specifies the monthly installment payments and other details, and finally adds the following sentence, which I will read to you verbatim:

> Buyer understands and agrees that full title to the item(s) sold shall remain vested in Seller until the price is paid in full, and that Buyer shall have no right, title or interest of any kind until such time.

We checked the Article 9 records for financing statements and found nothing before we made the loan to Zapp and perfected by filing ourselves. This credit manager, however, claims he doesn't have to comply with Article 9 because he has a title retention contract, not a security agreement. Is he right about this?[4]

*You are very pleased with yourself for being able to deal with this problem. You turn back to the Manual material that Jane Robinson left for you.*

———

## BANK OF NEW BABYLON
## LOAN OFFICER TRAINING AND
## OPERATIONS MANUAL

### CHAPTER 2: GENERAL COVERAGE OF ARTICLE 9

#### C. "Personal Property or Fixtures"

One critical determinant of the scope of Article 9 is the nature of the subject matter of the transaction at issue. Article 9 limits this coverage to personal property

---

**4.** [See Section 1–201(37) and Rev. Section 1–201(b)(35); Section 2–401; Section 9–109(a)(5); Section 9–110.]

and fixtures. Article 9 defines **fixtures** in Section 9–102(a)(41) as "goods that have become so related to particular real property that an interest in them arises under real property law."[5] However, you will search in vain in both Article 9 and Article 1 for a definition of **personal property**. The term is obviously intended to distinguish Article 9 security interests from interests in land, which are **real property** interests, a distinction underscored by the specific exclusion of real property interests in Section 9–109(d)(11). Moreover, it is clear from looking at the types of collateral that are defined in Section 9–102(a) that personal property is a very broad concept. The primary types of collateral with which you will be concerned (and there are a number of more esoteric ones) are listed below, along with the sections in the Code in which their definitions can be found:

| | |
|---|---|
| Accounts | Section 9–102(a)(2) |
| Chattel Paper | Section 9–102(a)(11) |
| Commercial Tort Claims | Section 9–102(a)(13) |
| Consumer Goods (a subset of Goods) | Section 9–102(a)(23) |
| Deposit Accounts | Section 9–102(a)(29) |
| Documents | Section 9–102(a)(30) |
| Equipment (a subset of Goods) | Section 9–102(a)(33) |
| Farm Products (a subset of Goods) | Section 9–102(a)(34) |
| General Intangibles | Section 9–102(a)(42) |
| Goods | Section 9–102(a)(44) |
| Instruments | Section 9–102(a)(47) |
| Inventory (a subset of Goods) | Section 9–102(a)(48) |
| Investment property | Section 9–102(a)(49) |
| Promissory Note (a subset of Instruments) | Section 9–102(a)(65) |

You should keep this list of types of collateral handy for future reference. While questions concerning the exact scope of each type can be referred to the Legal Department, part of your job as a loan officer is to be sufficiently familiar with these types of personal property to make an appropriate classification of the collateral in which the Bank claims a security interest in any given transaction.

## D.  "A Transaction, Regardless of Its Form, That Creates a Security Interest"

### 1.  In General

The term "**security interest**" is defined, not in Article 9, but in Article 1 as "an interest in personal property or fixtures that secures payment of performance of an obligation."[6] Usually, determining whether or not this definition is satisfied is reasonably easy. The use of the phrase "regardless of its form," however, is an indication, first, that it will not always be easy, and, second, that the parties' characterization of a

---

**5.** Fixture financing is subject to a specialized, fairly complicated set of Article 9 rules, to which we shall return later in this Manual.

**6.** See Section 1–201(37) and Rev. Section 1–201(b)(35).

transaction may not be decisive. For example, if, instead of using the label "security agreement" or "security interest," the parties to a transaction use a pre-Article 9 designation like "chattel mortgage" or "conditional sale," the effect is to create an Article 9 security interest.[7]

---

**Problem 2–2**

*Under this excerpt is a page with the following note:*

Sidney:

I've got a small matter I need you to handle quietly, because it involves some of President Pompous' poor relations out in the town of Traylor Park. It seems his nephew, Wally Winnebago, needed money about a year ago. He asked his drinking buddy, "Bud" Wiser, for a loan of $2,000, and Bud agreed to make it if Wally would pledge his car in return and pay it back in a year. So Bud gave Wally $2,000 in cash, and Wally signed over the title to his 1984 Chevy El Camino to Bud. There may also have been a bill of sale—I'm not sure. Wally also gave Bud the keys to the car and let him take it to his house. Last week, the loan was due. Fortunately, Wally's lot has improved and he has the money. But when Wally tendered $2,000 plus interest to Bud and asked for his car back, Bud refused. Bud says that, as far as he's concerned, the deal was an absolute sale and, unless Wally can produce something in writing that says otherwise, Wally is "just spittin' tobacco juice into the wind." Do you think there's anything Wally can do to get his car back?[8]

---

*Underneath Jane Robinson's note is another excerpt from the Manual.*

**BANK OF NEW BABYLON**
**LOAN OFFICER TRAINING AND**
**OPERATIONS MANUAL**

**CHAPTER 2: GENERAL COVERAGE OF ARTICLE 9**

### D. "A Transaction, Regardless of Its Form, That Creates a Security Interest"

#### 2. Leases

A more difficult problem in determining whether or not Article 9 applies arises if the parties to a transaction deliberately place a misleading label on it. This problem of

---

**7.** Pre–1998 version of Article 9 made this particularly clear by including, in Section 9–102(2), a laundry list of archaic security devices and then expressly subjecting them to Article 9. Section 9–109(a)(1) of the 1998 version omits the list of outdated devices but its drafters indicate, in Comment 2 to Section 9–109, that the changes in the 1998 version of Section 9–109(a)(1) are in the interest of brevity and are not intended to change its meaning.

**8.** [See Section 9–109(a)(1); Section 9–202; Comment 3 to Section 9–203.]

misleading characterization occurs most often in the context of transactions nominally characterized as **leases**. The U.C.C. contemplates both true leases, which are not subject to the requirements of Article 9, and transactions that are called "leases" but are really disguised sales coupled with the retention of a security interest. Section 1–201(37)[9] contains rules intended to provide criteria for making the distinction.

The distinction between true leases and disguised security interests is especially critical if the property that is the subject of the lease also becomes the subject of claims by creditors of the lessee. If a transaction is a true lease, the lessee's creditors can acquire no interest in the lessor's residual interest in the leased property, even if they have no notice that the property is leased rather than owned outright by the lessee. The true lease is thus another example of the problem of **ostensible ownership**. The property is in the possession of one who does not have full ownership of it, and there is a risk that creditors of the possessor will extend credit in ignorance that an unknown party claims a partial, or even a superior, interest in it.[10]

In contrast, if a transaction is a disguised sale, and the "lease" document really creates a security interest, the "lessor"/secured creditor must perfect its security interest, usually by filing a financing statement under Article 9 to protect itself. If the "lessor"/secured creditor does not do so, he or she may be subordinated to other creditors of the "lessee"/debtor who follow the appropriate steps to obtain a superior interest in the property.

The following example illustrates the ease with which the characterization of a transaction may be manipulated. Consider the same transaction structured in two different ways:

(1) Able agrees to sell a piece of printing equipment to Baker for $7,000. Baker is obligated to pay $700 as a down payment and the balance in 48 monthly installments of $160, which includes interest at 10% per annum. Able and Baker also execute an agreement labeled a "security agreement" under the terms of which, Able retains a security interest in the printing equipment until Baker has paid in full.

(2) Able agrees to lease a piece of printing equipment to Baker for 48 months. The arrangement, set forth in a document labeled a "lease", requires Baker to pay a nonrefundable deposit of $700 and then make monthly rental payments of $160. At the end of the rental period Baker can buy the printing equipment for $1.00.

Very little reflection is needed to see that both transactions have the same economic effect. That is, Baker pays the same amount of money over a 48–month period (with the exception of the $1.00) and ultimately acquires ownership of the

---

**9.** See Rev. Section 1–203.

**10.** Particularly in cases in which the property at issue consists of goods, virtually any division of the bundle of rights associated with the concept of ownership can create a problem of ostensible ownership because the possessor of the goods will have less than complete rights to them. If the owner of goods grants a security interest in return for a loan, or if a seller of goods on credit retains a security interest until the full price of goods is paid, the problem of ostensible ownership can arise. Indeed, consignments, or even mere bailments, can generate the problem. With respect to nonpossessory security interests, as noted in Chapter 1, Section V.B. of this Manual, the characteristic Article 9 solution to the problem of ostensible ownership is to require the secured party to take some action that provides notice of the security interest to actual and potential creditors of the debtor who is in possession of the property.

equipment. However, if one makes decisive the characterization the parties have given to the arrangement, Article 9 applies in the first case and not in the second. If the Bank had a perfected security interest in all of Baker's equipment, Baker was in default, and Able had not satisfied any of Article 9's requirements, the Bank's rights would be superior to those of both Able and Baker in the first case but subordinate to Able's in the second (at least until Baker paid the $1.00 and became the owner of the equipment). Differentiating functionally identical transactions in this manner, however, makes no sense, and Article 9 would not, in all likelihood, respect the parties' characterization of the transaction as a "lease" in case (2). The absence of any requirement that a true lessor give public notice of his or her residual interest, together with the ease with which a secured transaction may be disguised as a lease, has three implications for the performance of your job as a loan officer. First, at the time you are making a secured loan for the Bank and assessing the Bank's potential collateral position, it is imperative that you make some effort to ascertain which of the Debtor's apparent assets he really owns and which are merely leased. The latter, if subject to true leases, should not be considered part of a collateral base. Second, if a secured loan goes into default and it becomes necessary to repossess the collateral, you may find yourself in a priority dispute with a lessor of goods to the Debtor, a lessor about whom you had no previous knowledge. Third, in such a priority dispute, it will be important for you, in consultation with the Legal Department, to ascertain whether what the Debtor and the purported lessor have called a "lease" of goods really is a lease. If the purported lessor with whom the Bank has a priority dispute can be recharacterized as a disguised secured party, the Bank's chances for success in the priority dispute may be improved.

---

### Problem 2–3

*The last page in the folder is the following memorandum.*

#### MEGABANK, INC.
#### INTEROFFICE MEMORANDUM

TO:  S. Carlson
FROM:  J. Robinson *JR*
RE:  Cortex Industries, Inc.

We are contemplating a loan to a new client, Cortex Industries, Inc. Cortex is in the business of manufacturing large coils for the electric power industry. If we make the loan, it will have a ten-year repayment period, and we intend to take a security interest in all of Cortex's equipment. One of Cortex's larger pieces of equipment is a multiple coil-winding machine. Cortex has told our loan officer, Don Santo, that the coil-winding machine is leased. According to Don, Cortex leased the coil-winding machine when it was new, five months ago. The initial term is 48 months at a monthly rental of $2,000. Cortex has the option, at the end of the lease term, to renew the lease for an additional 48 months at a monthly rental of $1,000. At the end of the option period, Cortex has the further option to purchase the coil-winding machine for $1. The monthly payments during the initial term approximate the purchase price of the coil-winding machine, and we are told that the machine has an expected useful life of seven years. As you know, whether our security interest will reach the coil-winding machine turns on whether it is a true lease or a disguised sale and the retention of a security interest. Can you let Don know which you think it is so that he can properly calculate the loan-to-security ratio for purposes of making the basic credit decision?[11]

## Problem 2–4

*After researching the Cortex issue you see the following postscript at the bottom of the memorandum:*

P.S. The Cortex loan got me thinking about true leases versus disguised sales and security agreements, since the Bank is considering setting up a leasing department. It is my understanding that, if the facts of a transaction do not meet one of the litmus tests for finding a disguised sale and security interest in Section 1–201(37),[12] that issue "is determined by the facts of each case."

How important are the following factors (alone or in combination) when the issue must be decided by the "facts of the case?"[13]

1. We make the lessee responsible for all repair, taxes and insurance.

2. Our lease expressly disclaims all warranties of merchantability and fitness for a particular purpose.

3. The equipment is selected by the lessee from the manufacturer, purchased by us and then leased to the lessee, who receives it directly from the manufacturer.

4. The lease recites that it is a "true lease."

Assuming that we enter into leases that we believe are true leases, does it make sense to file a financing statement pursuant to Section 9–505?[14] Or would that be a factor a court would use to hold that the transaction is a disguised sale and security arrangement?

Finally, there is a bill pending in the Gilmoria legislature that would require a lessor either to place a conspicuous notice on the leased property stating that it is subject to a lease or to file a notice of the lease in the same central registry where financing statements are filed. According to the drafters of the bill, the intent is to protect the lessor's interest in the property against rival claims of perfected secured parties. Should we ask our lobbyists to support this bill?

---

**11.** [See Section 1–201(37) and Rev. Section 1–203.]

**12.** [See Rev. Section 1–203.]

**13.** [See Section 1–201(37) and Rev. Section 1–203 and L.C. Williams Oil Co. v. NAFCO Capital Corp., 130 N.C.App. 286, 502 S.E.2d 415 (1998).]

**14.** [See *Leasing One Corp. v. Caterpillar Fin. Services Corp.,* 776 N.E.2d 408 (Ind.App.2002).]

*At this point you feel you have put in a good day's work, and you call one of your classmates from law school, Randy Grossman, to meet for dinner. Randy has joined a large law firm in New Babylon as an associate. Randy started his job a week earlier than you started yours. You agree to meet and compare notes.*

*At lunch you begin by telling Randy about the lease issues with which you have been struggling. Randy confides in you that he is at his wit's end. Three different senior associates have assigned him three different matters, and he has been told that they are all "urgent." Not only has Randy had trouble juggling the assignments; he also has not mastered keeping track of his time for the "time sheets" he must fill out each day. He tells you that the time sheets are divided into six-minute intervals. He muses whether he should record the time he goes for a cup of coffee if he is thinking about the client's problem. You think to yourself that the decision to take the job with the Bank, rather than with a firm, was not so bad after all (although you do regret that the Bank does not give its employees stock options).*

*The next morning you come in and find a memorandum from your boss sitting on your desk. You can't figure out how it got there overnight. The thought makes you a bit nervous. You decide to put it aside for the moment because you would like to finish the Manual materials on the coverage of Article 9.*

## BANK OF NEW BABYLON
## LOAN OFFICER TRAINING AND
## OPERATIONS MANUAL

## CHAPTER 2: GENERAL COVERAGE OF ARTICLE 9

### I. The Inclusive Provision

### E. Sales of Accounts, Chattel Paper, Payment Intangibles, or Promissory Notes

As noted above, the simplest Article 9 secured transactions can often be conceived as divisions of the cluster of rights we associate with ownership between the secured party and the debtor. Not all transactions within the scope of Article 9 fit this simple model, however. For some forms of collateral, transfer of the whole bundle of ownership rights constitutes an Article 9 transaction. In particular, Section 9–109(a)(3) brings outright sales of **accounts**, **chattel paper**, **payment intangibles**, and **promissory notes** within the coverage of Article 9. These types of collateral are all the subjects of detailed Code definitions, and all consist of or include some form of payment obligation.[15]

Rights to payment in all of these forms are, of course, valuable assets, and those who own them often use them as collateral for loans under conventional Article 9

---

**15.** See Sections 9–102(a)(2), (11), (42), (61), and 65. See also the discussion in the Manual at Chapter 1, Section V.B.

security agreements. However, the owner of such assets might also sell them outright as a way of financing ongoing business operations instead of taking a loan and using them as security.[16] If the owner of these assets gives a security interest in them, there is a perfection requirement to alert any subsequent potential creditor that a prior creditor has a claim to these assets and the subsequent creditor should not rely on them in deciding whether to extend credit. Bringing outright sales of these assets under Article 9 requires buyers of the assets to provide a similar notice, thus protecting subsequent third parties.

Subjecting sales of accounts, chattel paper, promissory notes, and payment intangibles to the perfection and priority provisions of Article 9 does not, however, mean that the distinction between a sale of and a security interest in such assets has lost all importance. It can be important for a variety of purposes, including the application of the default and remedial rules of Article 9.

Subjecting the sale of accounts, chattel paper, payment intangibles, and promissory notes to the perfection and priority rules of Article 9 has an additional advantage. It facilitates a sophisticated and relatively recent financing mechanism known as **asset securitization**. Asset securitization is a way of reducing the credit and bankruptcy risks associated with a traditional security interest in these types of assets. In an asset securitization transaction, the income producing assets of a company, such as its accounts, are sold to a separate business entity known as a "special purpose vehicle" (SPV). The SPV then issues securities backed by the value of the accounts it so acquires. The funds raised by the sale of the securities are used to pay the original company for the accounts. The investors in the SPV (those who purchased the securities) obtain their return from the income generated from the collection of the accounts. More importantly, the assets transferred now stand on their own and are not affected by the general credit of the original company. Moreover, Article 9, in Section 9–318(a), makes clear that company that sold the accounts does not retain any interest of any kind in the accounts. This means that, even if the original company files for bankruptcy, it has no effect on the rights of the owners of the SPV to the income generated by the accounts. This insulation from the risk of bankruptcy is one of the principal attractions of asset securitization as a financing mechanism. Article 9 facilitates this mechanism, as the common law could not, by simultaneously preserving a distinction between mere security interests and outright sales and subjecting both to perfection requirements that alleviate potential problems of ostensible ownership.[17]

## F.  Consignments

Section 9–109(a)(4) provides that Article 9 covers a consignment. A "consignment" is defined in Section 9–102(a)(20), with certain exceptions noted below, as "a transaction, regardless of its form, in which a person delivers goods to a merchant for the purposes of sale." Note that the definition uses the term "delivers" rather than

---

**16.** Indeed, the Drafters of the Code recognized that the line between sales and the more limited grant of a security interest often blurred with respect to such assets. See Comment 4 to Section 9–109.

**17.** For an in-depth discussion of asset securitization see, Lois R. Lupica, *Asset Sec-*

*uritization: The Unsecured Creditor's Perspective*, 76 Tex. L. Rev. 595, 599–616 (1998). For a discussion of the Article 9 impact on asset securitization see, Steven L. Schwarcz, *The Impact on Securitization of Revised UCC Article 9*, 74 Chi–Kent L. Rev. 947 (1999).

"sells." That is because the comments to Section 9–109(4)[18] and Section 9–102(a)(20)[19] make clear that the fundamental nature of the consignment transaction is a **bailment**. A bailment is the transfer of possession of personal property by one person (the "bailor) to another person (the "bailee") that does not result in title being transferred from the bailor to the bailee. In the context of an Article 9 consignment, the bailor is called a "consignor"[20] and the bailee is called the "consignee."[21]

Consignments, like leases, raise the problem of ostensible ownership. That is, the debtor is in possession of, and may appear to own, assets that actually belong to a third party. In contrast to a lessee, however, a consignee is deemed to have the rights of the consignor and may pass them to a buyer or creditor.[22] As a result, creditors can claim an interest in the consigned goods and buyers can buy the goods from the consignee free of the ownership interest of the consignor.[23] If the consignor wishes to avoid losing a priority contest with a creditor of, or buyer from, the consignee, he or she must take the steps necessary for perfection of an Article 9 security interest, since Article 9 treats the consignor's interest as a particular variety of security interest.[24]

In general, the consignment is used as a transaction form when the consignor wishes the consignee to attempt to sell the goods consigned but the consignee does not want to take the risk that there will be no buyers. This situation may occur if the goods consigned are a new product just coming onto the market, specialty goods, or if the goods consigned are very expensive, such as antiques. To the extent the goods remain unsold, the consignee has the right to return them to the consignor.

The term consignment as used in Article 9 should be distinguished from two other types of transactions that are also sometimes loosely referred to as consignments. In the first, a potential seller of an item gives possession of the item to a potential buyer to allow the buyer to test it before making the purchase. If the buyer is not satisfied with the item, the buyer may send it back to the seller without obligation. This is different from the normal sales transaction, in which there must be a defect in the goods or the seller's delivery for the buyer to reject the goods. In effect, this kind of sale delays acceptance to allow for the testing period. This type of transaction, while sometimes called a "consignment," is covered by Article 2 in Section 2–326 and is referred to as a "sale on approval." Under Section 2–326(2), the buyer's creditors can make no claim on the "consigned" item until the buyer accepts it.

In the second type of transaction, a seller sells goods to a buyer for purposes of the buyer's resale. Again, however, in contrast to the normal sale (in which the buyer may return the goods only if there is a defect in the goods or the seller's tender) the buyer is given the right to return the goods even though they conform to the contract. More specifically, the buyer may return the goods if he is simply unable to resell them. While the effect of this transaction is very much like an Article 9 consignment and is often called by the same name, the Comments to Section 9–109(a)(4)[25] expressly state that it is not an Article 9 consignment. It is not a mere bailment for sale, but a present transfer of ownership, subject to the buyer's option to undo the transaction

---

**18.**  Comment 6.

**19.**  Comment 14.

**20.**  See Section 9–102(a)(21).

**21.**  See Section 9–102(a)(19).

**22.**  See Section 9–319(a).

**23.**  State law other than Article 9 covers the rights between the consignor and the consignee.

**24.**  See Sections 9–103(d); 9–319(b) and Comments 2 and 3.

**25.**  Comment 6.

later.[26] Like the sale on approval transaction, this type of transaction is covered by Section 2–326, and is referred to as a "sale or return." While in the buyer's possession, goods held under a sale or return arrangement are subject to the claims of the buyer's creditors just like any other property the buyer owns. (See Section 2–326(2).)

As noted above, the definition of an Article 9 "consignment" contains a few exceptions. Specifically, it excludes transactions in which creditors of the consignee would assume the goods do not belong to the consignee, in which the value of the consigned goods is less than $1,000, in which the consignor used the goods as consumer goods, and in which the consignor is attempting to create an ordinary security interest in the consigned goods.[27] As a result, with the exception of the last exclusion, state law other than Article 9 covers these excluded transactions.

## II.  The Inapplicability Provisions

### A.  Partial Exclusions

Section 9–109(c) lists types of transactions in which the requirements of Article 9 would normally apply, but some other statute, regulation, or treaty expressly governs some aspect of these requirements. For example, federal statutes cover security interests in some forms of personal property. Since federal law preempts any inconsistent state law, attempts at state regulation of such transactions risk futility and are probably unnecessary in any event. Security interests subject to such federal statutes are excluded from Article 9, but only to the extent the federal statute regulates them. Residual aspects of such transactions may be subject to Article 9 rules. Rules concerning security interests in patents are good examples of this.

Section 9–109(c) also gives effect to state or foreign statutes that expressly cover some aspect of creation, perfection, priority, or enforcement of a security interest in a particular type of collateral. The best example of this partial exclusion from Article 9 is the requirement, under the law of every state, that notice of a security interest in a motor vehicle must be recorded on the vehicle's certificate of title to protect the lender against subsequent creditors of the owner of the motor vehicle.

### B.  Full Exclusions

The full exclusions, i.e., the transactions completely outside the scope of Article 9, are found in Section 9–109(d). There are different reasons for excluding these transactions from the reach of Article 9. You will recall that Section 9–109(a)(1) confines Article 9 to security interests in personal property, and this implicit exclusion of real estate transactions (with certain limited exceptions) is made express in Section 9–109(d)(11). As noted earlier in this Manual, real estate law varies from state to state, and attempts to smooth out such variations with a uniform statute might have threatened the uniform enactment of the Code. The exclusion of most statutory liens in Section 9–109(d)(2) and of transfers of wage claims in Section 9–109(d)(3) are likewise based upon the assumption that such matters are legitimately subject to local

---

**26.** See Section 2–326, Comment 1.     **27.** Section 9–102(a)(2)(A)-(D).

variation and, as such, inappropriate for inclusion in a uniform statute. Some forms of personal property, such as judgments and non-commercial tort claims, do not normally serve as collateral in commercial financing arrangements, and assignments of these forms of property are accordingly excluded from Article 9 in Sections 9–109(d)(9) and (12).[28] Since it would not normally occur to anyone to give public notice of such assignments, it makes little sense to impose Article 9 requirements on them.

## C. Mixed Transactions

As noted above, Article 9 does not apply to the creation of a security interest in real property. If a lender lends money and takes a promissory note to reflect the debt and a mortgage on the real estate to secure payment of the debt, state law other than Article 9 regulates the effectiveness of the mortgage. However, the original lender may seek to borrow money and use as collateral the promissory note and the mortgage. Section 9–109(b) makes clear Article 9 would cover the creation of the security interest in the promissory note and mortgage even though the security interest in the underlying transaction represented by the mortgage is not covered by Article 9.

## III. The Applicability of Other Law

Whatever the reason for a particular full or partial exclusion, it is important for you, as a loan officer, to remember several important implications and qualifications of Section 9–109. First, the fact that a particular transaction is excluded from Article 9 does not imply that it is unregulated. To take the most obvious example, real estate transactions are notoriously subject to very strict formal and recording requirements. Secured transactions subject to federal statutes and state statutory liens also often have special formal or public notice requirements.

Second, it is not uncommon for one or more assets of a particular debtor to be subject to both an Article 9 security interest and some other claim excluded from the scope of Article 9. When such a priority conflict occurs, Article 9 may[29] or may not contain a rule resolving it. If not, the priority conflict must be resolved by a legal rule from a source outside Article 9. If you are involved in a transaction in which such a priority conflict arises, contact the Legal Department.

―――――

### Problem 2–5

*With the Manual material behind you, you now turn to your boss' memorandum.*

**28.** A non-commercial tort claim that qualifies as proceeds of other collateral is subject to Article 9 priority rules.

**29.** For example, although Section 9–109(d)(2) excludes statutory liens from the coverage of Article 9, Section 9–333 contains a priority rule that governs the conflict between some forms of statutory lien and Article 9 security interests.

## MEGABANK, INC.
### INTEROFFICE MEMORANDUM

TO:      S. Carlson
FROM:    J. Robinson *JR*
RE:       Bovine State Bank–McDonald file; Friendly Finance Question; and NB Mortgage Inquiry

Sidney: I tried to call you at about 6:30 p.m. When I couldn't get you, I asked Jerry to put these inquiries on your desk so that you would have them first thing in the morning. I will call you tomorrow afternoon and hopefully see you and properly welcome you the next day. *[At this point you realize that you may have to reconsider what you assumed was a full day's work.]*

The first issue results from a call I just got from Bubba O'Reilly. He's a loan officer for the Bovine State Bank. He's also a pain in the neck. Five years ago, when Megabank acquired Bovine, our beloved President, Peter Pompous, told Bubba he should feel free to call him or any of "his people" at any time day or night. Bubba hasn't stopped calling since. It's one picayune thing after another. And please don't suggest I refer him to the BSB legal department. Unfortunately, we are BSB's legal department. They're not big enough to have their own. All they have locally is an outside lawyer who does filings and recordings and a few other things we can't do. Frankly, I don't trust him to do much more.

It seems BSB loaned some money to a local farmer, Ald McDonald. McDonald grows evergreens that are sold as Christmas trees. McDonald does not sell them to tree retailers. Rather he advertises in the local newspapers that people can come to the farm to purchase and cut down their own trees. While this has been a reasonably successful business, McDonald has taken to day trading and has lost his shirt and probably his pants and boots as well. Needless to say he has stopped paying BSB. BSB, under a written security agreement, took a security interest in all of McDonald's "goods including farm products," which is properly perfected. Unfortunately, there is nothing left other than his land and the trees, none of which will be sold for some months. Chaste Bank has a mortgage on the land and, I am told has lent McDonald more than the land is worth. Our only hope is the trees. Are we protected?[30] Find out and call Bubba.

### Problem 2–6

I understand that you have already done some work for Dan Conseco regarding Friendly Finance. Ronald Righton has approached Friendly for a loan. Dan thinks the loan could be dicey as he has heard rumors from his friends in the District Attorney's office that Righton is being investigated for selling drugs. Righton has told the loan officer that he needs the money for a business venture, but does not want to disclose the nature of the business. Righton is one of the top insurance agents for Mutual Life Insurance Company and has sold numerous life insurance policies in the area. Righton

---

**30.** [See Sections 9–102(34) and (44); Section 9–109(d).]

has shown the loan officer at Friendly documentation verifying that his renewal commissions (commissions he receives when policies are renewed each year) average per year more than double the amount he wants to borrow. Righton has indicated that he is prepared to give Friendly a security interest in the renewal commissions, as well as the commissions he earns from selling new policies, to secure the loan. He has also agreed to quite a high interest rate. This is the first time this type of collateral has been offered to Friendly. Dan wants to know if we can take an Article 9 security interest in these commissions.[31] I want to know if we should make this loan in any event.

## Problem 2–7

The final issue I would like you to look into results from an inquiry by John Morgan at NB Mortgage. As you know, almost all of NB Mortgage's lending is to buyers of residential mortgages. However, NB Mortgage has been approached by George "Grim" Aesop with a proposition. Aesop has sold the old family homestead in Hamelin (a small town north of New Babylon) to William Piper on a land sales contract. According to John, a land sales contract (sometimes called a "contract for deed") is like a "rent to own" arrangement. That is, the buyer makes monthly payments to the seller that are applied to the purchase price of the property. However, the seller retains the title to the real estate until the full purchase price is paid and, if the buyer stops making payments before paying the full purchase price, the buyer forfeits all the payments made to that point. The full purchase price for the land is $150,000 and will be paid over ten years. Aesop would like to borrow $100,000 from NB Mortgage and give NB Mortgage a security interest in the payments. John would like to know two things. First, is the security interest in the payments covered by Article 9 so that he would need to meet its requirements?[32] Second, if Piper stops paying does NB Mortgage have any security for its loan under Article 9?[33]

———

*With heavy heart and bulging briefcase, you trudge to the library to find the answers to the questions your boss has raised. Without any prior request, your secretary, who is about to leave for the day, hands you a prepared list of ethnic restaurants that deliver until 1:00 A.M.*

**31.** [See Section 9–102(a)(2); Section 9–109(d); In re Berry, 189 B.R. 82 (Bankr.S.C. 1995).]

**32.** [See Section 9–102(a)(2); Section 9–109(b); Section 9–109(d); In re Ivy Proper-

ties, Inc., 109 B.R. 10, 13 (Bankr.Mass. 1989).]

**33.** [See Section 9–109(d)(11); Comment 7 to Section 9–109; Section 9–203(g).]

# Chapter 3

# CREATING THE SECURITY INTEREST

*You have been in your position for more than two weeks, and you are beginning to settle in. You have come to the conclusion that the Loan Officer Training and Operations Manual is a lifesaver. All those things that made no sense when you took secured transactions in law school, and even less in the bar review course, seem to be more clearly explained in the Manual. As a result, you have obtained a copy of the Manual, and it sits on your desk. You have resolved (much like your resolution to begin an exercise program) to read through it as soon as possible.*

*The next section in the Manual relates to the creation of the security interest. Since you have a little time on your hands, you begin to read it.*

## BANK OF NEW BABYLON
## LOAN OFFICER TRAINING AND
## OPERATIONS MANUAL

## CHAPTER 3: ATTACHMENT AND ENFORCEABILITY OF A SECURITY INTEREST

### I. Overview

The initial requirements for the creation of a security interest are found in Sections 9–203(a) and (b). The Code, however, does not use the term "creation." Rather, it states that if the requirements of the sections are met, the security interest will "**attach**" to the collateral and will be "**enforceable**" against the debtor and third parties. However, "attachment" is essentially dependent on meeting the requirements for "enforceability." Thus, for purposes of understanding how a security interest is created, one should focus on the criteria for "enforceability."

There are three requirements for enforceability, although the order in which they are met is normally irrelevant. Two of the three requirements are that the creditor give value (usually to the debtor) (see Section 9–203(b)(1)) and that the debtor have a sufficient interest in the property that is to be the subject of the security interest to have "rights in the collateral or the power to transfer rights in the collateral."[1] (See Section 9–203(b)(2).)

---

**1.** The phrase "or the power to transfer rights in the collateral to a secured party," according to Comment 6 to Section 9–203(b), is to cover exceptional situations in

The final requirement is formulated in the alternative. Under Section 9–203(b)(3), there are four alternatives: (1) authentication of a security agreement by the debtor; (2) the secured party's possession of the collateral pursuant to the debtor's security agreement; (3) the delivery to the secured party of collateral in the form of a certificated security pursuant to the debtor's security agreement; or (4) the secured party's "control"[2] of collateral qualifying as deposit accounts, electronic chattel paper, investment property, or letter of credit rights.[3] The function of this somewhat convoluted requirement is evidentiary. Satisfaction of any of the alternatives provides a way to test whether the debtor intended to grant a security interest, and a way to determine the property subject to the security interest. See Comment 4 to Section 9–203.

## II.  Attachment by Possession

The most common way that the third requirement is met is through a security agreement. What constitutes a valid security agreement for this purpose is covered in detail below. However, the alternative requirement of possession by the secured party merits brief discussion here. First, note that Section 9–203(b)(3)(b) requires that possession be "pursuant to the debtor's security agreement." Possession pursuant to an agreement that the owner is simply loaning the property to the possessor would obviously not meet the requirement. Moreover, because possession is a *substitute* for satisfaction of a more traditional statute of frauds (i.e., a requirement of a writing or electronic record), the requisite agreement should be provable by the testimony of witnesses.

If you are contemplating taking a security interest in certified securities, or deposit accounts, electronic chattel paper, investment property, or letter-of-credit rights, the rules are much more complicated. In such a situation, please contact the Legal Department.

Finally, the Drafters of the Code, by expressly referring to Section 9–313 in Section 9–203(b)(3)(B), make clear that actual physical possession by the secured party is not always necessary. Possession by a secured party's agent or bailee will suffice. Section 9–313 provides for perfection by possession and Subsection (c) expressly permits possession by an agent or bailee to be the equivalent of possession by the secured party. The rights and obligations of secured parties in possession of collateral, as well as possession by agents and bailees, are discussed in more depth in Chapter 4 of this Manual (which addresses perfection of a security interest by possession).

———

which a party has the power to transfer greater rights than he or she has at the outset. If this issue arises, please check with the Legal Department.

**2.** The steps required for "control" of each of the types of collateral listed are found in Section 9–104–Section 9–107.

**3.** All of these collateral types are defined in Section 9–102(a).

## Problem 3–1

*As you are contemplating the distinction between an agent and a bailee,[4] your phone rings. With a certain sense of relief, you answer.*

S.C.: Hello, this is Carlson.

D.C: Conseco here. I need you to handle a small item for me.

S.C.: Go ahead, shoot.

D.C.: Sidney, that's probably not a particularly good turn of a phrase here in Gilmoria. People take their Second Amendment rights very seriously, and they don't like lawyers much, and bankers are probably just behind lawyers. In any event, Friendly Finance often has repeat customers who borrow from us to make larger consumer purchases. Two of our customers Ryann and Les Welton purchased a diamond necklace and a diamond bracelet from one of our local businesses, Perez Fine Jewelry, about a year ago. The total cost was a little over $2,400, and we lent them the money on an unsecured basis. We set up a 36–month payment plan. At 21% interest, their monthly payments were $90.45. After making four payments, the Weltons stopped paying. We contacted them, and they finally came in. It seems that Les had been very sick and lost his job. He said he was feeling better and things were looking up. We agreed to give them two more months in which they would not have to make a payment, but interest would continue to accrue and would be added to the principal amount. Then they were to resume making slightly higher payments to cover the added interest. We also agreed that they would bring the necklace and the bracelet in to us and that we would hold them until the debt was paid. They brought the items in to us and restarted the payments as scheduled.

S.C.: So what's the problem?

D.C.: This morning I got a notice from a bankruptcy trustee indicating that the Weltons had filed in Chapter 7 bankruptcy. The notice included a turnover order[5] claiming that we had assets of the Weltons, namely the necklace and bracelet, which were property of the estate.[6] We thought we had a security interest in them, although there is nothing in writing. Are we right?[7]

## Problem 3–2

*You no sooner finish your conversation with Conseco than the phone rings again.*

S.C.: Hello, this is Carlson.

J.R.: Sidney, this is Jane. I need you to handle something.

S.C.: What is it?

**4.** Generally this distinction turns on the issue of control. The more control the secured party has the greater likelihood that the individual will be deemed an agent.

**5.** [See Section 542(a) of the Bankruptcy Code.]

**6.** [See Section 541(a)(1) of the Bankruptcy Code.]

**7.** [See Section 9–203(b)(3)(B) and In re Fish, 128 B.R. 468 (Bankr.N.D.Okla.1991).]

J.R.: I just got another call from Bubba O'Reilly.

S.C.: What's Bubba's problem this time?

J.R.: Apparently, Bovine has a local borrower out there in Desolation, a company called Fantastic Plastics, Inc. I haven't seen it, but Bubba says Bovine has a security agreement with Fantastic that covers everything they own. The basic problem is that Fantastic Plastics looks a little shaky financially. We think the business is fundamentally sound, but it's having cash flow problems, mostly because one of its inactive shareholders, Alvin Idle, has been borrowing money from the business. Anyway, the result is that Fantastic has been slow-paying suppliers and trade creditors.

One of the trade creditors is a company called Digilease, which leased a computer to Fantastic for a 5–year term. Fantastic is now four months in arrears on its lease payments, and the Credit Manager for Digilease, David Debit, recently paid a visit to the President of Fantastic, Ralph Resin. When David arrived, Ralph was looking at the file documenting Alvin Idle's indebtedness to Fantastic. In particular, Ralph had on his desk a promissory note (payable on demand) executed by Idle in favor of Fantastic. The face amount is $50,000, which is apparently the total amount Idle has borrowed from the company.

Here's where it gets weird, so pay attention. Ralph apparently got up and went into the next room to get David a cup of coffee. The two then had a very unpleasant conversation about Fantastic's overdue lease payments, and David left. At that point, Ralph noticed that the $50,000 Idle note was missing. Sure enough, the note turns up in the possession of Digilease. Digilease claims that the note was "pledged" to it to secure the lease payments and has demanded payment from Idle. Frankly, if they succeed, Fantastic's cash flow problems get worse. Also, I assume Bovine's security agreement covers the note, so Bovine's collateral position is weakened.

S.C.: This doesn't sound right to me.

J.R.: Me either. But I need you to tell me why it's not right. Here's my question. It's pretty clear from what Bubba says that Bovine's security agreement is broad enough to encompass the Idle note. Do we really have to treat Digilease as a rival secured party?[8] They have possession of the note, and that troubles me.

S.C.: It bothers me too.

J.R. Well, I'm in the middle of working on the financing for a major acquisition by one of the Bank of New Babylon's biggest customers, Corrosive Chemicals, Inc. So make this Bovine problem go away. I can't spend time on it.

*It is lunchtime and you meet your friend Randy for some Sushi at Ninja's. After the usual talk about mutual friends, Randy tells you about a problem that he is working on for his firm. It seems that his firm has represented a furniture manufacturing company for a number of years. The company was not doing well financially, and the firm recommended that the*

---

**8.** [See Section 9–102(a)(47); Section 9–102(a)(65); Section 9–313; Section 9–201(a); Section 9–203 and Comment 4.]

*company file in Chapter 11 bankruptcy. The firm obtained from the company a retainer of $15,000 in anticipation of the bankruptcy work to be done, which was placed in a special account at BNB. The company did indeed file in Chapter 11, but it could not devise a viable rehabilitation plan. The Chapter 11 was then converted to a Chapter 7 liquidation,[9] in which the firm participated only nominally, if at all. Randy tells you that normally, collecting the firm's fee would not be a problem. The work the firm did, which amounted to $13,500, was for the benefit of the estate, and the firm would normally have a high priority claim. According to Randy, the firm's claim would be called a claim for an "administrative expense."[10] The trouble is that when a Chapter 11 case is converted to Chapter 7, the Chapter 7 claims for administrative expenses are awarded an even higher priority. In this case, they will eat up all of the assets remaining after the secured creditors, including BNB, take and liquidate their collateral. When you ask him about the retainer, Randy tells you that the trustee takes the position that the funds are assets of the debtor company and that the Bankruptcy Court has issued a turnover order. It occurs to you that you might have a suggestion that would help Randy.[11]*

---

*It is obvious to you that one of the keys to success is the Manual. You turn to it again.*

## BANK OF NEW BABYLON
## LOAN OFFICER TRAINING AND
## OPERATIONS MANUAL

## CHAPTER 3: ATTACHMENT AND ENFORCEABILITY
## OF A SECURITY INTEREST

### III.   The Security Agreement Alternative

### A.   Overview

Article 9 defines a "security agreement" in Section 9–102(a)(73) as "an agreement that creates or provides for a security interest." This is not a particularly helpful definition. However, Comment 3.b. makes clear that a document or electronic record constitutes a security agreement if the transaction it memorializes provides for a security interest, even if the parties characterize the document or record in some

---

**9.** [See Section 1112(a) of the Bankruptcy Code.]

**10.** [See Section 503(b)(4) of the Bankruptcy Code.]

**11.** [See Section 9–102(a)(29); Section 9–104(a); Section 9–203(b)(3)(d); In re Viscount Furniture Corp., 133 B.R. 360 (Bankr.N.D.Miss.1991). A debate has been going on for some time about whether secured creditors should be able to take all of the assets of a business borrower as collateral. If they are permitted to do so, the effect in a bankruptcy is that the unsecured creditors get nothing. Some commentators have argued that a portion of any debtor's assets should not be subject to a security interest, so that there can be some payment to the unsecured creditors in the event of bankruptcy. See William J. Woodward, Jr., *The Realist and Secured Credit: Grant Gilmore, Common–Law Courts and the Article 9 Reform Process*, 82 Cornell L. Rev. 1511 (1997).]

other way (e.g., as a lease). You will recall that a security interest is defined in Section 1–201(37)[12] as "an interest in personal property or fixtures which secures payment or performance of an obligation."

It is also important to note that Section 9–203(b)(3)(A) requires a security agreement to have two further features if it is to be enforceable. First, it must provide "a description of the collateral." Second, the security agreement must be "authenticated" by the debtor. The Code defines "authenticate" in Section 9–102(a)(7) to include a traditional signature,[13] but the term is not confined to such signatures. The substitution of "authentication" requirements for a required signature permits the use of electronic records.

## Problem 3–3

*Once again, the phone rings. It's the boss.*

S.C.: Carlson here.

J.R.: I swear I feel like I'm being nibbled to death by ducks. Bubba called again. I thought you were supposed to keep him off my back.

S.C.: I told him he should direct his inquiries to me in the future.

J.R.: Too subtle. He's a slow learner. I really don't have time for this.

S.C.: What did he want?

J.R.: It seems Bubba has a little brother, Buford, who makes Bubba look like an overachiever. Buford is the credit manager for the local department store, Harold's of Desolation (not to be confused with Harrod's of London). Buford occasionally needs a little help, and he turns for advice to his "smarter brother, the banker"—meaning Bubba. And Bubba tries to help him when he can. Anyway, the immediate problem is that Buford has three delinquent accounts, all of which Bubba helped him "set up," whatever that means.

S.C.: Well, start with the simplest.

J.R.: Okay, that would be the Hewey family. The rather large Hewey family. These people bought a number of items from the store—some large, some small, some for household purposes, some for business use—but all on credit. Buford had Mr. and Mrs. Hewey sign a "Credit Agreement" that listed each item sold, itemized the prices of each, gave a price total, recited a down payment, listed a balance due, and specified the amount to be paid each month over a period of 12 months. The Heweys only made two payments and then stopped. Bubba wants to know if Buford can repossess the stuff they bought.[14]

S.C.: That's it? No other documentation? Nothing like our form security agreement or financing statement?

J.R.: Nope. Not with the Heweys. I've literally told you everything the "Credit Agreement" said. It's only about half a page. Now with the Deweys, you have a little more. You have the same, bare bones Credit Agreement,

**12.** See Rev. Section 1–201(b)(35).

**13.** See the definition of "signed" at Section 1–201(39) and Rev. Section 1–201(b)(37).

**14.** [See Section 9–102(a)(7); Section 9–102(a)(69); Section 9–102(a)(73); Section 9–203.]

with the buyers, the items sold, and the numbers obviously changed. But the Deweys also signed a standard financing statement covering "goods," and Buford filed it.

S.C.: Is there a reference to the Credit Agreement on the financing statement?

J.R: No. But the Deweys aren't paying either, and Bubba wants to repossess.[15]

S.C.: You said *three* accounts?

J.R.: Ah, nothing gets by you. There is also the Lewey account. Again the store sold them a number of items on credit, some for personal and some for business use. But instead of a "Credit Agreement," Buford had Mr. and Mrs. Lewey sign a standard form promissory note—the kind of simple installment note you find in all the formbooks. He probably got it from Bubba. Anyway at the bottom of the note, just above the signatures, is the following language—and I'm reading it to you *verbatim* now:

> "This note is secured by a UCC financing statement of this state."

S.C.: Is there really a financing statement?

J.R.: Yeah. Buford had a copy. It lists all the items sold, and Buford filed it.

S.C.: Does the note list the items sold?

J.R.: No. Just a total balance, a recitation of "value" received, and a promise to pay monthly installments of a specified amount. The installments, as I am sure you have guessed, have not been paid. Now, you deal with Bubba. And, please, please keep him out of my way. I really have to focus on the Corrosive Chemicals deal.

## Problem 3–4

*You are beginning to learn that interoffice mail is not necessarily a blessing.*

### MEGABANK, INC.
### INTEROFFICE MEMORANDUM

TO:        S. Carlson
FROM:      J. Robinson *JR*
RE:        Bank of New Babylon—Flawless Furniture Matter

Flawless Furniture, Inc. is a manufacturer of hardwood furniture. Its factory is located in the industrial section of New Babylon, and the company has applied to the Bank of New Babylon for a line of credit to finance its need for operating capital. Our loan officers have examined Flawless' financial statements, and the loan looks like a prudent business move. However, there is one potential legal problem I would like you to explore.

Our financial wizards have recommended that any loan to Flawless be secured by its inventory of furniture and raw materials. Obviously, if we are

**15.** [See Section 9–502(d) and Comment 2.]

to make a secured loan, we would like to have a first-priority security interest. The problem we face is that there is another creditor of Flawless that may qualify as a secured creditor. Five years ago, Flawless was in financial difficulty and failed to make a number of scheduled payments to raw materials suppliers. The supplier with the largest delinquent account, Mountain Lumber Company, was particularly aggressive in its collection efforts. Following the usual round of negotiations and threats of lawsuits, the lawyers for Flawless and Mountain worked out a compromise. The General Counsel for Mountain drafted a short letter, the relevant portions of which are quoted below:

> "We have conceptually agreed as follows:
>
> Debtor acknowledges its debt to Creditor of $207,535. Your indebtedness shall be evidenced by an installment note secured by a lien on all accounts receivable, inventory and raw materials now or hereafter existing which shall be evidenced by a standard form security agreement and shall be perfected by a financing statement to be filed upon the signing of this letter.
>
> When signed by you [president of Debtor] this letter will form the basis for Creditor preparing a financing statement, the installment note, and security agreement.
>
> This arrangement is in lieu of our filing suit to obtain a judgment against you."

The president of Flawless signed the letter. Mountain's General Counsel then drafted an installment note and a security agreement, which Flawless never signed. We are checking to determine whether a financing statement was ever filed. Since we do not know yet, assume that it was. However, we need you to answer the preliminary question whether Mountain has the status of a secured or unsecured creditor.[16]

---

*You have some leftover babaganush[17] from last night and you have brought it in for lunch. You heat up the pita in the microwave and sit down to read some more of the Manual.*

---

**16.** [See Section 1–201(3) and Rev. Section 1–201(b)(3); *In re Owensboro Canning Co.*, 46 B.R. 607 (Bankr.W.D.Ky.1985).]

**17.** Ingredients: 3 medium onions; 3 eggplants; 6 cloves garlic; salt; lemon salt; 1 cup yogurt; 3 large spoonfuls (about 1/3 to 1/2 cup) tahini (a sesame-seed sauce). Procedure: Make long cuts in eggplant skin; cook in 400–degree oven for 1 1/2 hours; cool and peel the eggplant; place eggplant in food processor for a short time until it is chunky, not smooth; add 6 cloves of minced garlic, yogurt, salt, lemon salt to taste; add tahini and drizzle a little olive oil on top.

## BANK OF NEW BABYLON
## LOAN OFFICER TRAINING AND
## OPERATIONS MANUAL

## CHAPTER 3: ATTACHMENT AND ENFORCEABILITY
## OF A SECURITY INTEREST

### III.   The Security Agreement Alternative

### B.   Collateral Description

Except in the case of pledges of certificated securities, the Bank of New Babylon does not normally take possession of collateral in which it claims a security interest. Our commercial finance affiliate, NB Commercial Finance, occasionally makes purchases of chattel paper and takes possession, but such arrangements are unusual for the Bank. In the usual case, therefore, attachment of the Bank's security interest will require an authenticated security agreement that provides a description of the collateral. Section 9–108(a) provides that a description "is sufficient, whether or not it is specific, if it reasonably identifies what is described." Sections 9–108(b)-(e) provide more specific guidance as to what constitutes sufficient or insufficient collateral description.

There are various ways to satisfy the collateral description requirement. If, for example, the Bank is financing the acquisition of a single large piece of industrial equipment, it may be appropriate to describe the machine in question quite specifically, e.g., by manufacturer, model and serial number. Section 9–108(b)(1) indicates that such a description is sufficient, though Comment 2 indicates that it is not necessary. Specific description becomes impractical, however, when the Bank is taking a security interest in all of the Debtor's property of a particular kind. For example, if the Bank loans money to a large automobile dealership and wishes to take a security interest in the hundreds of automobiles and light trucks on its lot, describing the collateral by make, model, and serial number would be foolish, for two reasons. First, the description would be too lengthy and cumbersome, as the vehicles are too numerous. Second, the description would rapidly become outdated as the dealership sold some automobiles and acquired others. The first problem can be solved, and the latter partially solved, by describing the collateral in more general terms. It may be possible to do this using the terms of ordinary speech, e.g., by describing the car dealership's assets as "all automobiles, trucks, and other motor vehicles held for sale or lease." Section 9–108(b)(2) would appear to validate such descriptions by ordinary "category." However, as noted earlier in this Manual, the Drafters of the Code divided the universe of personal property into certain defined **types**. (See the discussion in the section of this Manual titled GENERAL COVERAGE OF ARTICLE 9, I. The Inclusive Provision, C. "Personal Property or Fixtures.") Although use of these Code types is not mandatory, they are useful for purposes of formulating collateral descriptions, and Section 9–108(b)(3) indicates that a collateral description incorporating them is normally sufficient.[18]

---

**18.**   There are some exceptions to the general rule that the use of collateral types is permissible. They are set out in Section 9–108(e).

The utility of the Code collateral categories derives, in part, from the mere fact that they are defined, technical terms. However, the same fact also implies that care must be taken in using them, as the Code definition of a particular term may not invariably coincide with the word usage of the ordinary layman.

One final observation concerning collateral description is in order at this point. Section 9–203(b)(3)(A) contains an additional description requirement when the collateral is "timber to be cut." In such cases, a description of the land on which the timber is located must be included. Given the language in Section 9–108(a) to the effect that a description need only "reasonably identify" the real estate, a formal metes and bounds legal description would not appear absolutely necessary, but it would be prudent to use such a description if it is available.

---------

### Problem 3–5

*Reading the Manual is starting to give you a headache. The words are beginning to blur on the page and you are afraid that you are about to fall asleep. Perhaps it is the babganush or the fact that you stayed too late last night at the Do Drop Inn with Randy. You are beginning to think that Thursday nights are not actually the beginning of the weekend now that you have a real job. The phone rings, jerking you to attention.*

S.C.: Sidney Carlson.

B.O.: Hi Sidney.

S.C.: *[You immediately recognize the voice.]* Hello Bubba.

B.O.: I called Jane and she told me to stop calling her and to call you. It kinda hurt my feelings.

S.C.: Jane's just really busy these days. What can I do for you?

B.O.: Max Reginelli operates a machine shop here in Desolation. Over the years, we have made loans to Max to buy pieces of machinery. Max has always been "good pay." Last year he needed a new drill press for his business and we lent him the money and took a security interest in the drill press. I used our standard security agreement and I stated: "Collateral for this loan is Debtor's drill press, Serial Number 87439." Well Max has run into some hard times and has stopped paying. I went to see him and I told him I was real sorry but that we would have to repossess the drill press. Max has 10 drill presses in his shop and I looked at all of them. None of them have the serial number "87439," but the one that looks the newest has the serial number "87349." I obviously screwed up and transposed the numbers. Would you check out whether I have a problem and let me know?[19]

### Problem 3–6

*Proving that no good deed goes unpunished.*

**19.** [See Section 9–108; Section 9–203(b)(3)(A); *In re Pickle Logging, Inc.*, 286 B.R. 181 (Bankr.M.D.Ga.2002).]

## FRIENDLY FINANCE COMPANY
## INTEROFFICE MEMORANDUM

TO:  S. Carlson, Megabank Legal Dept.
FROM: Theodore Cleaver, V.P., Friendly Finance
RE:  Haldanish Loan

You were so helpful on the Zapp matter that Dan Conseco said I should see if you can help us on this one as well. Three months ago, we made a loan to a local internist, Dr. Haldanish, in the amount of $2,000. The purpose of the loan was to finance the good Doctor's acquisition of a large-screen TV set, in which we, as usual, took a security interest. I used our standard form security agreement, which characterizes the collateral as "any and all consumer goods acquired with the loan proceeds." Dr. Haldanish is actually our doctor and a good friend of the family, and I even helped him set the TV up in his den one Saturday afternoon. Then yesterday my son had an appointment with Dr. Haldanish, and he noticed the TV had been moved to the Doctor's waiting room. Dr. Haldanish explained that his old waiting room set had broken and that he had temporarily moved his den TV to the waiting room. Do we have any legal problems here?[20] He also mentioned that if the waiting room set were not repairable, he would leave the old den TV in the waiting room and buy a new TV for the den. Would this be a problem for us?

## Problem 3–7

*You can't find your boss today. But she can find you.*

## MEGABANK, INC.
## INTEROFFICE MEMORANDUM

TO:  S. Carlson
FROM: J. Robinson  *JR*
RE:  Bank of New Babylon—Tepper Industries File

Some years ago, before becoming BNB's borrower, the debtor, Tepper Industries, Inc. (Tepper), purchased a spa manufacturing business from Charger Corporation (Charger). In conjunction with the sale, Tepper executed a promissory note in favor of Charger. The note was secured by a security agreement which described the collateral as: "The furniture, fixtures, equipment, accounts, contract rights, leasehold, inventory, proceeds of the same or similar type hereafter acquired by the debtor, located at 7200 Hazard Ave., City of Westminster, State of California." At the time of the sale, Tepper and Charger had agreed that Tepper would use the Hazard Avenue premises (where the business was then located), rent free for 60 days after the close of the sale and that, after that time, the furniture, fixtures, equipment, and inventory of the business would be moved to another location. Within the 60

---

**20.** [See Section 9–102(a)(23); Section 9–102(a)(33); Comment 4.a. to Section 9– 102(a); Section 9–108(e)(2); Comment 5 to Section 9–108.]

days, Tepper relocated and moved all of the secured property to 2122 Chestnut St., Santa Ana, California. Charger was aware of the move.

Subsequently, the BNB made a loan to Tepper. Frankly, we were unaware of the Security Agreement in favor of Charger at the time. Tepper executed a security agreement in favor of the Bank covering all of Tepper's inventory, accounts, and equipment. Six months ago, Tepper filed a Chapter 11 petition. When Tepper purchased the business from Charger, the inventory had consisted of approximately 50 spas. Tepper, however, manufactured hundreds of spas per year. When Tepper filed its Chapter 11 petition, its inventory had turned over completely, and Tepper owned none of the initial spa inventory. Moreover, the equipment Tepper used to manufacture spas also changed after Tepper purchased the business from Charger, as Tepper purchased new equipment. In fact, the equipment Tepper owned when it filed in bankruptcy was all new equipment purchased after moving from the Hazard Avenue address. Finally, Tepper had purchased the furnishings and office equipment it owned when it filed bankruptcy after moving from Hazard Avenue.

I need you to answer several questions. Obviously, we are in a priority contest with Charger in the Bankruptcy Court. (1) Does Charger have a valid security interest at all?[21] (2) If so, in what assets of Tepper? In that regard, note that Charger described types of collateral rather than listing each item. Is that permitted under Section 9–203?[22] (3) Is the standard for determining whether a collateral description is sufficient subjective (requiring proof of what the parties believed it meant) or objective (determined by what a reasonable person would have believed it meant)?[23] As you know, things move quickly in bankruptcy, so please give these questions your immediate attention.

## Problem 3–8

*A letter from the Bovine State Bank is in your "in" box. You try to ignore it for as long as possible. When you finally look at it, it contains the following:*

### THE BOVINE STATE BANK
### DESOLATION, GILMORIA
### "Serving Desolation for Fifty Years"

### MEMORANDUM

TO:      S. Carlson, Megabank, Inc.
FROM:   Bubba O'Reilly, Bovine State Bank
RE:      McDonald, Chalmers and Perdido Loans

I have three questions for the Legal Department. The first two concern loans the Bovine State Bank is about to make. First, we wish to make an operating loan to a local hog farmer, Duncan McDonald, and we want to take

---

**21.** [See Section 9–203 Comment 5; *In re Tepper Industries*, 74 Bankr. 713 (B.A.P. 9th Cir.1987).]

**22.** [See Section 9–108(b)(3).]

**23.** [See Section 9–108.]

a security interest in all his pigs. I'm using our standard short form security agreement, but I'm not sure how I should describe the collateral. How does "all hog inventory, now owned or hereafter acquired" sound?[24] Does it matter that McDonald also slaughters and cures the meat from some of the hogs?[25]

Second we are also going to provide start-up and operating capital to Alice Chalmers, who is starting a new tractor and farm implement dealership here in Desolation. Again, I think our standard security agreement is fine, and I thought I would describe the collateral as "all farm equipment, now owned or hereafter acquired." Do you approve?[26]

Finally, we made a loan to our local locksmith, Perdido Key & Lock. The loan has not performed well for some time, and we've decided to foreclose. The owner, Sam Perdido, is being generally quite cooperative. The security agreement describes the collateral as "all accounts receivable, present and future." Sam is letting us collect his normal trade and consumer accounts. However, he is refusing to turn over a tax refund of $700 the business just received. Can we make him surrender the tax refund to us?[27] Please advise.

## C.  Authentication

### Problem 3–9

*As you are about to leave the office for the day one Friday, the phone rings. Naturally, it is your boss. You have the following conversation:*

S.C.: Carlson.

J.R.: Sidney, this is Jane. I'm out here in the City of Bucolic.

S.C.: Where's that?

J.R.: About 150 miles from New Babylon. Beyond that, you don't want to know. I'm here to oversee our local counsel's repossession of the inventory of City Hardware Co., one of the local Main Street stores.

S.C.: Why is the Bank loaning money to a hardware store in the sticks?

J.R.: I'm trying to remember. I think the owner is related to President Pompous. Anyway, local counsel is worried about something, and I need you to do the research to make him comfortable.

S.C.: What's the problem?

J.R.: Well, I hope there is no problem, since I documented this transaction when I first started with the Bank. When the initial loan was made, I was called in at the last minute by our loan officer with a request to "paper this deal." The initial loan was small and the borrower remote, so I just mailed a standard form security agreement covering the inventory of City Hardware Co. to its President. He typed "City Hardware Co." on the bottom of it and faxed it back to me. I filed it away and thought no more about it. Unfortunately, that's not all. We made a second loan sometime later and took a

---

**24.** [See Section 9–102(a)(34); Section 9–102(a)(48).]

**25.** [See Comment 4.a. to Section 9–102.]

**26.** [See Section 9–102(a)(33); Section 9–102(a)(48).]

**27.** [See Section 9–102(a)(2); Section 9–102(a)(42).]

security interest in City Hardware's equipment. By then we had email so I emailed the President a standard security agreement covering the equipment. He obviously hit the "reply" button, typed "OK," and sent it to me. We are about to go to court to get a writ of possession for the inventory and equipment, and I can't produce anything with a pen-and-ink signature. So you tell me. Do I have a problem? [28] Call me back soon. I need to get back to town. You get tired of fried okra[29] and grits after a while.

*[Does this mean you have to work over the weekend? Yes!]*

### Problem 3–10

*On Monday morning you are actually beginning to feel pretty good about your job. It was not too difficult to resolve the City Hardware problem, and, when you were here on Saturday, Mr. Houseman, the General Counsel, was in his office. Even better, he noticed you when you came in. He actually smiled and seemed to give an approving nod. While it was a pain to get up on a Saturday morning, you think it might be useful to do it a couple of times a month to give the impression that you are working hard. As you get your breakfast Dr. Pepper, the phone rings.*

S.C.: Carlson.

T.C.: Ted Cleaver here at Friendly Finance.

S.C.: Ted, what can I do for you? *[You have to restrain yourself from asking how Eddie Haskel is.]*

T.C.: I have a problem and I can't reach Dan Conseco. Eight months ago we made a loan to Peter Sullivan, Jr. for $5,000. As you know, that is a pretty big loan for us. Anyway, we asked for some collateral and he didn't have anything worth anything. However, his father, Peter Sr., had a relatively new truck that he owned free and clear. Peter Sr. offered to put up the truck as collateral for Peter Jr.'s loan. That was fine with us. We did a standard security agreement in which we described the truck and had Peter Jr. sign it. Well Peter Jr. stopped paying, so we went to Peter Sr. to either pay or surrender the truck. Peter Sr. told us that he talked to his lawyer and that his lawyer said we don't have a right to the truck. Can this be?[30] Please call Peter Sr. and set him straight.[31]

*You are beginning to worry. You have some time and you pick up the Manual rather than playing a computer game.*

**28.** [See Section 1–201(28); Section 1–201(30); Rev. Section 1–201(b)(25); Rev. Section 1–201(b)(27); Section 9–102(a)(7); Comment 9(b) to Section 9–102; Section 9–203(b)(3)(A).]

**29.** Ingredients: 1 pound fresh okra; 1/2 cup cornmeal; Cajun seasoning to taste; oil, bacon grease, lard, or a mixture. Wash the okra. Cut off the ends and slice the rest into rounds. Procedure: Mix the cornmeal and Cajun seasoning in a small paper sack; put the okra inside the bag, close the top, and shake until the okra is totally coated with the cornmeal; put the okra in hot oil in an iron skillet and cook, stirring occasionally, until done.

**30.** [See Section 9–102(a)(28); Section 9–102(a)(59); Section 9–203(b)(3)(A).]

**31.** [See Rule 4.2, Model Rules of Professional Conduct. It is available on the web at http://www.abanet.org/cpr/mrpc/mrpc_toc.html.]

## BANK OF NEW BABYLON
## LOAN OFFICER TRAINING AND
## OPERATIONS MANUAL

## CHAPTER 3: ATTACHMENT AND ENFORCEABILITY
## OF A SECURITY INTEREST

### III.  The Security Agreement Alternative

### D.  Future Advances and After–Acquired Property

Usually, the Bank wants the security interest in its collateral to secure not only the initial loan but also any future loan that the Bank may make to the debtor. These future loans are referred to in Article 9 as "future advances." Section 9–204(c) permits the parties to a security agreement to agree in advance that future as well as present advances will be secured by the collateral. No magic words are required, but the intention of the parties must be clear. Similarly, the Bank usually wants to include, as collateral for a loan, property that the debtor does not yet own but will ultimately acquire. This is particularly true when the collateral is a changing mass such as inventory. Again, Article 9, in Section 9–204(a), permits the parties to agree that the collateral will form a pool that includes "after-acquired property." Under Section 9–204(b), there are two express, but limited, exceptions to the right to claim after-acquired property. The first provides that a secured creditor can claim after-acquired consumer goods as collateral only if the debtor acquires rights in them within ten days after the secured creditor gives value. (See Section 9–204(b)(1).) The second provides that an after acquired property clause is not effective to attach a security interest to an after-acquired commercial tort claim. (See Section 9–204(b)(2).)[32]

---

### Problem 3–11

*One afternoon, as you return from lunch, you retrieve this voice mail message from your boss:*

Sidney, this is Jane. I am out here at Inferior Interiors, one of the Bank of New Babylon's problem accounts. Inferior sells cheap furniture and bric a brac to the condominium and motel market. About two years ago, the Bank extended Inferior a $500,000 line of credit for operating capital, and the current loan balance is $370,000 and some change. Inferior executed a security agreement in the Bank's favor at the time of the initial loan, and the agreement described the collateral as "all accounts receivable." The loan went into default three months ago, and my guess is that the business won't survive. I would like to begin direct collection of the accounts to liquidate the loan balance.[33]

My one nagging reservation is this. Inferior typically sells its inventory on 30, 60 or 90 days open credit. Since the loan was made two years ago,

---

**32.** Section 9–108(e)(1) requires that the description of the commercial tort claim in a security agreement or assignment be more specific than a description by Code collateral type. Commercial tort claims are defined in Section 9–102(a)(13).

**33.**  [See Section 9–607(a)(1).]

Inferior has already collected all of the accounts existing at that time. Its current accounts receivable were generated by much more recent sales. Is that a problem for us?[34] Do some quick research and call me back before I leave here at 5:00.

## E.   Rights in the Collateral

*The next morning, when you arrive at work, the following is waiting for you. You wonder if someone is working all night?*

### Problem 3–12

### BANK OF NEW BABYLON
### INTEROFFICE MEMORANDUM

TO:          S. Carlson—Megabank Legal
FROM:        P.L. Driver—V.P., Bank of New Babylon
RE:          Dee Construction Loan

Jane Robinson said I should refer this directly to you. As you may know, the Bank has made operating loans to Dee Construction, Inc. for a number of years. We have a first priority security interest in all of Dee's construction equipment to secure the outstanding balance, which now amounts to over $750,000. Essentially, the amount we will advance to Dee's depends upon the appraised value of its equipment at any given time. We do appraisals on the equipment at least every six months, and sometimes we do them quarterly.

Yesterday, I was in the process of conducting such an appraisal when I noticed signs on two of Dee's largest cranes. The signs were not that conspicuous. They were located inside the operator's cab, not on the outside of the cranes. I actually only saw them by accident. The signs read simply, "Lethargic Leasing Co." As it happens, I am familiar with Lethargic. As you may have guessed, its business is heavy equipment leasing. And indeed, our contacts at Dee confirmed quite readily that the two cranes were leased by Dee from Lethargic.

The problem is that the two cranes are the most valuable pieces of equipment on Dee's lot. Our last appraisal included them, apparently on the assumption that Dee owned them. Without the cranes, I reckon Dee's equipment is worth only about $350,000. Do we have a problem?[35] Would you suggest I take any action?

### Problem 3–13

*You are about to have the worst phone call of your budding career.*

S.C.: Carlson

J.R.: Sidney! You need to drop everything and focus on the assignment I'm about to give you.

**34.** [See Section 9–204; Comment 7 to Section 9–204; Section 1–205; Rev. Section 1–303; *In re Filtercorp, Inc.*, 163 F.3d 570 (9th Cir.1998).]

**35.** [See Section 9–203; Section 1–201(37) and Rev. Section 1–203.]

S.C.: Okay, but that means I'll have to keep Driver waiting on the Dee Construction problem.

J.R.: We can live with that. This is bigger.

S.C.: What happened?

J.R.: You've heard of All Inclusive Appliances?

S.C.: Sure. AIA is one of NB Commercial Finance's biggest customers. Appliance stores all over this state and a dozen others. One of the biggest appliance chains in this country.

J.R.: Yeah, well guess what. They just filed for bankruptcy.

S.C.: You're joking. Don't say stuff like that. It makes my skin crawl.

J.R.: No joke. We've known for some time that business was not great for AIA, but we really didn't see this coming. It looks like AIA has been lying to Finance, and the people who were supposed to monitor AIA just got complacent and dropped the ball. Needless to say, when we get surprised like this, heads can roll.

S.C.: Yeah, I guess this shouldn't happen unless we know about it first.

J.R.: You guess? Hey, shrewd deduction, Sherlock. Anyway, we need to try to protect the position of Finance and save the bacon of a few loan officers.

S.C.: How bad is it?

J.R.: Actually, I've seen a lot worse. The people at Finance are pros, and they've got a perfected first priority security interest in all of AIA's present and after-acquired inventory and accounts receivable. The security agreement and financing statement are flawless, as far as I can see.

S.C.: That is good news. How steep is the loan balance?

J.R.: You don't want to know. Eight figures, and the first number ain't a one or a two. The number crunchers are busy figuring out what our collateral is worth, so that's not really your problem. It looks like no one is disputing our claim to first priority as to most of AIA's inventory and accounts, but my guess is the undisputed collateral won't liquidate the loan balance.

S.C.: So what is my problem?

J.R.: Problems in the plural, my young friend. There are three disputes as to portions of the inventory with companies that supply appliances to AIA. The first is with a supplier of electric stoves called Generic Appliances, Inc. Generic is a manufacturer that produces stoves according to its buyer's specifications and then applies the buyer's brand name to the stoves. It makes Kenmore stoves for Sears, and it also makes stoves for AIA that are resold under the AIA logo. Our specific dispute concerns an order by AIA for 500 AIA stoves to be delivered in 5 installments of 100 each. Generic is apparently the only company more clueless about AIA's financial problems than we were, so the whole order was a sale on open account with payment for each installment due 30 days after delivery. The first installment of 100 was actually delivered to AIA 3 days ago and seems to me to be clearly captured by the after-acquired property clause of our security agreement.

However, counsel for Generic claims he has the right to reclaim them as an unpaid seller under Article 2.[36]

The second installment was literally shipped yesterday (F.O.B. Seller's plant, under the terms of the contract of sale), and it's pretty clear that Generic is trying to interrupt the shipment en route. Generic claims if the stoves never get to AIA, our security interest does not attach to them.[37] The third installment has been manufactured and is sitting in crates in Generic's warehouse, all of which are addressed to AIA. Naturally, Generic is refusing to ship.[38] The fourth installment has been manufactured and AIA logo has been applied to the stoves, but the stoves have not been prepared for shipment in any way. Again, Generic says neither we nor AIA has any claim to them. The raw materials for the fifth shipment have been purchased by Generic, and some of the stoves have been assembled. However, the AIA name is not on any of them, and counsel for Generic told me they intend to modify them slightly and sell them to Sears. I need you to see which of the five installments are subject to our security interest and which belong to Generic. Are we clear so far?

S.C.: Yes. I guess there's more.

J.R.: Right you are, Midnight Oil Burner. We also have a dispute about some Whirlpool dishwashers. Whirlpool is a lot more savvy than Generic and figured out three months ago that AIA was in trouble. At that time, Whirlpool's credit manager, Hart O. Stone, paid a little visit to AIA. Up to that point, Whirlpool had been shipping to AIA on 90 days open credit. Stone reduced the credit period to 21 days. He also had the President of AIA sign a little handwritten note on the back of a laundry ticket. It's really short, so I'll read it to you. It says, "Buyer acknowledges the delinquency in its account with Whirlpool and agrees to make full payment for all future shipments within 21 days of delivery. In addition, Buyer agrees that Whirlpool retains title to all products shipped to Buyer until full payment is made, and, until full payment, Buyer disclaims any interest in the products."

S.C.: That's a little weird.

J.R.: Ah, but the fun has yet to begin. One shipment of 100 Whirlpool dishwashers arrived at AIA 22 days ago. Another shipment the same size is all boxed up and sitting in Whirlpool's warehouse, ready for shipment to AIA. Whirlpool hasn't been paid for either one and is refusing to ship the second one. Stone is telling me we can't claim any interest in either shipment because of the little handwritten document, which he insists on calling his "little insurance policy." I never have liked that guy. Anyway, see if there's anything to what he says.[39]

S.C.: Okay. Please tell me that's all.

J.R.: Wrong again, Bleary-eyed One. There's also the little matter of 300 Maytag refrigerators. Maytag was even more suspicious of AIA's financial

---

**36.** [See Section 1–201(32) and Rev. Section 1–201(b)(29); Section 1–201 (33) and Rev. Section 1–201(b)(30); Section 2–401; Section 2–403; Section 2–702(2); Section 2–702(3).]

**37.** [See Section 2–319; Section 2–401.]

**38.** [See Section 1–201(37) and Rev. Section 1–201(b)(35); Section 2–401; Section 2–403; Section 2–501.]

**39.** [See Section 1–201(37) and Rev. Section 1–201(b)(35); Section 2–401; Section 9–109(a)(5); Section 9–110.]

health than anyone else and has refused to sell to AIA except for cash for the last three months. So two days ago, the Maytag truck pulls up to AIA and unloads the 300 refrigerators. The driver dutifully demands, and receives, a check for the full purchase price as agreed. And guess what happened next?

S.C.: Gee, I don't suppose the check bounced did it?

J.R.: Well done. There may be hope for you yet. And of course, the AIA treasurer lied to the Maytag guy. He represented that the check was as good as gold. So Maytag's counsel claims that, since it was agreed that this was a cash sale and payment did not occur, they have the right to take the refrigerators back. I think the fridges are captured by our security interest. Find out who's right,[40] and I need to know fast. The coffee's on me. By the way, President Pompous is over here, so don't screw it up.

S.C.: But no pressure, right?

## F.  Value

### Problem 3–14

*You are now beginning to regret that the good people at the Bovine State Bank know how to find you.*

### THE BOVINE STATE BANK
### DESOLATION, GILMORIA
### "Serving Desolation for Fifty Years"

### MEMORANDUM

TO:          S. Carlson
FROM:    Bubba O'Reilly
RE:          Bovine State Bank—Polly & Ester's Fabrics Loan and Grub 'N Go
                 Grocery Loan

I need you to help me with a couple of problem loans. The first one, Polly & Ester's Fabrics, involves a long-time customer of the bank that has fallen on hard times. Polly & Ester's Fabrics is a local corporation that manufactures clothing, primarily targeted at the traveling salesman market. For a number of years, the Bank loaned the company operating funds, in amounts that ran as high as $250,000, on an unsecured basis. About a year ago, when the unsecured loan balance was $100,000, I became concerned about the company's ability to repay. Internet shopping has really cut down on the business of traveling salesmen, and selling clothing to them just isn't the business it used to be either. Anyway, at that time, I got the company to grant the Bank a security interest in all of the company's present and after-acquired inventory and accounts receivable. I had the company sign the security agreement and the financing statement your predecessor sent me, and I filed the latter where she told me to file it. I thought everything was fine.

---

**40.** [See Section 1–201(32) and Rev. Section 1–201(b)(29); Section 1–201(33) and Rev. Section 1–201(b)(30); Section 2–403(1)(b).]

Last month, the good people at Polly & Ester's realized their situation was hopeless, and they filed a petition in bankruptcy. I didn't worry too much, as I thought we had plenty of collateral. I still think so. The loan balance is down to $75,000, and I figure the accounts are probably worth $50,000 and the inventory on hand about $60,000. But then the Mayor of the town of Desolation, Bobby Bellicose, somehow got the local bankruptcy judge to appoint his son, Bobby, Jr., trustee for Polly & Ester's. Bobby, Jr. is fresh out of law school down there in New Babylon, and he's never been a Trustee in Bankruptcy before. Last Wednesday, Bobby, Jr. and I both happened to be at Polly & Ester's, and I told him that, assuming the Bankruptcy Court approves, we intended to repossess our collateral. Bobby, Jr. then told me he intended to oppose any attempts at repossession because he believes our security interest is invalid. He said that you have to give value to have a valid security interest,[41] and that the Bank had made two mistakes. First, he said that because the loan balance was $100,000 when we took the security interest and the collateral was worth more than that, the Bank hadn't given adequate consideration. Second, he said that we took the security interest after we made the loan, and that he learned in Contracts class that "past consideration is no consideration."[42] My instincts tell me Bobby, Jr. is a smart aleck punk who doesn't know what he's talking about, but I need you to help me convince him (or the Court) that he is wrong.

My second problem is a brand new account. A week ago, the Bank signed a loan agreement with the owner of a local grocery store, Grub 'N Go Groceries. Essentially, the loan agreement gives Grub 'N Go a $250,000 line of credit to draw on, and it gives the Bank a security interest in the store's inventory, equipment, and fixtures. We perfected the security interest in the manner your predecessor instructed us. What we did not know at the time was that the store's owner, Jerry Greenleaf, had been at fault in a car accident two years ago and had been sued by a man who had been injured. The injured man got a judgment against Jerry for $200,000 the same day we signed the loan agreement with Jerry, although we did not know that. Two days later, before Jerry had even drawn on his line of credit with us, the judgment creditor got the sheriff to seize some of the store's equipment. (Jerry runs the store as a sole proprietorship, so he is the direct owner of everything in there.) The next day, since we didn't know about the levy, Jerry drew on our line of credit, partly to buy inventory and partly to replace the equipment that had been seized. I told the judgment creditor's lawyer we had a security interest in the equipment he had seized. He said that, because the Bank hadn't funded the loan until after the levy, the Bank was unperfected at the time, so that he has priority. Could that be right?[43] The equipment in question is old, and neither Jerry nor I much mind if it is sold, but I certainly would like to have first claim to the sale proceeds to keep Jerry's loan balance at a lower level for the moment.

---

**41.** [See Section 9–203.]

**42.** [See Section 1–201(44) and Rev. Section 1–204.]

**43.** [See Section 1–201(44) and Rev. Section 1–204; Section 9–317(a)(2)(B); Sec-tion 9–102(a)(52); *First Maryland Lease-corp. v. M/V Golden Egret*, 764 F.2d 749 (11th Cir.1985).]

## Problem 3–15

*At this point in your legal career, you have already learned that, when the telephone rings, it is never good news for a junior lawyer. The phone keeps ringing anyway, and you keep answering it.*

S.C.: This is Carlson.

J.R.: Sidney. Thank heavens you are in. I'm here at the Corrosive Chemicals closing, and I have a problem.

S.C.: Which means I have a problem, right?

J.R.: Yeah, but at least you have a job. Assuming you solve this problem.

S.C.: So what's happened?

J.R.: Well, let me start at the beginning. I think you know how this deal is to be structured. The Bank of New Babylon's customer, Corrosive Chemicals, Inc. wants to get into the oil recycling business. As it turns out, the cheapest way to do that is to buy an existing oil recycling company, Flippity Dipstick, Inc. over in Fort Toxin. Corrosive is buying all the stock of Flippity Dipstick, Inc. for a price of $100 million. The Bank is loaning Corrosive $5 million for a cash down payment. (Our loan is secured by other assets of Corrosive, including its New Babylon factory.) The Acquisition Agreement reflecting the purchase provides that Corrosive will pay the balance to the current shareholders, the Dipstick family, in monthly installments over a period of 10 years. As security, Flippity Dipstick, Inc., at the direction of Corrosive, will grant the Dipstick family a security interest in substantially all of Flippity Dipstick's assets.

S.C.: Sounds pretty straightforward to me. What could go wrong?

J.R.: Well, all the business types and all the lawyers are here for the closing, and the Dipstick family introduces the family lawyer. Some kid named Bobby Bellicose from out in Desolation, obviously out to impress his clients with what he knows. For some reason, he picks now to put on a show. He claims the security interest Flippity Dipstick, Inc. is to grant in favor of the Dipstick family is not enforceable because Flippity Dipstick, Inc. is getting no value in return. So the Dipstick family starts jumping up and down and screaming that, if the kid is right, they need a lot higher price and a lot more cash up front or this deal is dead. The Corrosive people are so ticked off they are trying to figure out whether to strangle their lawyers, their bankers, the Dipsticks or the kid. The kid has to be wrong. If he's not, we've got a dead deal here and one very angry customer. Not to mention the fact that half the deals I've done in the past year have a rather serious flaw. So find something that proves the kid wrong and call me back.[44]

---

*Yesterday you overheard the paralegal talking about a case with Jane Robinson. You heard her mention "proceeds." Preparation being the better part of valor, you turn to the Manual to remind yourself about the concept.*

**44.** [See Section 9–203; Section 1–201(44); Section 9–102(a)(28); Section 9–102(a)(59); Comment 2.a. to Section 9–102.]

## BANK OF NEW BABYLON
## LOAN OFFICER TRAINING AND
## OPERATIONS MANUAL

## CHAPTER 3: ATTACHMENT AND ENFORCEABILITY
## OF A SECURITY INTEREST

### IV. Creating a Security Interest in Proceeds

As noted in the introductory portion of this Manual, one of the great advantages of having a secured claim is that the secured creditor has substantial assurance that assets (in the form of the collateral) will be available to cover some or all the of loan if the debtor fails to pay. Yet, because the debtor generally retains possession of the collateral, there is the risk that the collateral will be transferred to someone else or destroyed. In fact, because of the latter risk, the Bank's security agreements always contain a provision that the debtor will properly insure the collateral and that, if the debtor fails to do so, the Bank may insure the collateral and add the cost of the insurance to the principal of the loan. Article 9 protects the secured party in two ways. First, unless Article 9 expressly provides to the contrary,[45] the security interest in the collateral continues notwithstanding the transfer of the collateral by the debtor to some third party. (See Section 9–315(1).) Second, Article 9 provides that the security interest in the collateral attaches to any identifiable "proceeds" of the collateral. (See Section 9–315(a)(2).) Proceeds are, in turn, defined in Article 9 to include virtually anything the debtor receives in return for the collateral. (See Section 9–102(a)(64)(A).) Proceeds are more specifically divided into "cash proceeds" (defined in Section 9–102(a)(9)) and "non-cash proceeds (defined in Section 9–102(a)(58)).

### Problem 3–16

*The phone rings again. This time, the voice at the other end is unfamiliar and sounds even younger than yours.*

S.C.: Carlson.

J.D.: This is Jimmy Drabb. You don't know me, but I'm a loan officer here at Friendly Finance. I've only been on the job a week here, and I have a problem.

S.C.: Let me stop you a second. The lawyer assigned to Friendly Finance is Dan Conseco. You should call him. I don't want to encroach on his turf.

J.D.: It's okay. He's on vacation somewhere in the Bahamas. And everyone else in my office is at a conference in Las Vegas. I'm actually here alone.

S.C.: Well, call my boss, Jane Robinson, and she'll assign you someone.

---

**45.** The situations in which Article 9 creates exceptions will be discussed in Chapter 5 of this Manual concerning priorities.

J.D.: I did. She assigned you. Apparently you're the most junior person.

S.C.: Tell me about it. What's the problem?

J.D.: Well, it's like this. Two years ago, Friendly Finance loaned $5,000 to a local cabinetmaker, Alex Boxx. Alex works out of a shop in his basement, and he needed the money to buy a bunch of power tools. We entered into a security agreement with Alex that gives us a security interest in all his business equipment, including the new stuff he bought. Alex has paid like clockwork since he borrowed the money, until this month. His payment was due 10 days ago, and I have been unsuccessful in reaching him by phone. So today I drove on out to his house to see what the problem is. It turns out Alex decided to get out of the cabinet business, and he's been getting rid of all his power tools.

S.C.: What do you mean, "getting rid" of them?

J.D.: Well, it depends on which item you're talking about. Alex sold his table saw on credit to a friend, John Rodriguez. The hand written sales agreement says that Rodriguez will pay for the table saw in six months. Rodriguez's father wrote on the sales agreement that he would guarantee Rodriguez's debt and signed it. Alex traded his gas-powered air compressor in at the local hardware store. For the compressor and some additional cash, he got a new riding lawnmower. Alex had a very fancy lathe, which he sold to another cabinetmaker for cash. He took some of the cash and bought a new television for his den. The rest of the cash he put in his general checking account at Bank of Amerigo. Oh yeah, and Alex's drill press actually got hit by lightning and was destroyed. I think his insurance company sent him a check.

S.C.: Does he have any of our original collateral left?

J.D.: Not much. Anyway, since I'm new at this and no one else is here, what should I do? Can I go after the power tools he sold? Do we have any interest in what Alex got for them?[46] I don't think we're going to see any more money out of this guy.

## Problem 3–17

*The next week, you receive an e-mail from the same loan officer.*

To:        S. Carlson, Megabank Legal
From:    J. Drabb, Friendly Finance
Re:        Boxx loan

Thanks for your help last week. I have some more information and another question. You remember the compressor that Alex traded for a

---

**46.**  [See Section 1–201(24); Section 9–102(a)(2); Section 9–102(a)(9); Section 9–102(a)(12); Section 9–102(a) (23); Section 9–102(a) (33); Section 9–102(a) (58); Section 9–102(a)(64); Section 9–102(a)(77); Comment 13.c. to Section 9–102; Section 9–203(f); Section 9–315 and Comment 3; *Tracing Principles in Revised Article 9 § 9–315(b)(2): A Matter of Careless Drafting, or an Invitation to Creative Lawyering?* 3 Nev. L. J. 135 (2002). See also *In re MJK Clearing, Inc.*, 286 B.R. 109, 122–123 (Bankr. D.Minn.2002).]

riding lawnmower? Let me run some numbers by you. When we made the loan and Alex bought the compressor, it was worth $1,000. When he traded it in used, the hardware store allowed him $500, which is probably about what it was worth. Alex added $600 of his own cash and bought the lawnmower for $1100. My question is, assuming our security interest attaches to the lawnmower, can we claim the full value of the lawnmower or just the $1000 the compressor was originally worth? Or maybe even just the $500 it was worth when he traded it in? Please advise.

## Problem 3–18

*Just to make your week complete, you hear from Bubba again.*

### THE BOVINE STATE BANK
### DESOLATION, GILMORIA
#### "Serving Desolation for Fifty Years"

#### MEMORANDUM

TO:        S. Carlson, Megabank Legal Dept.
FROM:   Bubba O'Reilly, Bovine State Bank
RE:       Brown Tree Farm Loan

As you may know, we do a fair amount of agricultural lending out here. I think you looked into the McDonald screw up. This is another tree case, but in this instance Farmer Brown is in the business of selling the trees he grows. I'm a little worried about Brown. We loaned him $75,000 last summer based on the fact that he had a lot of timber growing on his land. Each year, Brown cuts a portion of the trees, which he sells to a pulp mill under a standing ten-year contract. However, Brown has an old sawmill on a stream on his farm and he turns some of the trees into lumber, which he also sells. We had him execute a security agreement, although it was done while I was out of town, and it's not our standard form. In fact, it's the shortest agreement I've ever seen. Apart from identifying the parties, all it says is this: "Debtor hereby grants Bank a security interest in all of Debtor's present and future farm products." Is that enough to make our security interest effective?[47] Brown has some of the harvested timber sitting in a warehouse at the farm, as well as a batch of lumber produced at the sawmill. I don't know if we'll need to foreclose, but I need to be ready.

## Problem 3–19

*One day, upon your return from lunch, you find the following hastily scrawled note from your boss on your desk:*

**47.** [See Section 9–102(a)(34); Section 9–102(a)(48); Comment 4.a. to Section 9– 102; Section 9–108(a);Section 9–203; Section 9–204(a).]

*Sidney:*

*Remember that Inferior Interiors security agreement where the collateral description left something to be desired?*[48] *Even if that description was flawed, don't we have some argument that we can claim the after acquired accounts?*[49] *Give me a call and let's talk about it some more*

*J.R.*

**48.**  [See Problem 3–11, supra.]
**49.**  [See Section 9–315(a)(2).]

# Chapter 4

# PERFECTING THE SECURITY INTEREST

*You have just returned from a general staff meeting of the Legal Department. You are actually quite pleased with yourself since Jane Robinson mentioned how helpful you had been with the Corrosive Chemical deal. You are equally pleased that no one asked you a question. During the meeting there was an interchange between Jane Robinson and General Counsel Houseman regarding perfection of security interests. You decide that it might be useful to brush up on perfection, so you pull out your trusty manual.*

## BANK OF NEW BABYLON
## LOAN OFFICER TRAINING AND
## OPERATIONS MANUAL

### CHAPTER 4: PERFECTION OF SECURITY INTERESTS

## I. Introduction

### A. Overview of the Methods of Perfection

As noted in the "Brief Introduction to Perfection and Priorities" in Chapter 1 of this Manual, the status Article 9 calls "perfection" is critical for a secured creditor, primarily because it is the key to the enhanced priority it is possible for the secured creditor to achieve. In effect, perfecting the Bank's security interest is normally the only hope for prevailing in disputes with rival claimants to the collateral, including lien creditors, the trustee in bankruptcy, rival secured parties, and purported buyers of the collateral. In particular, as discussed earlier, perfection of the Bank's security interest will normally give it priority over a rival unperfected secured creditor, even if the unperfected secured creditor's interest arises earlier.

Article 9 generally provides that a security interest is perfected when it has attached and when any additional steps specified by Article 9 have been taken. See Section 9–308(a). The "additional steps" are found in Section 9–310 through Section 9–316. The additional steps required for perfection fall into four general categories. In most cases, the actions required provide some form of constructive notice of the secured creditor's interest in the collateral to third parties. The most common form of constructive notice is the **filing** of a **financing statement** in the appropriate public records. See Section 9–310(a). For some kinds of collateral, taking possession of the collateral can provide the requisite constructive notice. See Section 9–312 and Section 9–313.

A third form of constructive notice, **control** of the collateral, has assumed increased importance in recent years. The increased prominence of control as a perfection device is, in part, a reflection of the gradual encroachment of electronic media on the traditional province of writings and, in part, a reflection of the expansion of the types of assets that may be collateral under Article 9. For example, when the vast majority of investments in publicly traded corporations were represented by shares of stock embodied in physical certificates, (referred to in Article 9 as "certificated securities) possession sufficed as a method of perfection for investment securities. However, as the variety of investment products increased and more and more of them were reflected only in electronic records, often maintained by intermediaries of various kinds, possession became less and less practical as a perfection device. Therefore, it was necessary to define a category of collateral, "investment property," for which perfection of a security interest could be accomplished by control. See Section 9–106 and Section 9–314. With the potential emergence of electronic chattel paper, the drafters were required to define a method of control for electronic chattel paper and specify that method as a permissible mode of perfection. See Section 9–105 and Section 9–314(a). Finally, security interests in deposit accounts and letter of credit rights normally must be perfected by control. See Section 9–104, Section 9–107, Section 9–312(b) and Section 9–314. While security interests in forms of collateral that may or must be perfected by control will not arise often in your work as a loan officer, you should know which types of collateral permit perfection by control. Moreover, a reading of the definitions of control in Section 9–104 through Section 9–107 should reveal that "control" is not a unitary concept. The meaning of control varies with the type of collateral at issue. See Section 9–109(c). In a very limited class of transactions, there are no steps beyond attachment necessary for the perfection of a security interest. This limited class defines a fourth category of perfection often called **automatic perfection**. See Section 9–309.

As noted in Chapter 2 of this Manual, Article 9 does not apply to the extent another statute of this state or the United States expressly governs creation, perfection, priority, or enforcement of a security interest. Two significant exceptions to the use of one of the foregoing four perfection methods normally necessary to perfect a security interest arise as a result of the applicability of other statutes. First, for some types of assets, e.g., automobiles, there are state certificate of title statutes that require security interests to be listed on the certificate of title for any particular asset falling within the legislatively enumerated type. Such statutes effectively supplant the Article 9 perfection devices with the title notation requirement. See Section 9–311(a)(2) and (3). Second, there are some statutes, regulations or treaties of the United States that supply alternate perfection requirements. See Section 9–311(a)(1). Examples include the Copyrights Act, the Ship Mortgage Act, and the federal patent statute. However, while such statutes, regulations or treaties may govern the manner, duration and renewal of perfection, security interests perfected under them otherwise may be subject to Article 9. See for example, Section 9–311(c).

## B. Purchase Money Security Interests

One final concept must be understood before the perfection requirements can be considered in detail. That is the concept of a **purchase money security interest**. It is defined in Section 9–103.[1] Perhaps the simplest case of the purchase money secured creditor is the **seller** of goods who permits a buyer to purchase on credit and who reserves a security interest in the goods to secure the unpaid price. Such a seller is classified as a purchase money secured creditor under Section 9–103(a) and (b). However, a **lender** may also acquire the status of a purchase money secured creditor if the lender advances funds or otherwise gives value to enable the debtor to acquire rights in or use of the collateral and takes a security interest in the collateral to secure the loan balance. See Section 9–103(a)(2). For example, the Bank would qualify as purchase money lender (or "enabling lender") in a transaction in which the Bank took a security interest to secure repayment of a loan to a manufacturer for the purpose of an equipment purchase, the Bank issued the loan funds in the form of a check payable jointly to the manufacturer and the seller of the equipment, and the manufacturer endorsed the check over to the seller immediately prior to delivery of the equipment. The Bank's loan would enable the debtor to acquire **rights in** the collateral. Similarly, if a consumer purchased a refrigerator on "layaway," and the Bank advanced money to enable the consumer to pay the balance of the purchase price and obtain delivery of the refrigerator, taking a security interest in return, the Bank would qualify as a purchase money secured creditor because the Bank's loan would enable the debtor to acquire **use of** the collateral.

The purchase money status of a security interest has some impact on the requirements for perfection. However, the chief significance of the purchase money character of a security interest is that there are special priority rules pertaining to such interests. In some circumstances, a secured party with a perfected purchase money security interest takes priority over even a rival perfected secured creditor whose perfection is prior in time. These special priority rules will be explored in Chapter 5 of this Manual.

---

### Problem 4–1

*It seems your boss just cannot resist farming out your services.*

### NB COMMERCIAL FINANCE, INC.
### INTEROFFICE MEMORANDUM

TO: S. Carlson, Megabank Legal Dept.
FROM: R. Comstock, NB Commercial Finance
RE: Bud's Studs Loan

Jane Robinson said you have some free time, and, since we are swamped over here, I hope you can help me with a problem. As you probably know, our specialty at NB Commercial Finance is inventory and accounts receiv-

---

**1.** See Keith Meyer, *A Primer on Purchase Money Security Interests Under revised Article 9 of the Uniform Commercial Code*, 50 U. Kan. L. Rev. 143 (2001).

able financing. The above-referenced loan is one of our very few forays into equipment financing, and I'm feeling a little out of my depth. Bud's Studs is a manufacturer of steel studs used to frame the walls in commercial buildings. Essentially, Bud's takes sheet steel, slices it into eight or ten-foot lengths and bends the pieces into the shape of wall studs.

A large machine called a slitter performs the slicing and bending operation. About a year ago, Bud's needed a new slitter. The owner, Bud Rose, contacted a heavy machinery manufacturer, Acme Factory Supply. Acme agreed to sell Bud a new slitter for $50,000. Acme and Bud's entered into a written conditional sale agreement that called for a 20% cash down payment (i.e., $10,000) with the balance to be paid over a three-year period. Acme reserved a security interest in the slitter until the price is paid in full.

Bud came to us to borrow the down payment. We have been doing accounts receivable financing for Bud for years, so this loan was approved fairly quickly. We had Bud sign one of our standard form security agreements describing the slitter as collateral, and we then issued Bud a check for $10,000. Bud signed the check over to Acme.

At the moment, Bud's Studs is current in its payments to us, but its latest financial statement gives me some cause for concern. I'm not yet certain whether our security agreement or Acme's conditional sale agreement was signed first, and I don't yet know which of us filed first. I'll get back to you when I have a better picture of the sequence of events. As a preliminary matter, however, I need to know whether either Acme or NB Commercial Finance holds a purchase money security interest in the slitter.[2] Thank you for your attention to this matter.

## Problem 4–2

*Upon returning from the coffee machine, you notice that your voice mail light is on and you retrieve the following message:*

Hello, Carlson. This is Jimmy Drabb at Friendly Finance again. Mr. Conseco is still out of town and I need advice on how to paper a deal. A little less than two months ago, the proposed borrower, Susan Davidson, bought a dining room set on sale at Main Street Furniture. The price was $2,000, and the sale was on open credit with immediate delivery and "no payments due for sixty days." We are now approaching day 60, and Ms. Davidson does not have the cash to pay Main Street in full. Ms. Davidson has a steady job and a good income, and both the credit manager at Main Street and I think extending credit to her would be prudent. Main Street, however, does not particularly like long-term credit, so it looks like we will ultimately be the creditor, preferably on a purchase money secured basis. The question is, which of two possible ways should we do it? We could have Main Street enter into a conditional sale contract with Ms. Davidson now, and we could then pay Main Street and take an assignment of the contract. Or, we could just make a loan to Ms. Davidson, let her pay Main Street, and have her execute a standard form security agreement covering the dining room set. Which do you think would be better?[3] Or does it not matter?

---

**2.** [See Section 9–103.]

**3.** [See Section 9–103 and Comment 3; Section 9–310(c).]

### Problem 4–3

*That annoying little voice on your computer tells you that, "you've got mail," and you click on the following e-mail message:*

To:        S. Carlson, Megabank Legal
From:     Bubba O'Reilly, Bovine State Bank
Re:         Ledbetter Loan

Well, we just got this new e-mail system here at the Bank, and I don't know if I've quite got the hang of it yet. So if you don't get this, call me right away and I'll fill you in. Anyway, this friend of mine, August "Augie" Ledbetter wanted to buy this new Ford F–150 King Cab 4–door heavy-duty pickup truck with mag wheels. The dealer quoted him a price of $30,000 even, with 10% down, but Augie had to arrange his own financing. Augie had the $3,000 for the down payment, and he falls well within our criteria for an auto loan. So I approved a loan of $27,000, to be secured by the truck. Augie has his account here at the Bank, so, the day the loan was approved, I had $27,000 credited to Augie's general checking account, and Augie signed our standard security agreement. Augie had to leave on a fishing trip that afternoon, so he didn't actually get back to the dealer for another week, at which time Augie wrote a check for the full purchase price and took delivery. Our security interest is recorded on the certificate of title, so I think we have a perfected purchase money security interest in the pickup. But I was talking to your boss yesterday, and she said something bothered her about the way we did this deal. She couldn't put her finger on the problem, so she suggested I run it by you.[4] Personally, I think it's fine. We handle our car loans this way all the time.

## BANK OF NEW BABYLON
## LOAN OFFICER TRAINING AND
## OPERATIONS MANUAL

## CHAPTER 4: PERFECTION OF SECURITY INTERESTS

### II. Automatic Perfection

As noted earlier, there are some situations where a security interest is perfected without any additional step beyond attachment. We refer to this as **automatic perfection**. While automatic perfection is the exception rather than the rule under the Code, there are a number of such exceptions. Moreover the instances of automatic perfection do not share a single rationale.

For example, there are times when a security interest will be perfected by possession or is already perfected by possession, but (a) the collateral needs to be temporarily left in the debtor's possession to effect proper transfer or delivery, or (b) the collateral is temporarily turned back to the debtor to allow storing, shipping, collection, sale and the like. (See Section 9–312(e)–(h).) In both of these cases, the security interest is either perfected initially or remains perfected without the secured

---

**4.** [See Section 9–103(a)(1) and Comment 3.]

party filing a financing statement. However, the period of automatic perfection is limited to 20 days.

In some instances, the Code provision for automatic perfection is based on the simple fact that no one would think of filing a financing statement with respect to particular types of transactions. Automatic perfection is provided in order not to defeat the parties' expectations, and because there is little danger to third parties. The best example of this variety of automatic perfection is the assignment of less than a significant part of the debtor's accounts. (See Section 9–309(2) and Comment 4.) Assignments of beneficial interests in decedents' estates are similarly considered not to be commercial financing transactions and are automatically perfected. See Section 9–309(13) and Comment 7.

---

## Problem 4–4

*Drabb seems to have latched on to you. Contrary to the "Cheers" theme song, you want to go where nobody knows your name.*

### FRIENDLY FINANCE COMPANY
### INTEROFFICE MEMORANDUM

TO:        S. Carlson, Megabank Legal Dept.
FROM:    J. Drabb, Friendly Finance
RE:         Dweeb Loan

Mr. Conseco is back in town, but he's so busy he would like you to help me with this problem, if it's okay with Ms. Robinson. In the last few years, one of our better sources of business has been a local computer store, CompuSwamp, Inc. CompuSwamp uses us as a financing arm—if a customer cannot pay in cash or with a credit card, they refer the customer to us for financing, which we do on a secured basis if the customer meets our loan criteria. About a year ago, CompuSwamp sent us Malcolm Dweeb, a computer science teacher at the local high school. Dweeb wanted to buy a pretty fancy computer system for $4500. It included the usual components—a CPU, monitor, cables, speakers, printer, and a deluxe, pre-installed software package. We made the loan, set up a payment schedule, and had Dweeb sign a standard form security agreement that specifically described the computer system. Dweeb apparently took the computer system home and set it up in his family room. Two months ago, Dweeb lost his job. (I don't know the details—something about pictures downloaded from the Internet at school.) Yesterday, Dweeb filed a petition in bankruptcy. I can't find a financing statement in the file, and I don't think we filed one. The trustee in bankruptcy is claiming the computer system on behalf of Dweeb's estate.[5] Do we have priority over the trustee?[6] Please get back to me quickly.

---

**5.** [See 11 U.S.C. 544(a); Section 9–317(a)(2).]

**6.** [See Sections 9–102(a)(23), (33), (42), (44), and (75) and Comments 4.a. and 5.d.; Section 9–309(1); Section 9–310(b)(2).]

## Problem 4–5

*You have been confined to your office or the library all week, and it is thus almost a relief when the phone rings.*

S.C.: Carlson.

J.R.: So, Sidney, have we been keeping you busy? Don't answer that. I need a quick answer to a question.

S.C.: How come no one ever wants a slow and thorough one?

J.R.: Because fast and thorough is better. I'm out here at Sisters of Suffering Hospital, one of the Bank of New Babylon's larger health care clients. We have a blanket security interest in virtually all of the hospital's assets, tangible and intangible and have been providing operating financing for the hospital for a long time.

S.C.: I'm familiar with the credit line. What's the problem?

J.R.: Well, I don't really think it's a problem, just a need for some reassurance. As you know, one of the intangible assets in which we claim a security interest is the hospital's entitlement to payments from health insurers for services provided to insured patients. Basically, before services are provided to patients, the hospital has the patients assign their rights against the insurance companies in writing, and the hospital collects directly from the insurers. Those rights to payment are part of the Bank's collateral under our security agreement with the hospital, although I can't remember exactly how they're classified or how we describe them. Anyway, I'm in the hospital business office now, talking with Ben Counter, the hospital's Chief Financial Officer. I happened to mention our security agreement and financing statement, and he is concerned that the hospital doesn't file financing statements when it takes its patients' initial assignments of the rights to health insurance payments. I don't think he really needs to worry, do you?[7]

## BANK OF NEW BABYLON
## LOAN OFFICER TRAINING AND
## OPERATIONS MANUAL

## CHAPTER 4: PERFECTION OF SECURITY INTERESTS

### III. Perfection by Possession or Control

When the only reliable security device was the common law pledge, possession was the only way to perfect a security interest in personal property. Permitting perfection by possession or control is predicated on the plausible assumption that any subsequent party who intends to take a security interest in tangible assets of a debtor as collateral for a loan will want to see the assets in question before entering into the transaction. If the debtor cannot produce them because they are already in the possession of a third party under a pledge, the party seeking to obtain the security interest will be put on notice that inquiry as to the state of ownership of or claims in those assets is necessary. Even when the alternative approach of perfection by a

---

**7.** [See Sections 9–102(a)(2) and (46); Section 9–309(5).]

public notice was developed to accommodate debtors' needs to retain possession and use of collateral, the use of possession by the secured party (or a third-party on behalf of the secured party) was continued as a method of perfection in cases in which it was practical. Article 9 generally continues the use of possession or control of collateral by a secured party as a means of perfection. However, for some types of collateral, possession or control is not a perfection option. In contrast, for other types of collateral, possession or control is the only perfection option.

————

## Problem 4–6

*Late one Friday afternoon, you are about to leave the office for what appears to be your first totally free weekend in weeks. The phone rings. You contemplate the prospect of ignoring it briefly and then answer. You will live to regret it.*

S.C. Carlson

I.H.: Carlson. This is General Counsel Houseman.

S.C.: (Straightening in the chair.) Yes sir.

I.H.: I know we haven't met in person, but I hear good things about you from Robinson, Conseco and Comstock. Look, as you know, the American Bankers Association Convention starts here in New Babylon today and runs through Wednesday. I have to give a speech Monday night on Article 9 perfection requirements. We all have trouble keeping it straight. I need you to write the speech for me. I know that security interests in some types of collateral can only be perfected by filing, some only by possession, some only by control, and some by more than one method. I need you to sort out which collateral types are subject to which perfection methods. Be sure to cover all the following types of collateral: Accounts, Chattel Paper, Deposit Accounts, Documents, Instruments, Investment Property, General Intangibles (including Payment Intangibles), Goods, Money and Fixtures. I'd do it myself, but President Pompous and I are going to try to cut a few participation deals at the golf tournament over the weekend. And have it on my desk first thing Monday morning, won't you?[8] I'll need time to go over it.

S.C.: Yes sir.

*You are resigned to another Saturday in the office.*

## Problem 4–7

*On Monday morning you check your e-mail when you get to the office. Big mistake!*

TO:           S. Carlson, Megabank Legal Dept.
FROM:     Jimmy Drabb, Friendly Finance
RE:           Kruger loan

I have a question for you. We just loaned $5,000 to a fairly prominent coin collector, Randy Kruger. We had Randy execute a security agreement in

**8.**   [See Section 9–309–Section 9–314.]

favor of Friendly Finance giving us a security interest in his coin collection, which is described in great detail. The coins are currently in a safety deposit box at the local branch of Bank of Amerigo. Randy gave me both of his keys to the box. Is that enough to perfect our security interest, or do I need to do something more?[9]

## Problem 4–8

*You no more finish the e-mail when an envelope is delivered to your desk containing the following missive.*

### BANK OF NEW BABYLON
### INTEROFFICE MEMORANDUM

TO:  S. Carlson, Legal Dept.
FROM: P.L. Driver, V.P.
RE:  Ross Loan

Our borrower, Fletcher Worthington Ross, IV, is the prospective heir to one of the largest fortunes in the State of Gilmoria and the beneficiary of several family trusts administered by our Trust Department. Given Fletcher's spending habits, this often leaves him a bit short of cash in the few weeks or sometimes months, before he receives another trust distribution. As a courtesy to his family, we often make short-term loans to young Fletcher during these periods of cash deprivation. Little Fletch just came into the Bank this morning looking for another loan to "tide him over." He says he can put up 200 shares of Microsoft and his ordinary deposit account at Chaste Bank as collateral. I am happy to make the loan, and I assume I can use our standard security agreement to cover the stock and deposit account. But how do I perfect?[10] Will a financing statement do it? Little Fletch also wants to know whether giving us a security interest in the deposit account will keep him from drawing on the account. I told him there was no problem so long as it did not fall below the amount of the outstanding loan. Have I impaired my security interest?[11]

## Problem 4–9

*Once again, the phone rings just as you return from lunch. How do they know when you come back? You look around the office for a hidden camera.*

S.C.: Carlson

H.B.: Hello, Carlson, this is Hans Bigg from NB Commercial Finance.

S.C.: Have we met?

**9.** [See Section 9–313 and Comments 3 and 4; Section 1–201(24).]

**10.** [See Section 4–104(a)(5); Section 8–106; Section 8–301; Section 9–104; Section 9–109; Section 9–312(a); Section 9–313(a); Section 9–314; Bruce A. Markell, *From Property to Contract and Back: An Examination of Deposit Accounts and Revised Article 9*, 74 Chi–Kent L. Rev. 963, 984–988(1999); Ingrid Hillinger, David Batty, and Richard Brown, *Deposit Accounts Under the New World Order*, 6 N.C.Banking Inst. 1 (2002).]

**11.** [See Section 9–104(b) and Comment 3; Section 9–109(c)(13).]

H.B.: No. I'm a loan officer. I'm in the middle of a repossession, it's turned into a huge mess, and I can't find Comstock. Robinson told me to talk to you.

S.C.: Okay, what are you repossessing and where?

H.B.: Inventory. Furniture, to be more precise. We have a security agreement with a furniture store, Shiner's Recliners, giving us a security interest in their inventory of furniture. Shiner's has been in default for three months, and we lost patience with them. So early this morning, I rented a truck, hired the usual crew of people who can lift heavy things and showed up at the store to repossess our collateral.

S.C.: So far, so good. What's the problem?

H.B.: Well, we got here about 9:00 A.M. and had about half the furniture loaded into our truck by 11:00. I'm thinking, "Man, this is the first easy one in a long time." Just then, a deputy sheriff shows up and tells me to stop loading. I ask why. The sheriff says some jerk who slipped and fell on the showroom floor just got a judgment against Shiner's for a million bucks, and he's there to levy on the furniture. I tell him I'm repossessing under a security interest, and he asks to see a copy of our financing statement. That's when I discover we didn't file one. So we argue for an hour, and we're getting nowhere. I'm certainly not going to unload what's already on the truck, but when a man with a gun tells me to stop, I stop.[12]

S.C.: So would I.

H.B.: Wait, it gets worse.

S.C.: How? What more could happen?

H.B.: Well at noon, this lawyer for Shiner's shows up. He says he's just filed a petition in bankruptcy on behalf of Shiner's and that the Sheriff and I better leave. And he wants me to unload the furniture from the truck.[13] So the three of us argue for an hour and get nowhere. I hate this job. You better get over here and set these guys straight.

## Problem 4–10

*When you get back from your somewhat successful excursion to Shiner's Recliners, you find the following memorandum. It is another Driver special.*

### BANK OF NEW BABYLON
### INTEROFFICE MEMORANDUM

TO:     S. Carlson, Megabank Legal
FROM:   P.L. Driver, V.P.
RE:     Ali Baba's Rugs Loan

We have been providing operating capital to the above-referenced borrower for a number of years under a written security agreement that gives us a security interest in Ali Baba's inventory of oriental rugs. The loan balance varies, but it normally ranges in the high six figures to the low seven figures.

---

**12.** [See Section 9–313(b); Section 9–316(d) and (e); Section 9–601, Comment 4; Section 9–609.]

**13.** [See Section 9–313(d); Section 9–317; Sections 544(a), 547, and 362 of the Bankruptcy Code.]

Two years ago, Ali Baba's was in very shaky financial condition. We had (and continue to have) a valid financing statement on file, and, as far as I know, our security interest was (and is) first priority. However, as you may know, oriental rugs are fairly easy to move and have a habit of disappearing in the middle of the night. (They tell me some of Ali Baba's people are thieves.) So, to assure a minimum collateral base, we required Ali Baba to deposit 40 of the most valuable rugs for storage here at the Bank. The rugs were kept locked in our vault, except on those rare occasions that Ali Baba's brought in potential buyers, at which time we let Ali Baba employees display them in one of our conference rooms, always under the supervision of a Bank employee.

Six months into this arrangement, Ali Baba's informed us that, in order to preserve the rugs properly, it was necessary to air them in the sun and mothball them. So we released the rugs to Ali Baba's employees, who performed the preservation work and returned them to the Bank three days later. That was 18 months ago. The good news is that Ali Baba's financial position is now so strong, we feel comfortable turning the rugs back over to them. The bad news is that, when we surrendered the rugs two days ago, ten of them were missing. We really don't know what happened, as we did not count the rugs when Ali Baba's employees returned them 18 months ago. Now Ali Baba's claims an offset against the loan balance for the price of the missing rugs, which are worth about $25,000 each. Are we in trouble here?[14]

### Problem 4–11

*It is 4:30 in the afternoon and you get back to your desk with your afternoon snack of root beer (you do not need any more caffeine today[15]) and a bag of what appears to be cheese twists. You thought you had resolved the Shiner's Recliners problems. But no! There is an e-mail from Bigg.*

TO:          S. Carlson, Megabank Legal
FROM:    H. Bigg, NB Commercial Finance
RE:          Shiner's Recliners

I thought I should run this by you since you are familiar with this debtor's problems. Shiner's bankruptcy continues to be a mess. As you know, most of our advances to Shiner's were secured by furniture inventory. On one occasion, however, we loaned a small amount ($5,000) on the strength of two-dozen conditional sale contracts between Shiner's and its customers. Naturally, we took possession of the conditional sale contracts and informed the customers, in writing, that they should make their payments directly to us. One of the customers was a guy named Barry Slack, who was buying a $1500 sofa on time. Two months later, Slack stopped paying. That was eight months ago. I don't know why we never contacted Slack. He just fell through the cracks. Anyway, Slack has apparently skipped town. No one can find him. One of my people found the sofa, but Slack trashed it before he left, and it's now worth very little. Shiner's is disputing

---

**14.** [See Section 9–207, and *In re Bi-glari Import Export, Inc.*, 130 B.R. 43 (Bankr.W.D.Tex.1991).]

**15.** http://www.popsoda.com/soda-pop/dadoldfasroo.html

our claim in the Bankruptcy Court, claiming our balance should be reduced because we dropped the ball on Slack. Is there any truth to that?[16]

# BANK OF NEW BABYLON
# LOAN OFFICER TRAINING AND
# OPERATIONS MANUAL

## CHAPTER 4: PERFECTION OF SECURITY INTERESTS

### IV.  Perfection by Filing

Perfection by filing is the most common method of perfection under Article 9.[17] It is accomplished by the use of what Article 9 refers to as a "financing statement." The term "financing statement" is defined in a manner that expressly contemplates not only hard-copy files but also paperless electronic filing systems, should a particular enacting state so desire. See Section 9–102(a)(39) and (69). Consistent with the trend toward the use of electronic media, the requirement that a debtor sign a financing statement, once a part of Article 9, has been omitted. To protect the debtor's interest, a requirement that the debtor *authorize* the filing of the financing statement has been substituted. See Section 9–509. The debtor's execution of a security agreement automatically constitutes authorization to file a financing statement covering the collateral described in the security agreement. See Section 9–509(b). If, for any reason, a purported secured party is not authorized to file a financing statement, it is ineffective. See Section 9–510. However, if a secured party is authorized to file a financing statement as to certain collateral, but includes additional collateral, the financing statement is effective as to the authorized collateral but is ineffective as to the unauthorized collateral. See Comment 2 to Section 9–510.

In fact, apart from the special requirements for timber, mineral-related collateral, and fixtures, set out in Section 9–502(b), the Code lists only three requirements for an effective financing statement:

1.  The name of the debtor;

2.  The name of the secured party or his/her representative

3.  An indication of the collateral.

However, a loan officer who prepared a financing statement containing only the foregoing information would be seriously remiss in his or her duties. The reason is that the Code effectively imposes further requirements when it authorizes—indeed requires—a filing officer to reject financing statements that do not contain additional information. See Section 9–516(b) and Section 9–520(a). These additional requirements really make a proper financing statement a much more detailed document. The additional requirements include the addresses of the debtor and secured party and an indication either that the debtor is an individual or that it is an organization. In the case of an individual, the statement must specify which name is the debtor's last name. In the case of an organization, the financing statement must show the type of

---

**16.**  [See Section 9–207(a).]

**17.**  See generally Charles Cheatham, *Changes in Filing Procedures Under Revised Article 9*, 25 Okla. City U. L. Rev. 235

(2000) and Harry C. Sigman, *Twenty Questions About Filing Under Revised Article 9: The Rules of the Game Under New Part 5*, 74 Chi.-Kent L. Rev. 861(1999).

organization (corporation, limited liability company, partnership, etc.), the jurisdiction in which it was organized, and the organizational identification number, if any.

Failure to include the information specified in Section 9–516(b) both authorizes and requires the filing officer to refuse to accept it for filing under Section 9–520(a). Of course, it is possible that a careless filing officer might file a financing statement in spite of such incompleteness. If that happens, the plain implication of Section 9–502 is that the financing statement is effective if it contains the more minimal requirements imposed by that section. It should be obvious, however, that you, as a loan officer, should never place yourself and the Bank in a position in which you must count on a filing officer to be derelict in his or her duty. You should always include all information specified in both Section 9–502 and Section 9–516(b) in any financing statement. If you do not, a diligent filing officer may refuse to accept it, and the Bank's security interest may remain unperfected.

The Code tolerates minor inaccuracies in a financing statement. It contains a provision making a financing statement effective if it substantially complies with Code requirements, in spite of minor errors, as long as the latter are not "seriously misleading". See Section 9–506(a). The Code provides, at various points, more specific guidance concerning which errors make a financing statement seriously misleading.

Section 9–521 contains model forms, including the model form for the financing statement. See subsection (a).

----

## IV. Perfection by Filing

### A. Debtor's Name

### Problem 4–12

*With the dawn of a new day there is always new hope. In your case, the hope is that this will be a light day. That hope is about to be dashed as a result of the following memorandum that is sitting on you desk.*

**NB COMMERCIAL FINANCE, INC.**
**INTEROFFICE MEMORANDUM**

TO:       Jane Robinson, Megabank Legal Dept.
FROM:     Sal Vache, NB Commercial Finance
RE:       Review of Cavalier Files
          *Sidney: Help this guy out—JR*

As you may know, I am the replacement for Mose Cavalier, the loan officer who left in the wake of the Dismal Investments matter. Mr. Comstock asked that I undertake a review of all of Cavalier's existing files, and he said you had agreed to help us with less urgent legal questions while he handles the time sensitive matters. I have found several files that give me some cause for concern, and I will describe them in sequence below:

## Strickland Loan

This loan is unusual in that it is a simple equipment financing, which I am told we don't normally do. I do not see any record that Cavalier obtained prior approval for it. The debtor is an individual, James T. Strickland. Two years ago, the debtor purchased from Grady, Inc., a Caterpillar model VC60D forklift for $22,229.00. Strickland contributed a 10% down payment, and we provided the balance of the funds necessary for the purchase. Strickland signed a security agreement in standard form, listing the forklift as the collateral by make, model and serial number. A financing statement with the same collateral description was filed. Here's the difficult part. The financing statement lists the name of the debtor as "Strickland Builders Supply" and the address as "Box 240, Golden, Gilmoria. 38847." The financing statement was signed by James T. Strickland. My own investigation has revealed that "Strickland Builders Supply" is the trade name for a sole proprietorship owned by James T. Strickland. Is our security interest perfected by this financing statement?[18]

## Silverline Loan

This loan is secured by our usual security interest in present and after-acquired inventory and accounts receivable. The security agreement is flawless, as far as I can see. I have one concern about the financing statement. The debtor is a corporation, the true name of which is Silverline Building and Maintenance Co., Inc." The financing statement lists the name of the company as "Silvermine Building Maintenance Co., Inc." Is that close enough?[19]

## Happy Hog Loan

This one is very odd. The borrower in this case is a dealer in high-end motorcycles, Happy Hog, Inc. The security agreement gives us a security interest in the debtor's present and after acquired inventory and accounts receivable. The financing statement describes the collateral perfectly, and it uses the debtor's exact corporate name—Happy Hog, Inc. I have a receipt for the filing fee and a copy of the financing statement, stamped to indicate when it was accepted for filing. It looks to me like Cavalier did everything right. So I was flabbergasted when I got a call from E.Z. Ryder, the President of Happy Hog. He said an officer from Chaste Bank had just showed up to repossess some of the motorcycle inventory. Apparently, Happy Hog is a little short of funds, and the Chaste made a loan secured by inventory, upon which Happy Hog promptly defaulted. But Chaste's loan is two years later than ours, and so is its financing statement. When Ryder told Chaste's officer that, she said she had searched the UCC records, and we don't have a financing statement on file under the name "Happy Hog, Inc." or any close variant. I checked it out, and it turns out she's right. The moron filing officer took Cavalier's financing statement and filed it under our name, NB Commercial Finance.[20] To make matters worse, when I told the bank

---

**18.** [See Section 9–502; Section 9–503(a)(1) and (c); Section 9–506.]

**19.** [See Section 9–102(a)(70) and Comment 11; Section 9–503 and Comment 2; Section 9–506; *District of Columbia v.*

*Thomas Funding Corporation*, 593 A.2d 1030 (D.C.App.1991).]

**20.** [See Section 9–516(a) and Section 9–517. See also Section 9–516(b), Section 9–520(a), Section 9–516(d) and Comment 3.]

officer from Chaste about this she looked at it and called me back to tell me that the financing statement is defective in any event. The financing statement indicates that Happy Hog is a limited liability company when it is, in fact, a corporation.[21] I've talked to the bank officer, and she agreed to hold off while we each checked with our respective lawyers. I think you better get back to me on this one fairly quickly.

### Simpson Loan

This is another filing officer issue. This is an inventory financing arrangement with a car dealership, Simpson Motors, Inc. When I looked in the file, I found a copy of the financing statement. Unfortunately, it was the original. It was attached to a letter from the filing officer indicating that it was returning the financing statement and the filing fee because there was an error. Below that statement is a list of possible errors and the one checked was "improper filing fee." Sure enough, the check (uncashed) is also attached to the letter. When I looked at the filing fee schedule, it was clear that this was the correct filing fee, so the filing office just made a mistake. Unfortunately, when I checked the filing records I found a financing statement in favor of Bank of Amerigo covering the inventory. Is there any chance we can still have priority?[22]

### Problem 4–13

*The fun continues.*

## BANK OF NEW BABYLON
## MEMORANDUM

TO:      S. Carlson
FROM:    J. Robinson
RE:      High Roller Matter

High Roller, Inc. is a manufacturer of bowling balls with a factory on the south side of New Babylon. High Roller started up with a loan from the Bank 50 years ago and has been a good customer ever since. Obviously, we've amended and renewed various loan documents a number of times. Our most recent Loan and Security Agreement gives us a security interest in all of High Roller's present and future inventory, equipment, accounts, general intangibles, machinery, vehicles, raw materials, chattel paper, and just about anything else you can name. Our financing statement is current and uses both the same collateral description and the correct corporate name.

About a week ago, the original President of the company, David "Rip" Kegler, retired and turned the business over to his son, Sonny Kegler. Sonny has decided the future of the company lies in the economy end of the bowling ball market, and he is officially changing the name of the company to LowBall, Inc. My question is, do we need to file something because of the

---

**21.** [See Section 9–516(b)(5)(C)(ii); Section 9–502, and Section 9–338.]

**22.** [See Sections 9–516(a) and (d); Section 9–516(d); and Comment 3 to Section 9–516.]

name change?[23] If so, what? Can we mail it in?[24] What happens if we just do nothing? Give me a memo on this for future use.

### Problem 4–14

*Just as you complete the memo requested by your boss on the High Roller matter, you check your "in" box and find the following handwritten note from the boss (who has conveniently disappeared).*

*Sidney:*

*A thousand apologies. I got the facts on the High Roller matter from Rip, and either he didn't get it straight or Sonny wasn't entirely candid with him. I talked to Sonny today, and the deal is a little more complicated. Apparently, LowBall, Inc., is an existing company and competitor of High Roller. Sonny has cut a deal to merge High Roller into LowBall, with LowBall the surviving corporation. The Kegler family gets a nice premium, and Sonny gets a consulting contract. Anyway, tell me what happens to our security interest, if anything, as well as our relationship with LowBall.[25]*

*JR*

## B. Description of Collateral

### Problem 4–15

*You see a new name on your e-mail. You click on it in hopes that it is something diverting like a list of good lawyer jokes.[26] No such luck.*

TO:      S. Carlson, Megabank Legal Dept.
FROM:    Sharon Leiffer, Bovine State Bank
RE:       Some Direction

I have just started at the Bank and I asked Mr. O'Reilly about some questions regarding our financing statements. He suggested I contact you. He referred to you as the "expert."

1. If we discuss a loan transaction with an individual, but they have not yet signed a security agreement, can the Bank file a financing statement covering the expected collateral to insure the earliest possible priority date? Does it matter if I have discussed the description in the financing statement with the potential borrower and the potential borrower orally agreed to the filing?[27]

---

**23.** [See Section 9–503(a); Section 9–506; Section 9–507; Section 9–521(a).]

**24.** [See Sections 9–102(a)(18) and (74); Section 9–516(a).]

**25.** [See Section 9–203(d) and (e); Section 9–326; Section 9–508(b) and Comments 2 and 3.]

**26.** See http://cartalk.cars.com/timekill/archives/doc-law.html

**27.** [See Section 9–509(a); Harry C. Sigman, *Twenty Questions About Filing Under Revised Article 9: The Rules of the Game Under New Part 5*, 74 Chi.–Kent L. Rev. 861, 871–874 (1999) (Sigman).]

2. If we take a security interest in collateral specifically described in the security agreement, for example, as a "drill press," can I use "equipment" as the description in the financing statement since the drill press is equipment? Similarly, if the we have taken a security interest "equipment," can I describe the collateral in the financing statement as "inventory, equipment, and accounts receivable" in case we make a later loan and want to take a security interest in these other assets at a later time.[28]

3. If the answer to any of the above is no, what impact would my actions have on the validity of the financing statement?[29]

## Problem 4–16

*You've voice mail indicator light is flashing. You try to ignore it, hoping that it will go away. You actually begin to fantasize about contracting a non-fatal, non-painful disease that will require you to have one month's bed rest with no stressful interactions. You pick up the phone, dial in your code and hear: "You have three new messages."*

*The first message:*

Sal Vache from NB Consumer Finance here. One of our customers, Herman Hodad has a surfboard shop on the Coast of Gilmoria. He operates it as a sole proprietorship, and we have been financing his inventory since he started. We have a security agreement with him that grants us a security interest in his present and after-acquired inventory and accounts. We have a financing statement on file describing the collateral as "inventory, equipment, and accounts" and listing Herman individually as the debtor. About a month ago, Herman organized a corporation called The Board Room, Inc. ("TBRI"). He transferred all the assets of his shop to TBRI, and the business is going to continue under the corporation. Do I need to do anything?[30] I also have a second question on the Hodad loan. It seems Herman has a second lender, Remnant Finance Co. Their financing statement was filed after ours, but the description reads, "all inventory, equipment, and accounts, now owned or hereafter acquired, to secure all advances, whenever made." I also checked and their security agreement uses the same description. Does it matter that our description in the financing statement is less detailed than Remnant's? Call me back.[31]

*The second message:*

Sidney, it's Jane. We're doing a start-up loan on a new business, Biscuits.com, which is gearing up to sell dog food and assorted pet accessories over the internet. We're taking the usual blanket lien on everything they have or ever will have. My question is, can we just use a description like, "all personal property whatsoever, now owned or hereafter acquired, to

**28.** [See Section 9–509(a); Sigman at 871–874.]

**29.** [See Section 9–509(d)(2); Section 9–510(a) and Comment 2; Section 9–513(c); Sections 9–625(b) and (c)(4); Sigman, 871–874.]

**30.** [See 1–201(28) and Comment 28; Section 9–203(d) and (e); Section 9–315(a)(1); Section 9–326; Section 9–507(a) and Comment 3; Section 9–508(b) and Comments 2 and 3; *In re Bluegrass Ford–Mercury, Inc.,* 942 F.2d 381 (6th Cir.1991).]

**31.** [See Section 9–9–203(b); Comment 2 to Section 9–502; *Thorp Commercial Corporation v. Northgate Industries, Inc.,* 654 F.2d 1245 (8th Cir.1981).]

secure all advances whenever made," in the security agreement and financing statement? I'll be back in the office at 4:00. Call me then or leave me a voice mail.[32]

*And finally, a voice mail from your favorite rural banker:*

Hey Carlson. This is Bubba from the Bovine State Bank. Here's the deal. One of our local construction contractors, Buddy Diggs, has applied for a short-term loan to help him get the capital to finish a big job. I think he's a good risk, and he's offered us a security interest in a fairly new Caterpillar backhoe he claims to own outright. If he's telling the truth—and I think he is—the backhoe is worth a lot more than he wants to borrow. But I checked the UCC records, and the local branch of Bank of Amerigo has a financing statement on file under Buddy's name with a collateral description that reads, "certain construction equipment." Buddy says the backhoe isn't covered by the Bank of Amerigo security agreement. Is there any good way to verify that?[33] I'm really not on very good terms with the local folks at Bank of Amerigo.

# BANK OF NEW BABYLON
# LOAN OFFICER TRAINING AND
# OPERATIONS MANUAL

## CHAPTER 4: PERFECTION OF SECURITY INTERESTS

### IV. Perfection by Filing

### C. Place of Filing

The 1972 version of Article 9 offered states three options for the place to file a financing statement. The first provided for a central filing of financing statements. The second provided for a central filing in some cases and a local filing in others. The third required both a central filing and a local filing. A comment 2 to Section 9–501 points out, multiple places of filing increased the cost of the transactions and also increased the potential for error. The 1998 version of Article 9 provides, with limited exceptions, for central filing of financing statements. See Section 9–501.

---

### Problem 4–17

*There is nothing like a missive from Bubba first thing in the morning.*

**THE BOVINE STATE BANK**
**DESOLATION, GILMORIA**
**"Serving Desolation for Fifty Years"**

**MEMORANDUM**

TO:        S. Carlson, Megabank Legal Dept.
FROM:    Bubba O'Reilly, Bovine State Bank
RE:        Clark Loan

**32.** [See Section 9–502(a)(3); Section 9–504(2); *Lehigh Press, Inc. v. National Bank of Georgia*, 193 Ga.App. 888, 389 S.E.2d 376 (1989). Compare Section 9–108(b) and (c).]

**33.** [See Section 9–210; Section 9–625. But see Comment 2 to Section 9–502.]

Bovine State Bank is about to loan James C. Clark $400,000. While Clark does not have a job (he lists his profession as "heir"), he does have two operating oil wells on his 20–acre home site outside of Desolation. These wells are top producers and he sells the oil from the wells to Shell. He has signed a security agreement that gives us a security interest in the accounts receivable that Shell owes him. They pay on a quarterly basis. I have never done a transaction like this. Could you help me draft the financing statement, let me know what kind of authorization I need to get from Clark to file the financing statement, and where I should file it?[34]

## IV. Perfection by Filing

## D. Lapse

### Problem 4–18

*It is now January 9th, and you have just returned from your holiday break. The phone rings. It is your boss. The New Year is not starting well.*

S.C.: Carlson

J.R.: Jane here. I'm glad you are finally back. We have a problem.

S.C.: [Audible groan.] What is it this time?

J.R.: Gutenberg Printing Company, one of the last of the old line printers. Never really entered the computer age.

S.C: And I assume they owe one of our affiliates money.

J.R.: No, I just feel sorry for them and want you to observe a moment of silence. Of course they owe us money! Why do you think I'm calling?

S.C.: Give me the details.

J.R.: We start by going back five years from one week ago. On that day, the Bank of New Babylon loaned Gutenberg $250,000. By a security agreement dated the same day, the Bank took a security interest in three enormous printing presses used by the business. We filed a financing statement the same day describing the presses in great detail, including serial numbers.

S.C.: Sounds like everything was done by the book, so far.

J.R.: Well, it didn't stay that way. Jump ahead to seven months ago. You know P.L. Driver at the Bank?

S.C.: Of course. Pretty reliable guy.

J.R.: Normally, yes. On this occasion, his computer tickler file told him the Gutenberg financing statement needed attention. So he filed a continuation statement on June 17.

S.C.: Does that matter?

J.R.: That's what I would like to know. Anyway, on December 30, the sheriff showed up. A former employee has a $500,000 judgment against Gutenberg arising out of a workplace injury, and he had the sheriff levy on the presses. Apparently, the presses were too big for the sheriff to cart away, so he

---

**34.** [See Section 9–102(a)(6); Section 9–501(a); Section 9–502(b); Section 9–509.]

tagged and immobilized them. Everybody went home to celebrate the New Year.

S.C.: And we didn't know about any of this?

J.R.: Not until January 5, when I saw a notice of the sheriff's sale of presses in the paper. That's when I checked our filings and got very nervous. I assumed that I had the right to file another continuation statement and a new financing statement[35] and I did so because it was all I could think of. So do some research and tell me if we are o.k.[36]

# BANK OF NEW BABYLON
# LOAN OFFICER TRAINING AND
# OPERATIONS MANUAL

## CHAPTER 4: PERFECTION OF SECURITY INTERESTS

### V. Perfection as to Proceeds

It undoubtedly took very little time as an employee of the Bank for you to learn that the assets of both individual and business borrowers are seldom stable. A system of secured credit which confined a lender's security interest to the assets on hand when a security agreement was executed would, in many instances, offer the lender only fleeting and precarious protection. It would also place a heavy burden on the lender to monitor the business affairs of the debtor.

You are already familiar with one Article 9 response to this problem, viz., the broad authorization of the use of future advance and after acquired property clauses in Section 9–204. In addition, when a debtor transfers an asset that is part of the secured lender's collateral, Article 9 permits, with some exceptions, both the continuation of the secured lender's interest in the original collateral (Section 9–315(a)(1)) and the attachment of the secured lender's interest to the assets the debtor receives in exchange for the original collateral (Section 9–315(a)(2)). Indeed, the interest in the latter assets, which the Code calls "proceeds," arises automatically and need not be separately described in the security agreement. See Section 9–203(f).

In Section 9–102(a)(64)(A) the Code defines "proceeds" as "whatever is acquired upon the sale, lease, license, exchange, collection or other disposition of collateral." It also includes distributions on account of collateral, such as dividends on shares of stock the debtor has pledged (Section 9–102(a)(64)(B)). You should also note that since the definition of collateral includes proceeds (see Section 9–102(a)(12)(A)) what ever is acquired on the disposition of proceeds is also proceeds. The Code divide the class of proceeds into "cash proceeds," which includes "money, checks, deposit accounts, or the like," and the residual category of "non-cash proceeds." See Section 9–102(a)(9) and (58).

Thus, virtually anything that a debtor receives in exchange for or on account of collateral will be "captured" by the security interest of a secured lender, in the sense that the secured lender's interest will attach to it, provided that it is identifiable as

---

**35.** [See Section 9–512(a) and Section 9–509(b).]

**36.** [See Section 9–510(c); Section 9–515; Section 9–516(b)(7) and Section 9–520(a); Harry C. Sigman, *Twenty Questions About Filing Under Revised Article 9: The Rules of the Game Under New Part 5*, 74 Chi.-Kent L. Rev. 861, 886–888 (1999).]

proceeds of the original collateral. See Section 9–315(a)(2) and (b). In the non-inventory setting, for example, the proceeds may commonly take the form of cash or a check, or perhaps a tangible asset taken in trade. In the case of dispositions of inventory, the potential array of proceeds is quite varied and includes cash, open accounts, instruments, or chattel paper. The automatic attachment of the secured party's interest to the proceeds establishes his or her rights to these assets relative to the debtor.

Generally speaking, if the security interest in an item of original collateral is perfected, the Code continues perfection in its proceeds, at least temporarily. See Section 9–315(c). However, as a Bank officer, you should always bear in mind that the continued perfection may be only for 20 days. Thereafter, continued perfection may (or may not) require additional steps, depending on what form the proceeds take and how they are acquired. See Sections 9–315(d) and (e). Because the question of continuing perfection can become quite complex, it is normally prudent to consult the Legal Department.

---

### Problem 4–19

*More e-mail.*

TO:        S. Carlson, Megabank Legal Dept.
FROM:   Sal Vache, NB Commercial Finance
RE:        The Board Room, Inc. (formerly Herman Hodad)

First of all, thanks for your help on the name change problem. I have our new financing statement on file listing TBRI as the debtor and describing our collateral in the same way it is described in the security agreement, that is "all inventory and accounts, now owned or hereafter acquired." Herman, of course, is still running the place, and he still runs it in the same casual way. I swear, these beach bums are going to give me a heart attack. Anyway, I've been watching how he does business, and I have some questions. As you know, Herman sells surfboards, skim boards, boogie boards and the like. Some are cheap, but some of them cost thousands of dollars. Herman will sell them any old way he can. Like everyone else, he takes plastic, so some sales generate rights to payment from the credit card issuers. When he's lucky, he gets paid in cash, although some of the cash sits around for days in his safe. He does the same with the checks. When he gets around to it, he deposits the cash and checks into his deposit accounts. There is a special cash collateral account here at Finance into which he is supposed to deposit all proceeds from the sale of inventory. Sometimes he complies, but sometimes he deposits cash or checks into a general operating account he's had for years with the Bank of New Babylon, in which there are funds from other sources as well. Anyway, on a few occasions, he has sold very expensive boards to his friends, either on open account or based on a promise embodied in a simple promissory note. When he collects the accounts, the funds go into one of the two bank accounts. If someone he doesn't know as well wants to buy a board on time, he has them execute a conditional sale contract. My initial question is whether we can claim an interest in any of the assets Herman gets in return for boards. If we have an interest, do we have to do anything to perfect it?[37]

My other question relates to some equipment Herman has purchased recently. He's bought two new cash registers and two new computers for use in the business. He bought one cash register with a check drawn on the cash collateral account and one with a check drawn on the operating account. He bought one of he computers by signing over a note from one of his friends, and the other by endorsing a check from another customer. Can we claim an interest in any of this new equipment? Do we have to perfect it?[38] Please advise.

## Problem 4–20

*Your e-mail has become as bothersome as your telephone.*

TO:         S. Carlson, Megabank Legal
FROM:    J. Drabb, Friendly Finance
RE:         Bart R. Swapp Loan

I have a somewhat unusual transaction here, and the question it raises is one that Mr. Conseco could not answer off the top of his head. We financed Mr. Swapp's purchase of a computer system from CompuSwamp and took a security interest in it. Since it was pretty clear the system was for home use, we did not file anything. Mr. Swapp apparently grew tired of playing video games on the computer, and he traded it to his neighbor, Mr. Smith, for the latter's big screen television. I assume the TV is proceeds and that we have an interest in it, but I'm not sure if we need to do anything to perfect our interest. Can you help me out?[39]

# BANK OF NEW BABYLON
# LOAN OFFICER TRAINING AND
# OPERATIONS MANUAL

## CHAPTER 4: PERFECTION OF SECURITY INTERESTS

### VI.    Perfection of Property Subject to a Certificate of Title

For many years, automobiles and other vehicles have been the subject of special legislation providing for distinctive forms of evidence of ownership. This special treatment is a product of a combination of causes. In part, it is simply a function of the fact that, after a home, an automobile or truck may be the single most expensive

---

**37.** [See Sections 9–102(a)(2), (9), (12), (47), (58) and (64); Section 9–203(f); Section 9–310(a); Section 9–312, Section 9–314; Section 9–315; Section 9–501(a)(2); Bruce A. Markell, *From Property to Contract and Back: An Examination of Deposit Accounts and Revised Article 9*, 74 Chi–Kent L. Rev. 963, 984–988(1999); Ingrid Hillinger, David Batty, and Richard Brown, *Deposit Accounts Under the New World Order*, 6 N.C.Banking Inst. 1 (2002).]

**38.** [See Section 9–315; Section 9–331, Section 9–332; Section 9–102(a)(33); William Stoddard, *Tracing Principles in Revised Article 9 § 9–315(b)(2): A Matter of Careless Drafting, or an Invitation to Creative Lawyering?* 3 Nev. L. J. 115 (2002).]

**39.** [See Section 9–309(1) and Section 9–315(d).]

item an average person owns. In part, it is a reflection of the fact that automobiles and other vehicles are mobile and thus may be stolen and transported to a distant jurisdiction with relative ease. Finally, special legislative treatment of automobiles is, in part, a product of a desire to keep track of vehicles operated regularly within the boundaries of a particular state, in order to facilitate systems for appropriate taxation and owner identification.

Today, there is legislation in all states requiring, with some exceptions, that ownership of automobiles, trucks and motorcycles be evidenced by a special document (normally called a "certificate of title") issued by a state agency. In some states, farm equipment and mobile homes are likewise covered by certificate of title legislation. In addition, vehicles located permanently within a state are normally subject to a system of mandatory registration, which facilitates the collection of taxes and results in the issuance of license plates that must be placed on vehicles as identifying markers.

Normally, when an individual purchases a motor vehicle in a particular state, the relevant state agency issues a certificate of title and the vehicle is registered in that state at the same time. If the vehicle is purchased from a dealer, the dealer processes the necessary paperwork. If the sale is of a used car by a consumer, the buyer normally applies for a new certificate of title and changes the registration. When a vehicle owner permanently moves to a new state, that will typically trigger a requirement that the vehicle be re-titled or, at least, registered in the new state. In many instances, the old title certificate will be exchanged for a new one issued by the new state. In some instances, a copy of the original certificate of title may be sufficient to register the vehicle in the new state and obtain license plates.

Lenders very quickly seized on certificates of title as a way of giving notice that a vehicle was subject to a security interest. The buyer of a second-hand vehicle would normally want proof that the seller actually owned it. A lender preparing to advance funds on the strength of a vehicle would want similar proof. Exhibition of a certificate of title would normally be the response of the seller or borrower. If a prior lender could obtain a notation of its security interest on the title certificate, potential buyers or lenders would be on notice of it. Obviously, the effectiveness of title notation as a form of public notice would be enhanced if it were legally required as a condition of perfection of the security interest.

At this time, all states require that certificates of title be issued for all motor vehicles and that they be registered. Further, all states require that any security interest in an automobile, motorcycle, or truck be noted on the certificate of title.[40] In practice, as an additional safeguard for a lender who creates and obtains notation of such a security interest, the original certificate of title is actually held by the lender with the first noted security interest. If that lender's loan is satisfied, the lender so notes and delivers the certificate to any junior lender listed on the certificate or, in the absence of a subordinate lender, to the vehicle owner.

The Code generally defers to such certificate of title statutes for purposes of perfection of security interests in automobiles and other motor vehicles. Absent such a statute, a security interest in an automobile, which qualifies as a "good" under Section 9–102(a)(44), could be perfected either by filing or possession. See Section 9–310,

---

**40.** [See, e.g., the Uniform Motor Vehicle Certificate of Title and Anti–Theft Act.]

Section 9–312, and Section 9–313. In the case of an automobile that qualified as a "consumer good," a purchase money security interest would be automatically perfected. See Section 9–309. The Code, however, expressly provides that filing is neither necessary nor effective to perfect a security interest in collateral subject to a certificate of title statute, and makes compliance with the certificate of title statute, for nearly all purposes, the only way of perfecting such a security interest. See Section 9–311(a)(2) and (b).

Three qualifications to the generality of the preceding paragraph must be added at this point, however. First, some certificate of title statutes pertaining to goods other than motor vehicles provide for the issuance of a certificate of title as evidence of ownership but do not require notation of security interests on the certificate of title as a condition of perfection. Items covered by such statutes are not "covered by a certificate of title" within the meaning of the Code and are not subject to the special deferential Code rules just described. See Section 9–102(a)(10). Second, even as to forms of collateral (like automobiles, trucks and motorcycles) that are subject to a true certificate of title statute (in the Code sense), when such collateral is held as inventory by a debtor who deals in goods of the kind, filing in the normal U.C.C. records remains a necessary condition of perfection. See Section 9–311(d).

Third, the very mobility of motor vehicles requires additional Code rules to resolve problems created when vehicles (or other collateral subject to certificate of title statutes) moves from one jurisdiction to another. Generally speaking, the Code's choice of law rules make the state law (including the certificate of title statute) of a jurisdiction issuing a certificate of title apply for purposes of assessing whether a security interest is perfected and determining its priority. See Section 9–303(c). However, additional rules are necessary to settle choice of law and perfection questions that arise when collateral (e.g., boats or mobile homes) moves from a state which does not cover it with a certificate of title to one that does, or when collateral subject to a certificate of title statute in one state is permanently relocated to another state, perhaps triggering the new state's title or registration requirements. See Section 9–303, Section 9–313(b), and Section 9–316(d) and (e). This is discussed more fully in Chapter 6 of this Manual.

———

## Problem 4–21

*You are leaning back in your chair contemplating dinner. You are just teasing up the image of rare salmon with a ginger-orange glaze, a salad with field greens, toasted walnuts and goat cheese, some green beans (aldente), and a nice glass of pinot gris*[41] *when the phone rudely interrupts you.*

S.C.: Carlson

J.D: Hi Carlson. This is Jimmy Drabb at Friendly Finance. I have another strange one for you. This one involves a borrower who pulled the wool over our eyes.

**41.** *http://www.eatdrinkdine.com/.* Click on "Start With Food" then on "Seafood" then on "Salmon, Grilled." You will see a link to the recipe and a link describing the wine.

S.C.: How so?

J.D.: Well, he's sort of a double dipper. The guy's name is Barry Slick, and he had this Porsche Boxer. Red, naturally. Anyway, he needed money, so he borrowed $5,000 from his friend, Dave Ernst. Apparently, Ernst used to work for an inventory finance company, so he actually hand-wrote a security agreement and filed a financing statement describing the car by VIN number. Time went by, and Slick didn't pay when he was supposed to. So Ernst actually repossessed the car. Nice trick for a layman. Anyway, Slick still had the title certificate for the car, and he persuaded one of our loan officers to loan him $10,000. We took a security interest in the car and had it noted on the certificate of title. Slick didn't pay us either, so we went to repossess the car. Only one problem–no car. We've talked to Ernst, and he says his interest has priority. That can't be right, can it?[42]

**42.**  [See Section 9–310(b)(3) and Section     Section 9–316(d).]
9–311 and Comment 7; Section 9–313(b);

# Chapter 5

# PRIORITIES

---

## BANK OF NEW BABYLON
## LOAN OFFICER TRAINING AND
## OPERATIONS MANUAL

## I.  Introduction

It is a sad, but inevitable, fact that some of the borrowers whom you encounter in performing your duties as a loan officer will default on their obligations to the Bank. If, as is normally the case, the Bank's loan is secured, you may determine that the best avenue of collection is through the assertion of a claim against the Bank's collateral. Often, however, you will encounter another creditor or claimant who likewise seeks to appropriate the collateral in order to satisfy his or her claim. In cases in which the property consists of personal property, it is the function of the priority rules of Article 9 to determine which creditor or claimant has the superior right to appropriate collateral assets that are insufficient in value to satisfy all claims.

The priority rules of Article 9 vary depending, in part, upon the nature of rival claimants in the priority dispute at issue. Accordingly, succeeding sections of this Manual will include discussions of the priority rules governing disputes between (a) two or more secured creditors; (b) secured creditors and lien creditors; (c) secured creditors and buyers of the collateral; and (d) secured creditors and claimants under real estate law when the collateral consists of personal property that becomes attached to real property. An additional section will address special problems that arise when the defaulting borrower files in bankruptcy and the secured creditor's claim is challenged by the Trustee in Bankruptcy.

Of course, in applying the priority rules discussed in the following sections, you should bear in mind that priority disputes may also be affected by the attachment and perfection rules discussed in Chapters 3 and 4 of this Manual. If, for example, the Bank, as a perfected secured creditor, is involved in a priority dispute with a rival claimant who purports to be another perfected secured creditor with a superior position under the normal rules governing priorities between perfected secured creditors, the Bank may still prevail if we can demonstrate that the rival claimant's alleged security interest never attached properly or, though attached, was never properly perfected. In effect, such a demonstration would make the priority rules governing disputes among perfected secured creditors irrelevant and trigger the rule that, in general, perfected secured creditors prevail over unsecured creditors and unperfected secured creditors.

## II. Priority Disputes Between Two or More Secured Creditors

### A. The Standard Rule

It is sometimes said that the basic priority rule among secured creditors is "first in time, first in right." Even if this were the only Article 9 priority rule, this formulation would be an oversimplification badly in need of elaboration. Initially, one needs to know which critical events must be placed in a time sequence to determine who is "first in time." In the (extremely rare) case of a dispute between two unperfected secured creditors, for example, the critical event is the time of attachment. The secured creditor whose interest attached first has priority. See Section 9–322(a)(3).

In contrast, if one secured creditor is perfected and the other unperfected, the order of attachment ceases to have any significance. The perfected secured creditor prevails. See Section 9–322(a)(2). If both of the secured creditors are perfected, the critical event in the time sequence may be either filing or perfection. Conflicting perfected security interests rank in order of the earlier of filing or perfection, provided there is no period thereafter when there is neither filing nor perfection. See Section 9–322(a)(1). The most basic applications of the last rule may be illustrated as follows:

**Illustration 1:**

Debtor, as security for a $10,000 loan, grants a non-purchase money security interest in construction equipment to Secured Party 1 (SP1) on February 1. SP1 files a financing statement covering construction equipment the same day. On March 1, Debtor borrows $5,000 from Secured Party 2 (SP2) and grants SP2 a security interest in the same construction equipment. SP2 files a proper financing statement covering construction equipment the same day. Debtor repays neither SP1 nor SP2, and both seek to foreclose on the equipment at a time when it is worth $12,000.

Under Section 9–322(a)(1), SP1 has priority, and (ignoring, for a moment, the questions of interest, costs of sale, and collection costs) SP1 may appropriate the first $10,000 of the proceeds of the collateral to retire SP1's debt in full. SP2 will receive the remaining $2,000 in partial satisfaction of SP2's debt. Each secured party has both a filing date and a perfection date, although filing date and perfection date are identical in each case. Because SP1's filing and perfection date (February 1) precedes SP2's filing and perfection date (March 1), SP1 is "first in time" and entitled to priority.

The same result would follow if, instead of filing on March 1, SP2 perfected by taking possession of the collateral or somehow became entitled to automatic perfection. In that case, SP2 would have only a perfection date and no filing date, but SP2's perfection date would still be subsequent to the date of SP1's filing and perfection.

**Illustration 2:**

Debtor, in anticipation of a loan from SP1, enters into a security agreement with SP1 covering Debtor's construction equipment. On February 1, SP1 files an appropriate financing statement. On March 1, Debtor borrows $5,000 from SP2 and grants SP2 a security interest in the same construction equipment. SP2 files an appropriate financing statement the same day. On April 1, SP1 advances $10,000 to the Debtor.

Debtor repays neither SP1 nor SP2, and a priority dispute arises at a time when the equipment is worth only $12,000.

The result is the same as in the preceding illustration. SP1 has priority and may appropriate the first $10,000 in collateral value, and the remaining $2,000 in collateral value is allocated to SP2. Once again, SP2 has identical dates for filing and perfection, March 1. SP1, however, has a February 1 filing date and an April 1 perfection date (since perfection presupposes attachment and the latter cannot occur until the last remaining step—the giving of value—occurs on April 1.) However, since SP1's filing date precedes SP2's perfection date, and there is no subsequent time in which SP1 is neither filed nor perfected, SP1's February 1 filing date makes SP1 "first in time" and entitled to priority. See Comment 4, Example 1 to Section 9–322. Article 9 thus sets up a notice filing system, in which, once SP1 is the first to file, SP1 may make subsequent advances with the assurance of priority without the need for constant checking for subsequent filings like that of SP2. Once again, the result would not change if SP2's method of perfection on March 1 were something other than filing.

The foregoing illustrations are the simplest applications of the basic "first in time, first in right" rule that governs priority disputes between perfected secured creditors. Additional complications can arise where either or both secured creditors have used future advance or after acquired property clauses in their respective security agreements, as Article 9 expressly authorizes. See Section 9–204, Section 9–322, and Section 9–323. Moreover, it is critical to note that, in certain kinds of disputes between particular varieties of secured creditors, Article 9 departs from the standard "first in time" rule and establishes special superpriorities for favored classes of secured creditors even though their filing or perfection dates are not first in time. See, e.g., Section 9–324 (purchase money superpriority); 9–308 and Section 9–330 (possessory chattel paper superpriority). These special superpriority rules will be covered in subsequent sections of this Manual.

---

## Problem 5–1

*Your fear of your own telephone has now become pathological, particularly on Fridays.*

S.C.: Carlson.

B.O.: Hey, Sidney. Glad to find you in on a Friday afternoon. Bubba O'Reilly here.

S.C.: Are you in town?

B.O.: No, I'm out here in Desolation. We've got a little awkward situation here I need you to help me resolve.

S.C.: (Audible groan). What's the problem?

B.O.: Well, you probably remember young Bobby Bellicose, the mayor's kid turned lawyer?

S.C.: (Even more audible groan). How could I forget? Puts his mouth in "drive" while his brain is in "neutral."

B.O.: That's our boy. And he's right here with me. He and I have a little dispute over some beer vats. You may remember our local brewer up here, Swamp Fog, Inc.

S.C.: Oh yes. Brewers of Swamp Fog—"the beer that brings Desolation to you"—not to mention Nutria Sweet Brown Ale.

B.O.: Right. That last one wasn't very successful, which is one reason why we're here. Anyway, four years ago, when the brewery began its operation, we made a start-up loan to the company in the amount of $100,000. We took the usual blanket security interest in all the assets of the business— equipment, inventory, accounts, and everything else you can name. We had the company president sign one of our standard security agreements, which, as you know, has the usual after-acquired property clause and future advance clause. And we filed our usual financing statement on February 1 of that year.

S.C.: Sounds good so far.

B.O.: Yeah, I followed standard operating procedure on this one. About six months later, on July 5 the company borrowed another $50,000 from the local branch of Bank of Amerigo. They also made the loan on a secured basis, and their security agreement and financing statement are virtually carbon copies of ours. Frankly, at the time the business looked so good, I don't think Bank of Amerigo minded being second in line, and I didn't feel like the Bank of Amerigo loan created any problems for us.

S.C.: You knew about it?

B.O.: It's a small town, Sidney. Everybody knows everything. We all knew about it. In fact, the business looked so good, we advanced the company another $100,000 on August 1.

S.C.: So where are we now?

B.O.: Well, the Nutria Sweet Brown Ale project pretty much destroyed the company, and Swamp Fog is behind in its payments to us and to Bank of Amerigo. The inventory was sold long ago and is probably coursing through the blood of a thousand frat boys down there in New Babylon. The remaining accounts are uncollectable. Both Bank of Amerigo and our Bank are trying to find collateral to seize. About all that's left are ten large steel brewing vats, which have some value in the used equipment market. I think they're worth about $15,000 apiece. Our loan balance is about $165,000 so we're a little under water even if we take them all.

S.C.: What do you mean, "if"? Why wouldn't we take them all?

B.O.: Because young Bobby here says we can't. See, four of the vats were on hand when the company started that February. Two more were bought in May. The last four were bought in late July. Bobby says two things. First, he says because I knew about their July 5 advance, we only have priority in any of the vats to secure our initial $100,000 advance. Then he says, even if that's wrong, Bank of Amerigo and we have to share pro rata in the last four vats. I think that's crazy. We do things this way all the time. He says he'll only back off if you can show him exactly where it says we can have it all.[1] So talk to him, okay? Here. I'll put him on the line.

1.　[See Section 9–322 and Comments 2, 4 and 5; Section 9–323 and Comment 3.]

## Problem 5–2

*While you were on the phone with Bubba, your voice mail light went on. It turns out to be another old friend.*

Hello, Carlson. This is Jimmy Drabb at Friendly Finance. I have another somewhat unusual situation here, and Mr. Conseco suggested I talk to you. What I have is a rags to riches to rags story. On March 1, two years ago, the company made a consumer loan of $1,000 to a borrower named Rollo D. Dyce. The loan officer at the time had Dyce sign an old security agreement form that granted the company a security interest in "all of borrower's household goods, and any and all household goods acquired by borrower in the future." We filed a financing statement the same day. We didn't know it at the time, but, two weeks later, Dyce bought a "Pick 3" lottery ticket in the Gilmoria state lottery, and it turned out to have 3 matching alligators. So he won $5,000. He went out on March 15 and bought a used piano for $3,000. On March 16, he went down to the casino in New Babylon and promptly lost the remaining $2,000 of his lottery winnings at the blackjack tables. On March 30, he somehow talked Household Finance Company into lending him another $5,000. Household made him sign a security agreement granting a security interest in "all household goods in the borrower's possession, now or in the future." Household also filed a financing statement. Now Dyce has failed to pay both our company and Household. To tell you the truth, the only thing worth repossessing and selling is the piano. Dyce will surrender it willingly, and our company and Household will cooperate on its sale. Do we have priority over Household for the first $1,000 in proceeds of the piano?[2] Please call me as soon as you can.

## Problem 5–3

*You did not work at all this weekend. There was a Humphrey Bogart festival on one of the cable channels. You watched 10 films starting with "High Sierra" (1938), and moving through "The Maltese Falcon" (1938), "The Big Sleep" (1946), "The Treasure of Sierra Madre" (1948), "Key Largo" (1948), "The African Queen" (1951), "The Caine Mutiny" (1954), "Sabrina" (1954), "The Harder They Fall (1958), and topped off by "Casablanca" (1943). However, when you enter your office humming "As Time Goes By," (http://bogart-tribute.net/sounds.shtml) you find on your desk the following memorandum dated <u>Saturday</u>.*

### MEGABANK, INC.
### INTEROFFICE MEMORANDUM

TO:          S. Carlson
FROM:     J. Robinson
RE:           Bank of New Babylon—Noyes Matter.

Here's one you don't see every day. A high school classmate of mine, Lotta Noyes, now owns a road construction company called Noyes Paving, Inc. Three years ago February 20, the Bank of New Babylon loaned Noyes

---

**2.** [See Section 9–204(b)(1) and Section 9–108(e).]

Paving $50,000 in operating capital. Noyes signed a security agreement giving the Bank a security interest in two relatively new Caterpillar bulldozers, which were described by make, model and serial number in the agreement. With Noyes' consent we filed a financing statement on February 21 that described the collateral as "construction equipment." On May 1, without the Bank's knowledge, Noyes Paving entered into an "equipment lease" with the Franklin National Bank covering three Kubota backhoes. The lease provided that Noyes Paving, if not in default, could purchase the backhoes at the end of the lease term for one dollar. Franklin did not file a financing statement at the time.[3]

Later that year, Noyes Paving experienced some difficulty in keeping current on its payments under the security agreement with our Bank. The following January 30, I worked out an extension agreement extending Noyes Paving's time for payment. In consideration for the extension of time, Noyes Paving signed an amendment to the security agreement giving the Bank a security interest in "all of Noyes Paving's equipment, now owned or hereafter acquired." It went on to provide that the security interest secured payment of "all loans, advances, debts, liabilities, obligations, covenants and duties owing by Noyes Paving to the Bank of New Babylon." We did not file any additional financing statement at the time of the amendment of January 30. (Between you and me and the trees, we didn't even know about the backhoes at the time.)

Noyes Paving stabilized for about a year, but financial problems arose again in the early spring. By March, Noyes Paving was in default under the Bank's security agreement, as amended, as well as the equipment leases with Franklin. On May 21, Franklin repossessed the backhoes. We have repossessed the bulldozers and some other equipment, but it's all old enough that it won't bring enough at a sale to retire the Bank's debt. I would love to get my hands on those backhoes. Could we possibly have first claim to them? Please write up the usual brilliant memo, as I need something to show Pompous, who has taken an interest in this matter.[4]

## Problem 5–4

*Just when you thought it was safe to open your e-mail, the following appears:*

TO:       S. Carlson
FROM:  J. Robinson
RE:       Bank of New Babylon—Hooping Crane Matter

It seems nothing is ever simple. Rick Hooping is a subcontractor here in New Babylon. He owns half a dozen very large construction cranes and makes his living supplying and operating cranes for the contractors who build skyscrapers downtown. It all began two years ago in January, when the Bank loaned Dan half a million dollars and took a security interest in his

---

**3.** [See Section 1–201(37); Rev. Section 1–203; Section 9–505.]

**4.** [See Comment 2 to Section 9–315; Section 9–322; Section 9–323 and Comment 3; *James Talcott, Inc. v. Franklin National Bank*, 292 Minn. 277, 194 N.W.2d 775 (1972).]

equipment and accounts receivable, now owned and hereafter acquired. We perfected with a financing statement filed on January 10. Rick is in default, and it may become necessary to repossess and sell the cranes, which are still worth a lot.

There is a potential problem with one crane, however, a Kingfisher Model 1029. In looking through the Bank's files on this loan, I came across an old security agreement between Hooping and a Finance Company I have never heard of, Blue Heron Finance Company. The security agreement is dated a little more than 16 months before our transaction, on April 20, and it grants Blue Heron a security interest in the Kingfisher 1029 (which is described down to the serial number) to secure a $50,000 loan. The file also contains a copy of a financing statement apparently filed by Blue Heron on the same day, describing the collateral as "equipment." Our loan officer, P.L. Driver, apparently inquired as to the status of this loan at the time of our loan, as there is a letter dated January 3, from Blue Heron's President to Driver confirming that the Blue Heron loan balance has been paid off entirely.

Now comes the interesting part. In one of his conferences with Rick, Driver found out that Hooping borrowed another $100,000 from Blue Heron in November, some 11 months after our transaction. Blue Heron and Hooping wrote up a new security agreement exactly like the old one. I do not know if they also filed a new financing statement, but Driver is checking. It should be fairly obvious that the question I have for you is whether the Bank or Blue Heron has priority as to the Kingfisher.[5] Please respond ASAP.

—Jane


## Problem 5–5

*As you return from the library, that annoying voice on your computer announces that "you've got mail," and you retrieve the following e-mail message:*

TO:        S. Carlson
FROM:      J. Robinson
RE:        More on Hooping Cranes

This is an addendum to my previous e-mail. It seems there is a problem with another of the cranes, this time an Egret Model 575. Driver found another surprise in the Hooping file. In the year before our transaction, on July 1, Hooping apparently borrowed $50,000 from Pelican Finance Company. He executed a security agreement in favor of Pelican that granted Pelican a security interest in the Egret Model 575, which is described by serial number. There is no future advance or after-acquired property clause in the agreement. There is a copy of Pelican's financing statement (date stamped July 1) in the file, and it describes the collateral as "equipment." We do not yet know how much of the initial loan balance remains unpaid. To

**5.** [See Section 9–322; Section 9–323(a)     tion 9–513; Section 9–625(b) and (e).]
and Comments; Section 9–509(d)(2); Sec-

complicate matters further, on June 1 of the next year, Hooping borrowed another $35,000 from Pelican. This time, Hooping executed a second security agreement that grants Pelican a security interest in large diesel-powered generator, which Hooping apparently had acquired on March 30 of that year. The June 1 agreement recites that the generator secures Hooping's "debt to Pelican." We do not know if another financing statement was filed at this time, but there is no copy in our files. I need you to sort out our priority relative to Pelican, both with respect to the Egret crane and the generator.[6] Driver and I are going out to meet with Hooping, and I'll call you when I get back.

## Problem 5–6

*You have not had time to digest the Cranes problem when another e-mail from your boss arrives.*

TO:       S. Carlson
FROM:   J. Robinson
RE:       Bank of New Babylon—High Roller Matter

You remember Sonny and Rip Kegler and their bowling ball manufacturing company, High Roller, Inc.? We talked about this before.[7] Anyway, it turns out the merger of High Roller, Inc. into LowBall, Inc., was completed on August 1. We found out a little late, but I took your advice and got a financing statement on file under LowBall's name by October 1. You will recall that our security interest was pretty much a blanket floating lien.

Our most recent financing statement under High Roller's name was filed last February 15, and its collateral description is as broad as we need it to be. The same is true of our new financing statement under LowBall's name. It turns out, however, that LowBall already had a secured creditor, Van Winkle Commercial Finance. Van Winkle has a blanket floating lien on the assets of LowBall as broad as ours, and their financing statement was filed on June 1. I need a memo from you describing the relative priority between us and Van Winkle with respect to collateral in High Roller's hands on or before August 1, collateral acquired by LowBall between August 1 and October 1, and collateral acquired by Low Ball after October 1.[8] Have it on my desk by the end of the week.

---

**6.** [See Section 9–203; Section 9–204; Section 9–322; Section 9–323.]

**7.** [See Problems 4–13 and 4–14.]

**8.** [See Section 9–203(d) and Comments to Section 9–508; Section 9–507; Section 9–508; Section 9–325; Section 9–326.]

## BANK OF NEW BABYLON
## LOAN OFFICER TRAINING AND
## OPERATIONS MANUAL

### CHAPTER 5: PRIORITIES

## II.  Priority Disputes Between Two or More Secured Creditors

### B.  Purchase Money Security Interest Superpriority[9]

You will recall the discussion of purchase money security interests in Chapter 4 of this Manual. The purchase money status of a security interest is even more important with respect to priority than it was with respect to perfection. Assuming certain requirements are met, a purchase money security interest in goods (usually equipment or inventory) has priority over a conflicting security interest that has an earlier filing or perfection date. See Section 9–324. There are two policy reasons traditionally articulated for varying the normal "first in time, first in right" rule. First, a fresh infusion of loan funds, coupled with the debtor's corresponding acquisition of new assets, does not diminish the asset pool previously available to the prior creditor. Since the prior creditor was satisfied with the asset pool available at the time it originally made its loan, it is not disadvantaged by giving the creditor that has financed additional assets first claim to the new assets. Second, without a purchase money superpriority, the holder of a blanket floating lien who was first to file would have an effective stranglehold on the debtor. Absent a purchase money superpriority (or some other method of subordinating the initial floating lien), any new lender or supplier of inventory or equipment on secured credit would be subordinate to the first to file under the normal priority rule of Section 9–322(a). The subsequent lender or supplier might be reluctant or unwilling to extend credit doomed to second priority, at best. Without the purchase money superpriority, the debtor might thus be held hostage to the original creditor.

It should be noted that it is also possible to achieve a higher priority position by way of agreement with an otherwise superior party. Section 9–339 expressly permits one creditor to agree to subordinate its claim to that of another creditor. Frequently, voluntary subordinations will occur when the creditor with an existing secured claim does not wish to extend additional credit, but recognizes that it would be to its own benefit for the debtor to obtain a new loan. In order to encourage a new lender to extend credit, the existing creditor may agree to subordinate his own claim to the collateral to that of the new lender (either completely or partially).

---

### Problem 5–7

*You have grown tired of interoffice memoranda. As you pick up the next one, you wonder if you will ever talk to a live human being again.*

---

**9.**  Keith Meyer, *A Primer on Purchase Money Security Interests Under revised Arti-* cle 9 *of the Uniform Commercial Code,* 50 U. Kan. L. Rev. 143 (2001).

## MEGABANK, INC.
## INTEROFFICE MEMORANDUM

TO:         S. Carlson
FROM:       J. Robinson
RE:         Bank of New Babylon—Great Weight Freight File

I need some research on one of the Bank's forays into the world of equipment financing. Our borrower, Great Weight Freight, Inc., hauls freight up and down the river in barges. Great Weight's warehouse is on the Damp Street Wharf here in New Babylon. Great Weight's primary lender is Bank of Amerigo, which has a blanket security interest in substantially all of Great Weight's assets. Bank of Amerigo and Great Weight signed their security agreement about three years ago. It contains a collateral description that includes all the Code general collateral types, as well as well-drafted future advance and after-acquired property clauses. Bank of Amerigo filed an equally broad financing statement at the same time.

Two years ago, the president of Great Weight, a Mr. Prudhomme, applied to our Bank for a loan. It seems Bank of Amerigo had declined to advance further funds, and he needed some new equipment for his warehouse. The company looked pretty solid financially, and opportunities to acquire new customers at Bank of Amerigo's expense are never unwelcome. On October 1 of that year, the Bank agreed to lend Great Weight $15,000 for the purchase of a brand new fork lift from a local heavy equipment supplier, Lugg, Inc. On October 2, we cut a check payable jointly to Lugg and Great Weight, which Prudhomme endorsed and delivered to Lugg. The fork lift was delivered to Great Weight later that afternoon. On October 4, Prudhomme came to the Bank and executed a security agreement granting the Bank a security interest in the fork lift, which was described by make, model and serial number. He also signed a financing statement with an equally specific collateral description, which we filed on October 15.

A few weeks later, Prudhomme paid the Bank another visit. Apparently, he had really wanted two fork lifts all along, but had not felt able to afford the second one in October. In early November, Lugg took a used fork lift in as a trade, and they called Prudhomme. The price was right—$3,000—but Prudhomme was concerned about its condition. So, on November 5, Lugg delivered it to Great Weight's warehouse on the express understanding that Prudhomme could try it out for a few days and return it with no questions asked if he was not satisfied. Great Weight used it for two weeks, and Prudhomme was quite pleased with it. On November 19, he called Lugg and told them he would buy it. The same day, he came to us to borrow the money. Once again, we had him sign a security agreement describing the fork lift by make, model and serial number. We also prepared a financing statement, which we filed later—specifically on November 27. By that time, Great Weight was maintaining the business checking account with us, although it had close to a zero balance. So we credited Great Weight's account with $3,000, and Prudhomme drew a check in favor of Lugg.

Great Weight is now in default on its obligations to Bank of Amerigo, and Bank of Amerigo is threatening to repossess everything that is not nailed down. I assume that we have done everything we need to do to prime

Bank of Amerigo with respect to the two fork lifts.[10] I have a meeting Monday with the Assistant General Counsel of Bank of Amerigo, so I need you to verify that my assumption is correct.

### Problem 5–8

*As you return to your office from lunch, you notice that your voice mail light is on.*

Carlson. This is Roy Comstock at NB Commercial Finance. You remember that matter you worked on for Bud's Studs?[11] Well, I finally nailed down the time sequence for you. The conditional sale contract between Acme and Bud's was executed first, on October 1 of last year. Acme delivered the slitter on October 2. Our security agreement was signed on October 8, and we filed on October 9. That's the good news, because Acme did not file until the next day, October 10. I'm even more worried about Bud's than I was when you worked on the file, and, since the slitter has presumably depreciated by now, I suspect we are headed for a priority contest with Acme.[12] So call me back and let me know where we stand. Thanks.

### Problem 5–9

*Your e-mail has grown so bothersome that you seldom get to play solitaire on your computer these days.*

TO:         S. Carlson, Megabank Legal
FROM:      R. Comstock, NB Commercial Finance
RE:         Vaca & Sipes File

Thanks for your help with the Bud's Studs matter. Proving that no good deed goes unpunished, I have another one for you. O'Reilly from the Bovine State Bank persuaded us to get involved with this borrower because we do a lot of purchase money inventory financing.

The borrower here is Vaca & Sipes, Inc. (Vaca), a large (for Desolation) electronics dealer. Four years ago, he borrowed $100,000 in operating capital from the Provident Credit Association (PCA). PCA took a security interest in "all Vaca & Sipes, Inc. inventory, whether now owned or hereafter acquired." PCA filed a financing statement at the same time, and I can't find any flaws in either it or the security agreement.

A year ago, at Bubba O'Reilly's urging, NB Commercial Finance agreed to loan Vaca funds to bring in a new line of digital televisions. We modified our standard security agreement somewhat, but what Vaca signed (on August 1 of last year) granted us a security interest in "all inventory financed by NB Commercial Finance, no matter when acquired, to secure all advances, whenever made, as well as any other obligations owing to NB Commercial Finance." In a separate paragraph, I also took a security interest in the rest of Vaca's present and future inventory. Anyway, on

**10.** [See Section 9–103 and Comments; Section 9–322(a)(1); Section 9–324(a) and Comment 3.]

**11.** [See Problem 4–1, supra.]

**12.** [See Section 9–103; Section 9–322(a)(1); Section 9–324(a) and (g).]

August 3, I sent PCA a letter notifying them of our acquisition of a security interest in Vaca's inventory and later that day I filed a financing statement describing the collateral as "inventory." We made two advances to Vaca. The first, in the amount of $50,000, was made on August 30, and Vaca used it to buy the initial lot of 20 televisions. A second $50,000 advance was made on October 1, and Vaca used it to buy an additional 20 televisions.

As you can guess, however, Vaca has defaulted on both our loan and the PCA loan, and I'm stuck in Desolation fighting over televisions. The PCA lawyer is some young smart aleck named Bellicose. I claim that we have priority because we have a purchase money security interest. He says that doesn't help us in this case. Is that true?[13] In addition Bellicose claims that even if we would have priority if we had a purchase money security interest, we do not have that status for two reasons. First, he claims that we can not have a purchase money security interest if our security interest covers "other obligations to NB Commercial Finance" which include the usual things like insurance premiums we paid on Vaca's behalf, finance charges and late charges, and collection costs. Second, he contends the use of after-acquired and future advance clauses are incompatible with purchase money status.[14] Can you help me straighten this guy out?

### Problem 5–10

*You know something is wrong. You are beginning to look forward to missives from Bubba. You are considering checking into a clinic.*

### THE BOVINE STATE BANK
### DESOLATION, GILMORIA
### "Serving Desolation for Fifty Years"

### MEMORANDUM

TO:         S. Carlson, Megabank Legal Dept.
FROM:    Bubba O'Reilly, Bovine State Bank
RE:         Doug's Rugs File

I need your help again, as I have a situation I haven't encountered before. We have a borrower, Doug's Rugs, that operates a carpet and rug shop here in Desolation. Doug opened four years ago, and the Bank provided the startup and operating capital. We have an ordinary security interest in his present and after acquired inventory and accounts receivable to secure all advances, whenever made. We filed an appropriate financing statement at the time we made the loan.

Most of Doug's inventory is either ordinary mass-produced residential carpet he buys from domestic manufacturers or more expensive woven rugs

---

**13.** [See Section 9–324(b).]

**14.** [See Section 9–103. Compare *South-trust Bank of Alabama v. Borg–Warner Acceptance Corp.*, 760 F.2d 1240 (11th Cir. 1985) with *Pristas v. Landaus of Plymouth, Inc.*, 742 F.2d 797 (3d Cir.1984). See also McLaughlin, " 'Add On' Clauses In Equip-ment Purchase Money Financing: Too Much Of A Good Thing," 49 Ford.L.Rev. 661 (1981) and Wessman, "Purchase Money Inventory Financing: The Case for Limited Cross–Collateralization," 51 Ohio St. L.J. 1283 (1990).]

he buys from foreign wholesalers. His credit rating is quite good, and he buys from both the manufacturers and wholesalers on open credit. I think we can safely assume we have a first priority security interest in all of this ordinary inventory.

Our advances to Doug are based on a percentage of his eligible inventory, and my question concerns whether we should include some rather unusual rugs in the calculation. A few years ago, a very small religious cult, the Dream Weavers, moved into an old house up in the hills behind Desolation. They grow their own food and have very little contact with the outside world. Until recently, however, I did not know that they raise a little spare cash by weaving and selling beautiful handmade rugs. The quality really is comparable to some of the foreign rugs, and none of them sells for less than $1,000. Anyway, they sell these rugs through Doug's Rugs on a consignment basis. Each time one of the Dream Weavers brings in a rug, they sign a "Consignment Agreement," which gives Doug the absolute right to return the rug if it doesn't sell and provides that it "remains the property of the Dream Weavers." Doug is an honest guy and is paying on time. However, I had a somewhat ugly experience when one of the Dream Weavers showed up while I was doing a field check of Doug's inventory. He told me, "Keep thine ugly mitts off mine rug." He obviously thinks that, if Doug ever went out of business, his right to the rug would be superior to ours. Could he be right?[15] If so, those rugs shouldn't be used in the "eligible inventory" formula, should they?

### Problem 5–11

*The phone rings. It is Sharon Leiffer from Bovine State Bank.*

S.L.: Hi. Sidney.

S.C.: Hi Sharon. Lost any collateral lately? *[This is what passes for humor among secured transactions professionals. This should worry you.]*

S.L.: Very funny. I have an interesting problem and I need some advice. I got a call from Ruth Fender, the president of Fender's Benders. Fender's Benders manufactures machines that are used to form steel rods and plates into various shapes for the construction industry. Fender says the company needs a loan of $50,000 to get it over a rough spot. It is offering a security interest in its equipment. I have checked and there is approximately $85,000 in value there. Unfortunately, both Chaste Bank and Bank of Amerigo have filed financing statements covering the equipment, with Chaste being first. I have also learned that Chaste is owed $40,000 and Bank of Amerigo is owed $35,000. When I spoke to the people at Chaste, they encouraged me to make the loan and said that they would agree to subordinate their claim to ours if we would do so. This makes no sense to me, but who am I to argue? What I need to know, is if we make the $50,000 loan to Fender's Benders and Chaste signs an effective subordination agreement, as between Chaste, Bank of Amerigo, and us, who would get what if Fender's Benders went into

---

**15.** [See Section 9–102(a)(20); Section 9–103(d); Section 9–319(a); Section 9–324(b).]

bankruptcy (a distinct possibility). To keep it simple, assume the above figures remain accurate at the time of default.[16]

## BANK OF NEW BABYLON
## LOAN OFFICER TRAINING AND
## OPERATIONS MANUAL

## CHAPTER 5: PRIORITIES

## II.  Priority Disputes Between Two or More Secured Creditors

### C.  Priority as to Proceeds

Like the original collateral, proceeds may be claimed by a variety of rivals, and priority contests can arise. Obviously, all secured creditors with a claim to the original collateral may assert a claim to the proceeds as well. In addition, priority contests between a secured creditor claiming an asset as proceeds and another secured creditor claiming the asset as original collateral often arise. Businesses that sell goods, for example, often have separate inventory and accounts receivable lenders. When the debtor sells an item of inventory on open account, the inventory lender may claim the account as proceeds, while the accounts receivable lender claims it as original collateral. If the sale of inventory generates either chattel paper or accounts, the inventory lender may face a rival claimant who is denominated a purchaser of the accounts or chattel paper, since outright sales of accounts and chattel paper fall within Article 9. The possibility of priority disputes requires Article 9 rules governing both the perfection of security interests in proceeds and priority rules for resolving contests among perfected security interests.

Generally speaking, the Code provides that the time of filing or perfection as to original collateral is the time of filing as to proceeds, and that priority disputes involving conflicting perfected security interests in proceeds are resolved under the usual "first in time of filing or perfection" rule. See Section 9–322(a)(1) and (b)(1). However, the exceptions to this generalization are both numerous and complex, and advice of the Legal Department will normally be necessary in the case of such priority contests.

———

### Problem 5–12

*You have begun to hear rumors of a shake-up in the Department. One of the secretaries told you that Pompous was unhappy, which made Houseman unhappy. You do not know if it is true, but you have decided to keep your head down. There are three memoranda on you desk that seem to be about the same sorts of issues, and you would like to get them all finished before you leave for the day. From a quick glance, it looks like a long day.*

**16.**  [See Section 9–339 and *ITT Diversified Credit Corp. v. First City Capital Corp.*, 737 S.W.2d 803 (Tex.1987).]

## NB COMMERCIAL FINANCE, INC.
## INTEROFFICE MEMORANDUM

TO:        S. Carlson, Megabank Legal Dept.
FROM:     R. Comstock, NB Commercial Finance
RE:        Wild Bill's Computers Bankruptcy

One of our borrowers, Wild Bill's Computers, filed a petition in bankruptcy last Friday. Wild Bill's was one of the first computer stores in town, and, like a lot of small operations, it just could not compete with the computer superstores over the long haul. NB Commercial Finance has provided operating capital to Wild Bill's for the last three years. At the inception of the relationship, we entered into a security agreement giving us a security interest in "all of Wild Bill's inventory, now owned or hereafter acquired, to secure all advances, whenever made." We filed a financing statement with the same collateral description at the same time. About a year ago, Wild Bill's borrowed $50,000 from Chaste Bank. The loan is secured by a blanket lien on virtually all of Wild Bill's assets, perfected by a financing statement with the same description, filed at the time.

Fortunately, we saw the handwriting on the wall and conducted an on-site audit of Wild Bill's assets two days before the petition was filed. Wild Bill's inventory was low, as suppliers cut the company off a month ago. The inventory he had on hand was probably only worth $25,000. However, Wild Bill's sold a lot of computers on credit, and its accounts on hand at the time of our audit had a face value of $50,000. I talked to Bill himself this morning, and he said the only change was that he had sold a $5,000 system for cash. He apparently used the cash to buy some diagnostic equipment for his repair shop and a revolving display rack. Anyway, I need you to find out who is acting as Wild Bill's trustee in bankruptcy and talk to him. (Robinson said you could use a little time out of the library.) Obviously, we would like to realize on our collateral as soon as possible. Our loan balance is down to $85,000, so I hope we won't end up under water by much. I assume we have first priority in everything.[17] Let me know if you see any problems. Thanks in advance for your help.

## Problem 5–13

## BANK OF NEW BABYLON
## INTEROFFICE MEMORANDUM

TO:        S. Carlson, Megabank Legal Dept.
FROM:     P.L. Driver, V.P. Bank of New Babylon
RE:        Bank of New Babylon—PastBlast, Inc. File

The Bank's customer, PastBlast, Inc., is a pressure-washing contractor specializing in cleaning and restoration of large buildings, especially those with historic significance. The Bank provides ongoing operating capital financing to PastBlast, secured by a perfected security interest in PastBlast's equipment, inventory, and accounts receivable. The security agreement has

---

**17.** [See Section 9–102; Section 9–315; Section 9–322.]

the usual future advance and after-acquired property clauses. Our most recent financing statement was filed about three years ago coving equipment, inventory, and accounts receivable. When PastBlast became the successful bidder for the pressure-washing subcontract on the Old Armory restoration project in July of last year, its President, Melvin Splash, came to us seeking a $20,000 loan to assist in the purchase of two new industrial pressure washing machines. The loan did not seem to me to be prudent at the time, and we declined to advance any funds.

Apparently, that same month PastBlast then persuaded the seller of the pressure washers, JetStream, Inc., to extend seller financing. PastBlast traded in one of its old pressure washers as a down payment on two brand new JetStream Supersoakers. JetStream had PastBlast execute a "title retention contract," which reserved a security interest in both of the new pressure washers in favor of JetStream until the price was paid in full. A financing statement, describing the collateral as "pressure washing equipment," was filed 8 days later.

About six weeks ago, PastBlast finished the Old Armory job, and its business has slowed down considerably. Apparently, it now has more pressure washers than it needs. Exactly 30 days ago, PastBlast sold both of the new Supersoakers. One was sold to another contractor, Sparkle, Inc., for $8,000 in cash. PastBlast used the cash to replenish its inventory of detergents and bleach, which had fallen to low levels because of the Old Armory job. PastBlast now has about 100 50–gallon drums of the stuff lying around its shop. The other Supersoaker was sold to a different contractor, CleanTeam, Inc. CleanTeam gave PastBlast a check for $1000 as a down payment, and PastBlast deposited it in its ordinary operating account the next day. (The account balance was $6,000 immediately before the deposit. Since then, PastBlast has written only one check I know about—to New Babylon Public Service, Inc., in the amount of $3,000, for overdue utility bills.)[18] The rest of the $8000 purchase price was to be paid by CleanTeam in monthly installments of $500 each. Interestingly, PastBlast used the JetStream title retention contract as a model and had CleanTeam execute an identical agreement reserving a security interest in the Supersoaker in favor of Past Blast.

PastBlast appears to me to be quite shaky financially. I am meeting with Mr. Splash tomorrow in order to explore ways of reducing his loan balance. However, I need a target figure, and, to calculate that, I need to know which of the remaining assets of PastBlast are subject to a first priority security interest in the Bank's favor and which assets are subject to prior security interests of others.[19] Please advise.

**18.**  [See Universal C.I.T. Credit Corp. v. Farmers Bank of Portageville, 358 F.Supp. 317 (E.D.Mo.1973).]

**19.**  [See Section 9–103; Section 9–315; Section 9–322; Section 9–324(a); Section 9–327; Section 9–340.]

## Problem 5–14

### NB COMMERCIAL FINANCE, INC.
### INTEROFFICE MEMORANDUM

TO:           S. Carlson, Megabank Legal Dept.
FROM:      R. Comstock, NB Commercial Finance
RE:            Charm of the Farm Implement Co.

I need your help with a situation that has turned somewhat messy. NB Commercial Finance has a customer, Charm of the Farm Implement Co., which, as the name suggests, is a dealer in various kinds of farm machinery, including White–Case and Massey Ferguson lines. The current loan balance is about $1.1 million, and it is secured by an ordinary security interest in Charm of the Farm's existing and after-acquired inventory. Our financing statement was filed on May 1, two years ago. Charm of the Farm borrows money secured by its accounts with one of our competitors, Heavy Duty Finance Co. Heavy Duty's financing statement (covering all accounts, including after-acquired collateral) was filed two years ago on July 1.

In March of last year, Charm of the Farm became an authorized John Deere dealer. Its John Deere inventory was financed by a subsidiary of the manufacturer, John Deere Acceptance Corporation ("JDAC"). JDAC makes loans to Charm of the Farm to enable it to acquire a variety of John Deere products, ranging from very expensive tractors and combine harvesters to smaller items like plough blades and tilling attachments. JDAC filed a financing statement describing the collateral as "inventory manufactured by John Deere" on March 15. About a week later, I received a letter from JDAC informing us that JDAC intended to commence purchase money financing. Actual deliveries of John Deere machinery did not start until April 1 of last year.

At the moment, Charm of the Farm is in default to all of its lenders. I can sort out most of the priority questions myself, including the relative priority with respect to the inventory still on Charm of the Farm's premises. However, I need you to help me with some priority questions concerning the proceeds of sales of John Deere inventory within the last month.

Specifically, two John Deere tractors were sold, one to a farmer named McDonald and another to a farmer named Johnson. In each instance, the buyer made a cash down payment of $10,000, which was deposited in Charm of the Farm's ordinary operating account at Bank of Amerigo. (I have heard, off the record, that that account is now down to about $500.) In each case, the buyer then signed a conditional sale contract reserving a security interest in the tractor in favor of Charm of the Farm until the remaining $65,000 of the purchase price was paid in installments over five years. A week or so later, McDonald wanted a tilling attachment, which he bought with a $2500 check. I do not know what happened to the check. Charm of the Farm may be holding it in its safe, or it may have been deposited in an account somewhere. Johnson, in the meantime, wanted a snow removal blade for his tractor. Johnson is apparently a more favored customer than McDonald, and Charm of the Farm sold the $1000 blade to him on open account. I'm not sure whether he has made any payments on the account or

not. As I acquire further information, I will call or e-mail you. But this
should be enough to get you started.[20]

## Problem 5–15

*After you take your first weekend off in what feels like five years, you
return to find that you have 47 e-mail messages, 46 of which are unread. This
is the first.*

TO:          S. Carlson, Megabank Legal Dept.
FROM:        R. Comstock, NB Commercial Finance
RE:          Cheatin' Heart Mobile Homes

As you know, the largest volume of our business is inventory and
accounts receivable financing. However, for the last five years, we have
dramatically expanded our direct financing of chattel paper. One of our
customers is Cheatin' Heart Mobile Homes, Inc., a mobile home dealer
located in Traylor Park, a somewhat remote suburb of New Babylon.
Cheatin' Heart's own customers are often unable to secure financing from
the more risk-averse urban banks, so Cheatin' Heart often extends seller
financing under conditional sale contracts, usually with a five-year term. We
buy Cheatin Heart's conditional sale contracts at a discount deeper than we
can get from other customers and take possession of them when we deliver
our check. We then collect from the mobile home owners directly. So far,
we're making decent money.

Last week, I got a call from "Honest" Joe Lincoln, Cheatin' Heart's
owner. He said one of his lenders, Double Wide Finance Company, was
giving him trouble. Apparently, Double Wide has been lending to Cheatin'
Heart on a secured basis for several years. I haven't seen their security
agreement or financing statement yet, but Lincoln assures me it's a standard, non-purchase money inventory financing arrangement. Unless I find
out otherwise, you should assume Double Wide has an ordinary security
interest perfected by a financing statement covering inventory that was filed
before ours. Anyway, Cheatin' Heart is in default to Double Wide, and
Double Wide has asked Lincoln to permit it to collect some of Cheatin'
Heart's accounts and chattel paper directly. I assume I will get a call or a
letter demanding we surrender the chattel paper we are holding. I assume I
do not have to honor it and that we have priority.[21] Double-check that for
me, will you? Thanks

—Roy

## Problem 5–16

*The next day, you receive another e-mail from the same source:*

TO:          S. Carlson, Megabank Legal Dept.
FROM:        R. Comstock, NB Commercial Finance
RE:          Charm of the Farm and Cheatin' Heart Files

I have some new information for you on both of the matters I previously
referred to you. As the saying goes, I have good news and bad news. The

---

**20.** [See Section 9–315; Section 9–322;
Section 9–324(b); Section 9–327; Section 9–
330; Section 9–331; Section 9–332; Section
9–340.]

**21.** [See Section 9–330 and Comments;
See also PEB Commentary No. 8.]

good news is on the Charm of the Farm matter. You will remember that both McDonald and Johnson made $10,000 down payments on their John Deere tractors. Their checks were deposited in Charm of the Farm's operating account, which I erroneously believed to be located at Bank of Amerigo and substantially depleted. It turns out the account is at our affiliate, the Bank of New Babylon, and it may still have a substantial balance. Has the Bank loaned Charm of the Farm any money? It occurs to me that it may have a security interest in, or right of set off against, the account.[22]

The bad news is on the Cheatin' Heart matter. It turns out Double Wide Finance Company's security interest is not a plain vanilla inventory security interest. I had a look at Double Wide's security agreement this morning, and it purports to cover equipment, inventory, accounts, and chattel paper, including after acquired property in all categories. The financing statement is equally broad. The amount Double Wide will finance is determined by a percentage of "eligible collateral," which is defined in the agreement to include specified percentages of property in all four categories. I don't know if this will affect your analysis or not, but I thought you should know.[23]

One more thing. One of the pieces of chattel paper we bought was an installment sale of a mobile home to a guy named Johnny Paycheck. He apparently sent Cheatin' Heart a letter complaining about defects in the mobile home and telling them to "take this trailer and shove it," stopped making his payments, abandoned the mobile home, and took off for some snooty New York suburb. Cheatin' Heart has reacquired possession of the mobile home and intends to resell it. Can we claim any interest in this thing?[24] Please advise.

## II.   Priority Disputes Between Two or More Secured Creditors

### D.   Accessions and Commingled Goods

### Problem 5–17

*You are eating your afternoon snack of microwave popcorn directly from the bag and drinking a Dr. Pepper. As you get butter marks on the following memorandum, you wonder how many calories you are consuming:*[25]

**22.** [See Section 9–104; Section 9–324; Section 9–327; Section 9–340; Bruce A. Markell, *From Property to Contract and Back: An Examination of Deposit Accounts and Revised Article 9*, 74 Chi–Kent L. Rev. 963, 984–988(1999); Ingrid Hillinger, David Batty, and Richard Brown, *Deposit Accounts Under the New World Order*, 6 N.C.Banking Inst. 1 (2002).]

**23.** [See Section 9–330 and Comments.]

**24.** [Compare J.I. Case Co. v. Borg–Warner Acceptance Corp., 669 S.W.2d 543 (Ky.

App.1983) with Crocker National Bank (Credit Alliance) v. Clark Equipment Credit Corp., 724 F.2d 696 (8th Cir.1984). See also Section 9–330(c)(2).]

**25.** It is a myth that popcorn is always a good snack when dieting. The number of calories in popcorn depends on the method of preparation. In a four-cup serving, air-popped has 92 calories and no grams of fat. It also has no taste. If you pop it with oil, it goes up to 164 calories and 8 grams of fat. Most microwave brands have between 140–180 calories and 7–17 grams of fat.

### THE BOVINE STATE BANK
### DESOLATION, GILMORIA
#### "Serving Desolation for Fifty Years"

#### MEMORANDUM

TO:        S. Carlson, Megabank Legal Dept.
FROM:    Bubba O'Reilly, Bovine State Bank
RE:        Swamp Thang Boat Tours

As you may know, commercial fishing was once a major part of our economy up here in Desolation, but, as the pollution in our local rivers has increased, many of our fisherpersons (aren't you proud of me) have been forced to find other ways to make a living. In May of last year, one such fisherperson, Dell Carp, came to the Bank with an idea for a new business. He wanted to adapt his old fishing boat and start giving tours of the Great Gaseous Swamp, which covers about half of this county. We thought the idea would probably work, so the Bank made a start-up loan to Carp in the amount of $25,000, secured by a blanket lien on all present and after acquired assets of the business, including "...all boats or other aquatic vehicles, now owned or hereafter acquired, and all additions, attachments, accessories and replacements thereto and thereof." We filed our financing statement on May 15. Carp started giving tours in the old boat in June under the trade name, "Swamp Thang Boat Tours."

Business was a little slow at first, and Carp decided that his chances of success would be improved if he installed on air conditioner in the observation cabin of the boat. On July 1, he paid $100 down and signed a conditional sale contract on a Trane marine air conditioner. Under the terms of the conditional sale contract, the balance of the $1,000 purchase price was to be paid in installments over two years, and the seller, Shivers of Desolation, reserved a security interest until the price was paid in full. As far as I can tell, Shivers never filed anything. The air conditioner was installed on July 5.

Business picked up a little, and Carp was starting to make good money when the engine on his boat failed. On August 1, he went into Monster Marine Motors here in Desolation and ordered a new one, priced at $5,000. Monster Marine likewise had Carp sign a conditional sale contract to secure the price, but Monster filed a financing statement describing its collateral as "one Mercury marine engine, serial #856123TRB" on August 25. Monster had installed the engine on August 10.

By November, Carp's business was failing. In a final effort to save it, Carp borrowed $10,000 from Greenslime Finance Company and gave them a security interest in the boat. He used the money to decorate the boat a little and advertise his tours locally and in New Babylon. Greenslime filed on November 10.

As you probably guessed, Carp is now in default to everybody and does not even have gas money for the boat. Both the Bank and Greenslime would like to repossess the boat, and Shivers and Monster are claiming superior interests in the air conditioner and the motor. Can you sort this out for me?[26] Thanks.

### Problem 5–18

*Every once in a while, a voice mail message can make your blood run cold. This one arrived just as you finished the library research on your last assignment:*

Hello, Carlson. This is Bubba. Hey, I had another thought on the Swamp Thang matter. I can't remember if we have a certificate of title statute for boats in this state. I know some states do. Does it make any difference?[27] Call me.

### Problem 5–19

*Yesterday you boss called to tell you how pleased she was with your work. She said that you were a "quick study," and that you "had a good touch with the people you dealt with." That makes it easier to face this next memorandum:*

### BANK OF NEW BABYLON
### INTEROFFICE MEMORANDUM

TO:        S. Carlson, Megabank Legal Dept.
FROM:      P.L. Driver, V.P.–Bank
RE:        Flannery's Cannery File

You may be familiar with this borrower. Flannery's Cannery is one of the last manufacturing operations still located in downtown New Babylon. The Bank has been financing its operations forever. Our most recent security agreement is dated April 1 of last year, and it gives us a floating lien on virtually all the assets of the company, including, in pertinent part, "all canned goods inventory, now owned or hereafter acquired." Our financing statement was filed on April 2.

In recent years, Flannery's has tried to take advantage of St. Patrick's day by boosting its production of specialty Irish-style canned goods in February and March. Last January, its management decided this year's promotional item would be Mother Flannery's Famous Corned Beef Hash, a new product. On January 15, Flannery's received a delivery of 50,000 pounds of potatoes from Blarney Produce, a local food wholesaler. Blarney insisted that Flannery's sign a security agreement covering the potatoes to secure their $15,000 price, which Flannery's did on January 16. Blarney filed a financing statement the same day. On January 18, Flannery's took delivery of 25,000 pounds of dried corned beef (also priced at $15,000) and executed a similar security agreement in favor of the seller, Leprechaun Livestock. Leprechaun filed January 19. Flannery's persuaded somebody–I don't know who–to sell them about $10,000 worth of onions and $5,000 worth of spices and preservatives at about the same time. At the end of January, Flannery's

---

**26.** [See Section 9–317(e); Section 9–322; Section 9–324(a); Section 9–335.]

**27.** [See Section 9–335(d) and Comment 7.]

ran the corned beef hash production line for about a week and produced 20,000 cases of the stuff out of the foregoing ingredients.

One thing I should tell you about Mother Flannery's Famous Corned Beef Hash. It's a truly vile concoction, and about half of it didn't sell. The remaining 10,000 cases are collectively worth about $18,000. Fortunately, the Bank's loan balance is down to $6,000, but Flannery's went into default last week. Blarney and Leprechaun haven't been paid at all. It looks like Flannery's won't be in business much longer. I've worked out a deal with Blarney and Leprechaun. If we can get Flannery's to surrender the canned goods, Blarney will arrange a sale to another food wholesaler and we will split the proceeds according to our priorities in the goods. How much will each of us take, assuming my estimate of the value is correct?[28] Thanks.

## III. Priority Disputes Between Secured Creditors and Lien Creditors

### A. In General

#### Problem 5–20

*Your voice mail light is on again.*

Sidney. This is Cleaver at Friendly Finance. I've got a problem and you were the first person I thought of. It involves a local travel agent, Fly By Night Tours. About six months ago, another loan officer authorized a loan of $10,000 to Fly By Night. We have a security agreement giving us an ordinary security interest in existing and after acquired equipment. I first opened the file earlier today, when I got a call from the President of Fly By Night, "Skip" Towne. Some lawyer for a guy with a judgment in a contract dispute against Fly By Night was out there with a sheriff threatening to seize some of Fly By Night's computers. That's about all they have by way of equipment. Skip wanted me to talk them out of the levy, and I told them we had a security interest in the computers and that they should back off. They went ahead with the levy anyway, and, at about that point, I found the original financing statement Skip had signed stapled to the back of our file. It looks like we never filed it. To make matters worse, Skip wasn't entirely candid with me. It turns out, he had authorized his own lawyer to file a bankruptcy petition on behalf of Fly By Night a week ago. Although Skip wasn't aware of it when the levy occurred, the attorney filed the petition yesterday. Is there any way to save anything from this wreck?[29]

#### Problem 5–21

*Your search for a way to remove your e-mail address from the directories of others has failed.*

TO: S. Carlson, Megabank Legal Dept.
FROM: J. Drabb, Friendly Finance
RE: Divot File

**28.** [See Section 9–322; Section 9–324(b); Section 9–336 and Comments.]

**29.** [See Section 9–102(a)(52); Section 9–317(a)(2); 11 U.S.C. 301, 544(a), 547(b), and 362.]

You may be familiar with Steroid Sporting Goods, Inc., as it has several stores in greater New Babylon. Steroid is one of several local companies that steers its customers to us if they want to buy expensive items on long-term credit. (They prefer cash, checks or credit cards.) Basically, Steroid e-mails us the customers' financial data from the store, and we call them back with an approval number if we decide to make the loan. Steroid has a stack of form conditional sales contracts that it can use to document such transactions, as well as form financing statements. Once a conditional sales contract and financing statement are executed, they mail them to us, along with an assignment, and we buy the debt and security agreement at an agreed discount. We file financing statements, if necessary, upon receipt of such contracts.

On the first of this month, Steroid sold a state of the art set of golf clubs to the golf pro at the New Babylon Country Club, Mulligan Divot. Divot signed the usual conditional sale contract that day, and took the clubs to work. We received the conditional sale contract on the third. On the fifth, some guy whom Divot once hit with a golf ball, and who had a tort judgment against him, had the sheriff show up at the Club and seize the clubs. What should I do? Oh, one more thing. The judgment is a big one, and Divot says he may have to file bankruptcy. How would that affect us?[30] Please advise. I'm not in a rush unless you are.

## Problem 5–22

*It is Saturday morning. You received this memorandum late yesterday and have been struggling with it ever since. You promised to meet Randy for lunch but you doubt if you will make it.*

### BANK OF NEW BABYLON
### INTEROFFICE MEMORANDUM

TO:        S. Carlson, Megabank Legal Dept.
FROM:    P.L. Driver, V.P., Bank of New Babylon
RE:         Anna's Bananas File

One of the longtime clients of this Bank, Anna Peele, started a banana importing company, Anna's Bananas, Inc., about a year and a half ago. Her initial investment capital came from her family fortune. However, in January of last year, she came to us for ongoing operating financing. The Peeles are quite experienced in business, and so she had quite a detailed business plan. We set up an arrangement giving her the right to draw specified amounts on a specific date each quarter, with further advances to be discretionary with the Bank. More specifically, the Loan and Security Agreement which the Bank and Anna's Bananas executed on January 15 gave Anna's Bananas the right to draw $50,000 on January 15, $25,000 on April 15, $25,000 on July 15, and $50,000 on October 15. While we did not close the door to further advances, we did not commit irrevocably to them either.

**30.** [See Section 9–103; Section 9–109; Section 9–110; Section 9–317(e); Section 9–514; 11 U.S.C. 362(a)(4), 362(b)(3) and 546(b).]

In order to secure all advances, whenever made, the Bank took a security interest in substantially all the assets of Anna's Bananas, now owned or hereafter acquired. We promptly filed an appropriate financing statement. The business appeared to us to be prospering, and all the quarterly advances under the agreement were made as scheduled. In addition, in response to a request from Anna, we advanced an additional $25,000 on September 15.

In retrospect, that was probably a bad move, and I am afraid we did not do a good job of monitoring this debtor's operations. While Anna's Bananas did not default on our loan until October 30, it had apparently been slow-paying or defaulting on debts owed to trade creditors and others almost from the beginning. One of the trade creditors, a foreign supplier named Republic Bananas, got a $50,000 judgment against Anna's Bananas. On July 14, Republic had the local sheriff levy on some of the equipment Anna's Bananas uses to unload bananas from ships at the wharf. As the equipment in question is too large to move easily, the sheriff levied by immobilizing and tagging it.

We did not know about the levy, and, because it was not terribly unusual for the equipment to be idle during our site inspections, we did not notice the tags. Anna's Bananas missed its first payment to us on October 30, and the company filed in bankruptcy on November 5. With the permission of the Bankruptcy Court, we have liquidated most of our collateral, although inventory as perishable as bananas is not worth too much. About all that is left is the banana unloading equipment, which both Republic and we claim. It's worth about $100,000, which is almost exactly the amount of our outstanding loan balance. As you know, under our payment allocation formula in the Loan and Security Agreement, payments and collections are credited first towards the oldest advances. So the outstanding balance really reflects our last three advances. Republic's counsel claims that is a problem for us. I don't understand. Why would it be?[31] Please advise.

### Problem 5–23

*Another voice mail from Ted Cleaver. You are beginning to think of him as Bubba lite.*

Hi Sidney! I know I keep calling you but you are the only one who doesn't yell. This problem involves Ray Suarez is a local welder. He needed to buy a new piece of welding equipment. Two weeks ago, he came to see us but he had not yet picked out the equipment. We had him sign a security agreement covering present and future equipment and we filed a financing statement covering equipment. We told Suarez to come by to see us when he picked out the welding equipment and we would consider making the loan. It turns out that Ray not only picked out the piece of equipment but last week he bought it on open account and brought it back to his shop. Unfortunately for him, the sheriff was waiting to execute on a $10,000 judgment against Ray and he seized the piece of equipment. Unfortunately for us, Ray did not tell us this fact when he showed up the next day with the bill of sale and asked for the loan. The cost of the equipment was $5,000 and we gave it to

---

**31.** [See Section 9–323, especially Section 9–323(b).]

him. He paid for the equipment but now he can't pay us and this is the only piece of equipment that has any real value. Is there any argument that we have priority over the judgment creditor?[32]

## Problem 5–24

*You can take the boy out of the country, but you can't take the old country boy out of your e-mail.*

TO:         S. Carlson, Megabank Legal Department
FROM:    Bubba O'Reilly, Bovine State Bank
RE:         Dell File

This e-mail stuff is really convenient. I have another problem for you. About five years ago, we loaned a local farmer, N.A. Dell, $50,000 to buy a tractor. We had Dell sign a standard form security agreement listing the tractor as collateral and describing it by serial number. We filed a financing statement with the same collateral description, and we recently kept it in force with a continuation statement. The loan balance is now down to about $8,000, but that is more than the tractor is currently worth by about $2,000.

Dell has not paid us anything in three months, and he will not return my calls. So last Thursday, my brother Billy and I took a ride out to the farm in Billy's flatbed truck. I figured that, if Dell couldn't come up with some money, or at least a payment plan, I'd repossess the tractor and sell it on the courthouse steps. Well, it turns out Dell has been having trouble with the tractor. In the last three months, he's taken it to Cronic Tractor Repair three times. The first two times, the repair charges amounted to $500 and $800 respectively, but Danny Cronic let Dell take the tractor home on Dell's assurance that he'd pay Danny out of the egg money. This last time, the tractor needed an additional $1200 worth of repairs, and Danny refuses to give Dell the tractor until he is paid in full. Dell claims that Danny's charges are too high, and that the first two attempts to fix the tractor were so inept he should not have to pay. We went to see Danny, and he won't surrender the tractor to us either. He claims he has some kind of garageman's lien on it and doesn't have to let us have it. Do you know anything about this?[33]

## Problem 5–25

*The phone rings. It is the boss.*

J.R.: Sidney, do remember the Gutenberg Printing Company problem that you did some research on back in January?[34]

S.C.: I have a vague recollection, something about some printing presses and a lapsed financing statement. I am sure I have the file here.

J.R.: That's the one. Well, as you can imagine, there is a priority dispute between the Bank and the lien creditor. Would you go back over the facts

---

**32.**  [See Section 9–317(a).]          **34.**  [See Problem 4–18, supra.]
**33.**  [See Section 9–333.]

and let me know whether our claim of first priority was lost due to the lapse in the financing statement?[35]

## BANK OF NEW BABYLON
## LOAN OFFICER TRAINING AND
## OPERATIONS MANUAL
## CHAPTER 5: PRIORITIES

### III. Priority Disputes Between Secured Creditors and Lien Creditors

### B. Federal Tax Liens[36]

When one of the Bank's borrowers fails to make the payments required under our loan and security agreement, we often find that the borrower has defaulted on obligations to other creditors as well. As no one seems inordinately fond of paying taxes, the Internal Revenue Service ("IRS") is often one of these unpaid creditors. A taxpayer's liability for federal taxes begins as an ordinary unsecured claim, much like any other. However, as a creditor, the IRS has a distinct advantage, as it can invoke the benefit of a special non-consensual lien created by the Federal Tax Lien Act, the most critical provisions of which are found at 26 U.S.C. 6321–6323. It is thus possible for the Bank, as an Article 9 secured creditor, to become a party to a priority dispute with the IRS claiming under a federal tax lien.

Much as Article 9 has separate requirements for making a security interest enforceable against the debtor (i.e., attachment) and for making it enforceable against third parties (i.e., perfection), the Federal Tax Lien Act has separate requirements for the initial creation of the federal tax lien and the functional equivalent of perfecting it. The creation of the lien requires three steps: assessment of the tax, a demand for payment, and a refusal to pay. 26 U.S.C. 6321, 6322. Once these steps are taken, the lien dates from the time of assessment (i.e., the first step) for purposes of enforcement against the debtor/taxpayer. *Id*.

"Assessment" may occur at different times, depending on whether the taxpayer concedes his liability for the tax at issue on his/her tax return. If the taxpayer does acknowledge such liability, assessment may involve nothing more than an administrative entry in the records of the IRS district director's office, and it may occur relatively quickly. If, on the other hand, the taxpayer contests liability, assessment cannot occur until the IRS has issued a notice of deficiency, the taxpayer has had an opportunity to respond, and the taxpayer either acquiesces in an adjustment or exhausts his administrative remedies. In such a case, assessment may take a long time. Once it is accomplished, however, and the remaining two steps have been taken, the nonconsensual lien that arises in favor of the United States is absolutely general, i.e., it covers "all property and rights to property, whether real or personal, belonging to such person." 26 U.S.C. 6321.

Because it is so broad, the federal tax lien's potential for conflict with rival claimants to the taxpayer's property—Article 9 secured creditors, buyers, or rival non-

**35.** [See Section 9–515(c) and Comment 3.]

**36.** Timothy Zinnecker, *Resolving Priority Disputes Between the IRS and the Se-* *cured Creditor Under Revised U.C.C. Article 9: And the Winner Is . . . ?* 34 Ariz. St. L. J. 921 (2002).

consensual lien creditors—is particularly great. The priority rules governing such contests are a combination of rules created by the Federal Tax Lien Act itself and the state law rules (including Article 9) to which it sometimes (but not always) defers. Note initially that the steps required for creation of the federal tax lien by Sections 6321 and 6322 do not necessarily provide notice of the lien to possible third party rival claimants. A federal tax lien may thus be a secret lien even if it is enforceable against the taxpayer. However, Section 6323(a) provides that the federal tax lien is not valid against purchasers, holders of security interests, mechanic's lienors, or judgment lien creditors unless notice of the federal tax lien has been filed in accordance with Section 6323(f). The latter subsection permits the states to designate by state law the office in which a federal tax lien filing is to be made, and specifies the office of the Clerk of the U.S. District Court for the district in which the property at issue is located in the event a state fails to make such a designation. (Most states have, in fact, taken the opportunity to designate the place of filing, and there is even a uniform model statute available for that purpose.) Real property is deemed located at its physical situs, while personal property, tangible or intangible, is deemed located at the residence of the taxpayer. See Section 6323(f)(2).

Section 6323(a) is not quite as generous to secured creditors as it appears on first reading. While it appears to subordinate an unfiled federal tax lien to any security interest, perfected or unperfected, that illusion is dispelled by the special definition of "security interest" in Section 6323(h)(1). Under this special federal definition, a security interest in property does not exist until the property exists, the secured party has parted with "money or money's worth," and the security interest has become protected under state law against a subsequent judgment lien. The combined effect of Sections 6323(a) and 6323(h)(1) is thus to subordinate the unfiled tax lien only to *perfected* secured creditors.

Section 6323(b) contains a list of rival claimants who, for various policy reasons, take priority over a federal tax lien even if the tax lien has been the subject of a public filing under Section 6323(f). They include purchasers of motor vehicles without actual knowledge of the tax lien (Section 6323(b)(2)(A)), those with possessory repair liens of the type that are also protected under Section 9–333 of Article 9 (Section 6323(b)(5)), and purchasers of personal property at retail in the ordinary course of business (Section 6323(b)(3)). None of these exceptions are of any assistance to a perfected secured creditor in a priority contest with a *filed* tax lien.

Because Section 6323(a) provides that a tax lien is not valid against a (perfected) secured party "until" notice of the tax lien is filed, it is a fair inference that a secured party who perfects his security interest before a federal tax lien is filed takes priority over the tax lien with respect to property in existence at the time the tax lien is filed. However, because the special federal definition of "security interest" in Section 6323(h)(1) confines the "existence" of a security interest to property that exists and to value that has been given, the normal future advance and after-acquired property features of the Article 9 security interest are in jeopardy unless specifically protected by other provisions of the federal statute. Security interests in property which the debtor has not yet acquired, or which secure advances that have not been made, *at the time of the tax lien filing*, do not yet "exist" within the federal definition. Fortunately for the Bank, there are two specific provisions that provide limited protection for the usual incidents of the Article 9 floating lien.

The more general of these provisions, Section 6323(d), applies to perfected Article 9 security interests regardless of the form the collateral for the security interest takes. It provides some protection for a security interest that "comes into existence" after a tax lien filing provided it is protected, as of the tax lien filing, against a lien creditor under state law (i.e., if the security interest is already perfected). Section 6323(d)(2). However, because protection of the secured party is confined to property subject to the tax lien at the time of filing (Section 6323(d)(1)—(i.e., t o property that is already property of the debtor)—6323(d) does not preserve the priority as to after-acquired property normally available under Section 9–322 to a perfected secured party with an after-acquired property clause. All that Section 6323(d) preserves is part of the Article 9 secured creditor's *future advance* priority. Specifically, a security interest which comes into "existence," in the federal sense, because of an existing secured party's advances made after the tax lien filing, has priority over the tax lien only if the advances are made before the 46th day after the tax lien filing. Moreover, if secured party has actual notice or knowledge of the tax lien filing within the protected 45–day period, that period of protection is cut short. Note that the 45–day period of protection under the federal statute partially parallels the 45–day future advance priority accorded the Article 9 secured party over ordinary lien creditors under Section 9–323(b). However, while the federal period of protection against the tax lien is subject to reduction by the acquisition of actual knowledge, the Article 9 period of protection against ordinary lien creditors is not; rather, it may be extended by the absence of actual knowledge of the rival interest.

The more specific provision, Section 6323(c), is, in one sense, more generous to a perfected Article 9 secured party. It preserves both a portion of the after-acquired property priority and a portion of the future advance priority the Article 9 secured party otherwise expects. However, it is restricted to security interests in particular forms of collateral, as well as to a few other privileged forms of agreement. Specifically, Sections 6323(c)(1) and (2) provide limited protection against a filed tax lien for parties to a "commercial transactions financing agreement." To qualify as the requisite type of agreement, the "qualified property" must be "commercial financing security." Sections 6323(c)(1)(A) and (2). This means that the property in dispute (the collateral) must be "paper of a kind ordinarily arising in commercial transactions," (e.g., chattel paper), accounts receivable, mortgages, or inventory. Security interests in all of these forms of collateral qualify for protection; purchases of all of them except inventory also qualify. Section 6323(c)(2)(A). The security interest that comes into existence (in the federal sense) under a commercial transactions financing agreement because of the operation of a future advance or after acquired property clause is given priority for a limited period of time, provided the security interest is perfected at the time of the tax lien filing. Section 6323(c)(1)(B). The priority protection extends to after-acquired property (in the form of commercial financing security) acquired before the 46th day from the tax lien filing. The secured party's priority protection also extends to future advances made before 46 days from the tax lien filing. The 45–day period of protection for after-acquired property is not expressly made subject to termination if the secured party acquires actual notice or knowledge of the tax lien. As under Section 6323(d), the opposite is true with respect to future advance protection; actual knowledge or notice of the tax lien within the 45–day protected period will cut it short.

Thus, the federal tax lien must be regarded as a substantial threat to the normal priority accorded an Article 9 security interest. It can cut off future advance and after-acquired property priority in ways that an ordinary lien creditor cannot. However, if an Article 9 secured party achieves priority over a federal tax lien in any of the ways discussed above, that priority extends not only to the debtor's obligation for the loan principal, but to interest, expenses of collection and enforcement, insurance, etc., to the extent that state law grants them the same priority as the principal obligation. Section 6323(e).

# BANK OF NEW BABYLON
# LOAN OFFICER TRAINING AND
# OPERATIONS MANUAL

## CHAPTER 5: PRIORITIES

## IV.  Priority Disputes Between Secured Creditors and Buyers

### A.  Introduction

Normally, when the Bank takes a security interest in tangible collateral, the collateral will be left in the debtor's possession and the Bank will perfect its security interest, if necessary, by filing a financing statement. The reasons for this are fairly obvious. If the security interest is in the inventory of a retailer or wholesaler, the inventory must normally be displayed at the debtor's place of business to have any prospect of sale. If the security interest is in the equipment of a manufacturing company, the debtor needs to use the equipment to produce whatever products it is in business to make. In neither case is a possessory security interest in favor of the Bank a practical alternative.

Of course, if the collateral is left in the debtor's possession, it is always possible that the debtor will sell it to a third party. In some instances, this is precisely what the Bank wants the debtor to do. When the Bank lends money to a wholesaler or retailer secured by the debtor's inventory, the debtor's only source of funds for repayment is typically the proceeds of collateral sales. The proceeds may take the form of cash proceeds produced by direct cash sales, or the immediate proceeds may be accounts (generated by open credit sales) that are subsequently liquidated to produce cash. In other cases, typified by the security interest in a manufacturer's equipment, the Bank does not anticipate that the debtor will sell the collateral and will normally insert a provision in the underlying security agreement prohibiting such sales without the Bank's consent. Even in that event, however, the debtor may sell the collateral in violation of the agreement. All of these potential scenarios make it necessary for Article 9 to have rules governing priority disputes between secured parties and buyers of collateral from the initial debtor.

The Article 9 priority rules governing such disputes begin with a presumption in favor of the secured party. Section 9–201 opens with a general statement that, unless the Code provides otherwise, a security agreement is valid according to its terms between the parties, against purchasers of the collateral, and against creditors. Under Sections 1–201(9), (32) and (33),[37] buyers are a subclass of the broader category, "purchasers." Section 9–315(a)(1) reinforces this general presumption by providing that a security interest continues in collateral notwithstanding its sale or other

---

**37.**  Rev. Sections 1–201(b)(9), (29), and (30).

disposition unless the secured party consents to the disposition. Finally, Section 9–507(a) continues the effectiveness of a financing statement as a method of perfection even if the debtor in whose name it is filed transfers the collateral to another party.

What at first appears to be a rosy picture for the secured party, however, is soon complicated by other provisions. The presumption of the continued effectiveness and priority of a security interest in collateral transferred by the debtor turns out to be riddled with exceptions. Sections 9–317(b)–(d) subordinate an unperfected security interest to a broad range of potential transferees of the collateral. Section 9–320(a)–(d) and Section 9–323(d) operate to cut off the effectiveness of even a perfected secured party's interest against certain protected transferees. The patchwork of situations in which a secured party is superior or subordinated to a buyer of the collateral can become quite complex, and a loan officer faced with such a dispute should normally seek the advice of the Legal Department.

---

## IV. Priority Disputes Between Secured Creditors and Buyers

## B. Unperfected Secured Creditor Versus a Buyer

### Problem 5–26

*You have still not managed to disable the annoying little tone in your computer that indicates an e-mail message has arrived.*

TO:      S. Carlson, Megabank Legal Dept.
FROM:   Bubba O'Reilly, Bovine State Bank
RE:      Two Problems

a. *Voice of Desolation*

You may not have known this, but Desolation is one of the few small towns with two local newspapers. One of them, the *Voice of Desolation*, is the more *avante garde* publication and a longtime customer of our Bank. We have been providing operating capital since the newspaper opened its doors in the 1960's under a series of security agreements and corresponding financing statements giving us a security interest in the *Voice's* equipment. Unfortunately, the *Voice* has fallen on hard times and will probably cease doing business within a couple of weeks. We saw this coming, so our loan balance is down to about $25,000.

This morning, I got two pieces of very bad news. First, our most recent financing statement covering the *Voice's* equipment lapsed six months ago. I really don't know how we dropped the ball on this one. Anyway, I also learned that the owner of the *Voice* has been offering his equipment at bargain basement prices to various other papers and magazines around the state. The largest single asset of the business is a relatively new computer-driven press that I have assumed to be worth about $30,000 on the used market. I am told that, yesterday, the owner of the *Voice* signed a contract to sell the press to his crosstown rival, the *Desolation Trumpet*, for $15,000. It must be a little galling for him, because the *Trumpet* is a really stiff publication without even any comics or advice columns. Anyway, delivery is supposed to take place next Thursday. I am more than a little worried that the owner of the *Voice* (who no longer returns my calls) is going to skip town with the cash, which he may or may not already have received. Is there anything I can do to protect the Bank?[38]

b. *Pickholtz Pots and Pans*

Priscilla Pickholtz is the owner of Pickholtz Pots and Pans, which, as the name indicates, is the place in Desolation for all of your cooking equipment needs. Pris has been a long time customer of the Bank and we often make loans to her. In February, she contacted me about the purchase of a new fancy electronic cash register. She purchased the cash register for $6,000 on February 6, using a cashier's check from us that was made out to Pickholtz Pots and Pans and the seller of the cash register. I think we had her sign a security agreement the same day. We filed our financing statement, which appears to be accurate, on February 24. I did not think much about this transaction until yesterday when I went into Pickholtz Pots and Pans to buy an anniversary present for my wife (four beautiful muffin pans), and I noticed that Pris was using an old manual cash register. When I asked her about the new electronic model, she told me that she could not understand how to use it and after a week had sold it to Lapides Old Tyme Photographers. They are one of those places where they dress you up in period costumes and take sepia tinted pictures. I have one on my mantle as a Union General. Pris still owes us most of the money on the loan. I am not particularly worried since I think she is OK financially, but I was wondering if we lost our security interest in the cash register when Lapides bought it? Would you check this out and let me know?[39]

# IV. Priority Disputes Between Secured Creditors and Buyers

## C. Perfected Secured Creditor Versus a Buyer

### Problem 5–27

*The morning had started out reasonably well. You didn't spill your vanilla latte in the car and the muffin was reasonably fresh. Then Drabb sends you an e-mail.*

TO:     S. Carlson, Megabank Legal Dept.
FROM:   Jimmy Drabb, Friendly Finance
RE:     CompuSwamp Customers

As you may remember, this company often refers people who want to buy computers over time to us for financing. We have about a dozen new customers, each of whom is buying a computer system worth in excess of $2,000 and each of which is borrowing all but a 10% down payment from us. We're taking security interests in each system under our standard form security agreement. Mr. Conseco is insisting that I file financing statements

---

**38.** [See Section 1–201(9); Rev. Section 1–201(b)(9); Section 1–201(25); Rev. Section 1–202; Section 9–317(b).]

**39.** [See Section 9–317(e).]

on each customer, although I can't for the life of me figure out why. Could you tell me why?[40] After what you said before, I thought it was unnecessary.

## Problem 5–28

*Some days you are so busy you almost forget to open your "snail mail." When you remember, you wish you had forgotten.*

### FRIENDLY FINANCE COMPANY
### INTEROFFICE MEMORANDUM

TO:        S. Carlson, Megabank Legal Dept.
FROM:     Theodore Cleaver, V.P., Friendly Finance
RE:        Ahab loan

This one is so complicated that Drabb, Conseco and I have to diagram it to keep everything straight. Our customer is a guy named Ahab, and he borrowed $25,000 from us to buy a used boat from a local dealer, Float Yer Boat, Inc. ("FYB"). We thought this was going to be a plain vanilla transaction, so we had Ahab sign our standard security agreement, which describes the boat by make, model and serial number. Our financing statement, filed at the same time, describes the collateral in the same way. Things turn out to be far from simple. We have pieced together the following history.

The boat in question started out in the hands of another dealer a year ago. The dealer, Bilgewater Enterprises (Bilgewater), had subjected its entire present and after-acquired inventory to a perfected security interest in favor of Tidewater Finance Company. A month after acquiring it, Bilgewater sold the boat to a man named Bligh. Bligh had only the 10% needed for the down payment, so he executed a retail installment contract that granted Bilgewater a security interest in the boat until the price was paid in full. Bilgewater filed a financing statement under Bligh's name.

Six months later, Bligh apparently got tired of the boat and sold it to FYB for cash. Needless to say, nobody got Bilgewater's permission or even notified the company. FYB apparently did not check for financing statements under Bligh's name. Two months later, along comes Ahab. Ahab bought the boat using our loan for the purpose. We checked for financing statements under FYB's name, and found only evidence of an inventory security interest in favor of Chaste Bank, which we weren't worried about. Now, there seems to be an epidemic of default. Ahab missed his last payment, and we were trying to decide whether to repossess or grant him an extension. Then Ahab told us he received a demand from Tidewater that he surrender the boat to them. Apparently, Bilgewater is in default on its agreement with Tidewater, and Bligh is in default on the retail installment contract to Bilgewater. The boat seems to be adrift on a sea of bad credit, and we fear it may go under. Please advise as to which of us has priority.[41]

---

**40.** [See Section 9–309(1); Section 9–320(b).]

**41.** [See Section 1–201(9); Rev. Section 1–201(b)(9); Section 9–315; Section 9–320; Section 9–322; Section 9–324; Section 9–325. See also Richard Nowka, *Section 9–320(a) of Revised Article 9 and the Buyer in the Ordinary Course of Pre–Encumbered*

**BANK OF NEW BABYLON**
**LOAN OFFICER TRAINING AND**
**OPERATIONS MANUAL**

**CHAPTER 5: PRIORITIES**

## IV. Priority Disputes Between Secured Creditors and Buyers

### C. Perfected Secured Creditor Versus a Buyer

#### 1. Farm Products Exception and the Food Security Act of 1985

One of the most important exceptions to the presumption that a security interest follows the collateral even if the debtor disposes of it[42] is the provision in Section 9–320(a) that a buyer in the ordinary course of business[43] takes free of a security interest created by his seller, even if the security interest is perfected and the buyer knows of its existence. Because of this provision, the purchaser of clothing or tools from a retail store need not worry about the possibility that the store's inventory is subject to a perfected security interest in favor of the store's lender.

The "ordinary course buyer" exception, however, has its own exception. (See Section 9–320(a)). The ordinary course buyers who enjoy protection from the normal rule that security interests survive disposition do *not* include buyers of farm products from those engaged in farming operations. Thus, if a lender perfects a security interest in a farmer's crops or livestock, and the farmer subsequently sells the crops or livestock to a grain elevator or packing house, the lender's security interest continues in the hands of the transferee (Section 9–320(a)), and perfection may be preserved by Section 9–507(a). If the farmer defaults, the lender may be able to repossess the crops from the elevator or the livestock from the packing house. If the grain elevator or packing house has resold the farm products in question, the lender may pursue a claim against them for conversion of the collateral.

Moreover, even the transferee who buys from the grain elevator or packing house may not escape. In the hands of the grain elevator or packing house, the crops or livestock are inventory, not farm products,[44] and the normal "ordinary course buyer" rule of Section 9–320(a) would normally cut off an existing security interest in the goods. However, the original lender's security interest was not *created by the transferee's seller* (i.e., the grain elevator or packing house). It was created by the agreement between the original lender and the farmer, and the normal ordinary course buyer rule is therefore inapplicable. As a result, the original lender's security interest also survives the second sale from the grain elevator or packing house to the transferee.

Because farmers typically borrow to finance their operations, the farm products exception to the ordinary course buyer rule creates a significant threat that professional buyers of farm products (like grain elevators or packing houses) will be forced to pay for them twice—once to the farmer under the contract of sale and once to the

---

*Goods: Something Old and Something New*, 38 Brandeis L. J. 9 (1999–2000).]

**42.** See Section 9–315(a)(1).

**43.** See Section 1–201(9); Rev. Section 1–201(b)(9).

**44.** See Sections 9–102(a)(34) and (48).

farmer's secured lender when the farmer defaults. In fact, litigation between secured agricultural lenders and professional buyers of farm products was once quite common.

When the Code was the only source of law for resolving such disputes, the arguments raised by the parties tended to follow a recurring pattern. A buyer of farm products faced with a conversion suit or a demand for possession by a secured agricultural lender could not resort to the ordinary course buyer rule. So the farm products buyer turned to the other major exception to the rule that security interests survive the debtor's disposition of the collateral. The farm products buyer argued that the secured agricultural lender authorized the sale of the collateral to him, and this authorization cut off the security interest under the express terms of Section 9–315(a)(1). Of course, many agricultural lenders inserted provisions in their security agreements with farmers prohibiting the sale of farm products collateral in the absence of express written authorization, and such a provision might effectively rebut the farm products buyer's contention that the sale was authorized. However, the contractual relationship between a farmer and a secured lender is often a long and/or recurring one, and, in many instances, secured lenders quietly acquiesced in sales by their farmer/borrowers as long as the proceeds were promptly remitted to the secured lenders. If a farm products buyer were fortunate enough to encounter and establish such a practice, he might argue that the sale was authorized by a course of dealing or usage of trade under Section 1–205[45], or that the provision requiring express written consent to sale was ineffective under a common law theory of waiver, implied consent, ratification or estoppel. The litigated cases eventually formed a patchwork of inconsistent authority.[46]

In 1985, Congress intervened to protect buyers of farm products by passing the Food Security Act, 16 U.S.C. 1631. While the details of the Act are too complicated to be pursued here, its core is Section 1631(d), which provides generally that one who buys farm products in the ordinary course of business from a person engaged in farming operations takes free of a security interest created by his seller. Congress has thus pre-empted and eliminated the Article 9 farm products exception to the ordinary course buyer rule. A secured agricultural lender who wishes to avoid this result and preserve his security interest in farm products notwithstanding their sale by a farmer must do one of two things. An agricultural secured lender in any state may preserve a post-sale security interest by giving a written notice to the farm products buyer in advance of the sale. Section 1631(e)(1) specifies the information the pre-sale notification must contain and the time it must be given. The second alternative requires that the state in which the farm products at issue are produced enact a statute providing for a central filing system for farm products. The central filing system contemplated is distinct from the Article 9 filing system and requires more detailed information, more extensive indexing, and periodic notifications by the Secretary of State to registered buyers of farm products. See Sections 1631(c)(2) and (e)(2). If an agricultural secured party makes an effective filing, a registered buyer should receive notice from the Secretary. If a buyer has not registered, and the secured party has made an effective filing as to farm products, the sale does not cut off the secured

---

**45.** Of course, the secured lender could argue under Section 1–205(4) that express terms, including requirements of written consent to sales, are controlling even in the face of contrary courses of dealing or usages of trade.

**46.** See *Clovis National Bank v. Thomas*, 77 N.M. 554, 425 P.2d 726 (1967) and *Five Points Bank v. Scoular–Bishop Grain Co.*, 217 Neb. 677, 350 N.W.2d 549 (1984).

party's interest in the farm products. Obviously, the means of escape from the ordinary course buyer rule of Section 1631(d) are sufficiently cumbersome that a rational agricultural secured party might prefer to acquiesce in the loss of his or her security interest upon the sale of farm products by his farmer/debtor and rely on his claim to the proceeds of sale under Section 9–315.

---

### Problem 5–29

*Drabb is becoming a real pain.*

TO:        S. Carlson, Megabank Legal Dept.
FROM:    J. Drabb, Friendly Finance
RE:        Complications on Schott Loans

Sidney:

You may remember that Steroid Sporting Goods, Inc., is one of the local businesses that steers customers our way when they want long-term credit. About a year ago, we made a loan of $1,000 to a local businessman, Harvey "Buck" Schott, so he could buy a couple of guns for recreational use. Specifically, he used our loan to buy a Belchdeath 30.06 hunting rifle and a Savage 12–gauge shotgun from Steroid. We had Buck execute our standard Purchase Money Security Agreement. Buck is an avid hunter, but only in his spare time, so we knew the guns were consumer goods. Accordingly, we did not believe that we needed to file a financing statement. Unfortunately, Buck's business failed about six months ago. He stopped making payments to us shortly thereafter, but we have given him some latitude. What we did not know, of course, was that he would sell the guns. He sold the rifle to a dealer, Hot Lead, Inc., who, in turn, sold it to another recreational hunter, Ernie Hemingway. Buck sold the shotgun to his neighbor, Chuck Heston. I do not think we will see any more money out of Buck. Is it possible for me to pursue our collateral in the hands of Hemingway and Heston?[47]

### Problem 5–30

*Yesterday you bought the "Buns of Steel®" video. You thought it might make it easier to sit through the interminable meetings that Houseman has been holding lately. You tried it last night and you are not sure you can physically get into your chair to pick up the memorandum that is sitting on your desk.*

### BANK OF NEW BABYLON
### INTEROFFICE MEMORANDUM

TO:        S. Carlson, Megabank Legal Dept.
FROM:    P.L. Driver, V.P., Bank of New Babylon
RE:        Drafting Assistance—Rust Belt Gears Matter

**47.**  [See Sections 9–320(a) and (b).]

The Bank has a new customer, Rust Belt Gears, Inc., the primary business of which is the manufacture of transmission parts for sale to automobile manufacturers. Rust Belt has changed lenders because of a dispute with Bank of Amerigo, which used to finance Rust Belt's operations. We are in the process of drafting a security agreement that will give us a security interest in a most of Rust Belt's assets, including its existing and after-acquired equipment. (Needless to say, we will also file an appropriate financing statement.)

There is one aspect of the transaction that requires advice from you. Some of Rust Belt's equipment is somewhat old and adapted for production of transmission parts for Ford models that are no longer made. The equipment does have some value in the second-hand market, however, and Rust Belt would like to sell it and use the proceeds to acquire new equipment. We have no objection to that, and we are quite capable of drafting an after-acquired property clause that will capture any new equipment. However, we want our security interest to continue in the old equipment unless we specifically release it at the time of sale. This will enable us to insist either on payment of a portion of the proceeds to the Bank or on earmarking the proceeds for new equipment that will feed our after-acquired property clause. The question is how we can accomplish our goal.

In the past, I have handled situations like this in one of two ways. In one instance, I included a clause in a security agreement that read, "Debtor is hereby authorized to sell the following pieces of equipment [described by serial number] subject to the security interest created by this agreement." On another occasion, I included a clause that read, "Debtor shall not dispose of any equipment subject to the security interest created by this agreement without the express written consent of Secured Party." When asked for such consent, I would send a letter that contained this language: "Debtor may sell the following equipment [described by serial number] to [buyer's name], free and clear of the Secured Party's lien, provided the proceeds of sale are immediately paid over to Secured Party." I need you to tell me which of these possible provisions best protects the Bank's interest. In particular, I need to know what happens, in either case, if Rust Belt just sells a piece of equipment, deposits the money in a commingled account, and uses the proceeds to pay ordinary trade creditors. Will we be able to pursue the equipment in the hands of the transferee?[48] Will we be able to pursue the sale proceeds into the bank account or into the hands of trade creditors?[49]

## Problem 5–31

*The next day, you receive a voice mail message from the same Vice President.*

Hello, Carlson. Driver here. It turns out my concern over Rust Belt Gears is not unrealistic, although my current problem is not with Rust Belt. We have another borrower, Champion Distillery. If you will forgive me for putting it indelicately, Champion makes cheap whiskey, gin and other spirits for what can only be described as lower end of the market. The Bank has a

**48.** [See Section 9–315(a)(1) and Comment 2.]

**49.** [See Section 9–332.]

perfected security interest in Champion's equipment, and the security agreement prohibits sale of any of the equipment without the express written consent of the Bank. Sixty days ago, Champion sold one of their bottling machines to another distiller, Tippler's House of Hootch, for $60,000. Champion neither sought our consent nor informed us of the sale. I'm sure that, by now, the sale proceeds have been dissipated. Our loan balance at the time of sale was $20,000. Thirty days later, we advanced Champion another $20,000. One of my loan officers went out to Champion to do a field inspection the next day and noticed the bottling machine was missing. When he inquired about it, the plant manager told him of the sale. Unfortunately, the loan officer did not tell me, and I authorized another $20,000 advance to Champion three weeks later. Champion is in default, and I doubt I can squeeze much more money out of the company. I have submitted a demand to Tippler's that they either surrender the bottling machine to us or pay us its reasonable value, which would retire our loan. Tippler's counsel wrote back, insisting our security interest is confined to the $20,000 initial balance. Could that be right?[50] Call me.

### Problem 5–32

*Vice President Driver is becoming more bothersome than a relative who needs money. This time, he finds you by e-mail:*

To:         S. Carlson, Megabank Legal Dept.
From:       P.L. Driver, V.P., Bank of New Babylon
Re:         Hott Industries

Since you have become our resident expert on customers who sell their equipment out the back door, let me run a strange one past you. On January 1, of this year, we loaned $30,000 to Hott Industries, Inc., a potato wholesaler. (You may have seen Hott Potatoes in the local grocery stores.) We took and perfected a security interest in Hott's existing and after-acquired inventory, accounts, and equipment at that time. On April 1, without our knowledge, Hott borrowed an additional $20,000 from Bank of Amerigo and granted Bank of Amerigo a security interest (presumably junior to ours) in Hott's equipment. On May 1, without informing us or Bank of Amerigo, Hott sold one of its potato sorting machines to a competitor, Quayle's House of Spuds. On July 1, in continued blissful ignorance of the sale, we advanced an additional $40,000 to Hott. I believe the potato sorter is worth about $70,000 at the moment. I think we will have to pursue our claim against the machine, as I doubt Hott has any of the sale proceeds left. The company has ceased doing business, its remaining inventory has rotted, and its remaining accounts are uncollectible. As between our Bank, Bank of Amerigo, and Quayle's, how will the value of the potato sorter be allocated?[51]

**50.** [See Section 1–201(27); Rev. Section 1–202; Sections 9–323(d) and (e).]

**51.** [See Section 9–322; Sections 9–323(d) and (e).]

**BANK OF NEW BABYLON
LOAN OFFICER TRAINING AND
OPERATIONS MANUAL**

## CHAPTER 5: PRIORITIES

## V. Priority Disputes Between Secured Creditors and Real Estate Interests (Fixtures)

Article 9 does not govern the creation or perfection of consensual or non-consensual liens on real estate. See Section 9–109(d)(11). Nevertheless, it is quite possible for an Article 9 secured party to become embroiled in a priority contest with another party who claims an interest in the secured party's collateral under real estate law. This happens most commonly when a secured party takes a security interest in goods that are then attached to real estate, or when a secured party takes a security interest in goods already attached to real property. The rival real estate claimant may be the outright owner of the real property, the holder of a consensual real estate lien on the real property (e.g., a mortgagee or holder of a deed of trust), or the holder of a non-consensual real estate lien (e.g., a judgment lien creditor or a mechanic's lienor). The real estate claimant may be one whose interest in the real estate precedes the attachment of the secured party's interest in the goods in question, or the real estate claimant may be a party who subsequently acquired a real estate interest.

The possibility of such priority contests arises because there are circumstances in which property that begins as "goods" (by the Code's or any other definition) can become so intimately connected to real estate that it passes with a conveyance of the realty. The degree of integration of the goods into the realty can be either complete or partial. Building materials, such as bricks, lumber, structural metal, cement and the like are personal property before incorporation into a structure, and a seller of building materials or a lender who finances the operations of such a seller may have an ordinary Article 9 security interest in them. However, once such materials are incorporated into a building, their character as personal property is lost entirely. Following such incorporation, no Article 9 security interest in them may arise, and any pre-existing Article 9 security interest in them is lost. See Section 9–334(a). An unpaid seller of such materials may have a materialman's lien on the real estate for their value, but real estate law will decide the priority of that lien in relation to other interests in the realty.

Some goods that become affixed to realty, however, do not lose their personal property character completely, even though they will ordinarily pass to a buyer of real estate if the realty is sold. Goods that are so related to realty that an interest arises in them under real estate law are called "fixtures." See Section 9–102(a)(41). The Code does not purport to set out the criteria for determining when a particular good becomes a fixture. That task is left to state real estate law. Those criteria vary somewhat from state to state, but the most consistently important factors include the intentions of the parties, the degree of physical affixation of the personal property to the real estate and the ease of its removal, the reasonable expectations of a buyer of the real estate, and the degree to which the personal property is or becomes crucial to the functioning of the enterprise conducted on the real estate.

A consensual security interest in fixtures may arise in more than one way. Article 9 permits the creation of a security interest in fixtures, or goods that are to become fixtures, by satisfying the usual requirements of Section 9–203. See Section 9–334(a). However, Article 9 also expressly recognizes the validity of an encumbrance on fixtures that is created under real property law. See Section 9–334(b).

In some exceptional instances, the perfection of a security interest in fixtures may be accomplished by filing a conventional financing statement. See Sections 9–334(e)(2) and (3). More commonly, however, the perfection of a security interest in fixtures requires a special filing (called a "fixture filing") in the real estate records in the office where mortgages and other real estate interests are recorded. See Section 9–102(a)(40). In addition to satisfying the minimum requirements for a normal financing statement, a fixture filing must indicate that it covers fixtures, indicate that it is to be filed in the real estate records, and contain a description of the real estate to which the fixtures are or will become related. See Section 9–502(b). The standard version of Article 9 does not expressly determine whether the description must be a formal legal description sufficient, for example, for inclusion in a real estate mortgage. Optional language may be enacted to make it clear that such a description is required. *Id.* Under certain circumstances, a real estate mortgage containing the requisite information may suffice as a fixture filing. See Section 9–502(c). If the Article 9 debtor does not have an interest of record in the real property to which the collateral is or becomes attached, the fixture filing must contain the name of the record owner. See Section 9–502(b)(4). This requirement may be triggered, for example, if the debtor is a lessee making improvements or a contractor supplying and installing goods in a building.

The priority rules for deciding contests between an Article 9 secured party and an owner or encumbrancer of real estate are somewhat complex. However, they begin with a rather simple presumption. Unless the Article 9 secured party can find a specific rule creating an exception, the Article 9 secured party's interest in fixtures is subordinate to that of an owner or encumbrancer of the related real estate (other than the Article 9 debtor). See Section 9–334(c). There are, however, several specific provisions delineating the circumstances under which the Article 9 secured party is entitled to priority. See Sections 9–334(d)–(f).

---

### Problem 5–33

*Occasionally, you make new friends. This is not always cause for rejoicing.*

### NB MORTGAGE CO., INC.
### INTEROFFICE MEMORANDUM

TO:          S. Carlson, Megabank Legal Dept.
FROM:        John Morgan, NB Mortgage Co, Inc.
RE:          Bates, Lord, and Salmon Files

I do not believe that you and I have met, as I have been working in our suburban offices and seldom get downtown any more. Jane Robinson said you had some free time and were ready for some more complicated problems. So I have three files I need you to work on. The first involves one of New Babylon's new crop of high-tech entrepreneurs, Gil Bates. Bates has a million-dollar house in the village of Nouveau, which has become the hottest suburban real estate market of greater New Babylon. We hold a first mortgage on the property with a loan balance of half a million and some change. We took the mortgage about 5 years ago when Bates bought the house, and you may assume we recorded it properly. The mortgage covers the land and building and all additions, accessions, fixtures and improvements that may be added or made.

Recently, Bates added a state-of-the art solar heating and cooling system to the house. The system includes solar panels, a variety of electric generating and storage hardware, compressors, ductwork, and a centralized computer control system, all of which are permanently affixed to the house. Bates bought the system—on credit, of course—from New Age Plumbing and Heating of Nouveau. New Age and Bates signed a security agreement reserving a security interest in the system in favor of New Age until the $50,000 purchase price was paid in full. The agreement was signed on June 1. The system was installed on June 3. New Age made what appears to me to be a flawless fixture filing on June 15.

I don't know if you follow the NASDAQ, but anyone who does knows that Bates' company hasn't been doing too well for the past year. Its poor performance is reflected in the stock price, and Bates' own financial position seems to be deteriorating as well. On July 15, Bates borrowed $100,000 from Bank of Amerigo and granted Bank of Amerigo a second mortgage on the house. The Bank of Amerigo mortgage, like our own, covers not only land and building, but all additions, accessions, fixtures, and improvements as well. Bank of Amerigo recorded the mortgage on July 16.

Last week, the price of stock in Bates' company hit a ten-year low. Since most of his wealth is tied up in the stock or stock options, he seems to have no cash at all. It appears he may default on all of his loans. We may have to foreclose. I am satisfied our mortgage on the house and land has first priority. I am less certain about the new solar heating and cooling system. Please do some research and let me know whether NB Mortgage, Bank of Amerigo, or New Age has priority with respect to that system.[52]

The second file involves a piece of commercial real estate, an eight-unit apartment building. The building is owned by Landis Lord, who makes his living in residential real estate leasing. NB Mortgage holds the first mortgage on the property to secure a current loan balance of $210,000. Once again, it is our standard form mortgage covering land and building as well as all additions, accessions, fixtures and improvements. Lord granted the mortgage to us three years ago, and it was properly recorded at that time.

Last year, the furnace in the building broke down and could not be repaired. Lord obtained a new one from Swelter Heating and Cooling, Inc. Swelter had Lord sign a Conditional Sale Contract granting Swelter a security interest in the new furnace to secure the purchase price. The Conditional Sale Contract was signed on October 1, and a financing state-

---

**52.** [See Section 9–334.]

ment describing the furnace was filed in the Secretary of State's office on October 10. The furnace was actually installed on October 4 and 5.

The Lord loan was actually one of our most trouble-free until November. On November 1, one of Lord's former tenants obtained a negligence judgment against Lord in the amount of $5,000,000. It seems the guy had been injured using the pool at the apartment building and claimed in was Lord's fault. Anyway, on November 15, the tort judgment creditor filed a judgment lien in the real estate records. As if that weren't harassment enough, he also got a writ of execution from the Superior Court and had the local sheriff come out to effect a seizure of the new furnace. I persuaded the sheriff to levy by tagging the furnace instead of disconnecting it, and I have told the lawyer for the tort judgment creditor that I think we have a prior interest in everything—the apartment building and the furnace as well. I need your help getting him to back off, and I need it quite soon. So do some quick research and sort out the priorities between NB Mortgage, Swelter, and this tort claimant.[53]

Finally, I need some help with a file that looks a lot like the Bates file. It's another case in which we hold a residential real estate mortgage on a fancy house out in Nouveau, and the owner, Walt Salmon, installed a new solar heating and cooling system. The system was even supplied by New Age, but this time New Age sold the system to the installation subcontractor, Elite Renovations, Inc. Elite granted New Age a security interest in the system to secure the price, and New Age once again made a satisfactory fixture filing in Elite's name within a couple weeks of installation. New Age never dealt with Salmon—Elite billed him directly. Unfortunately, Elite is having financial difficulty and defaulted on its obligations to New Age. New Age is making threatening noises, and I need to know if they have a right to repossess the system. Please advise.[54]

## Problem 5–34

*Just when you thought your boss had farmed out your services complete-ly, you find another item in your mailbox. A hand-written note, how quaint!*

---

**53.**  [See Section 9–334.]                    **54.**  [See Section 9–334.]

*Sidney:*

*I'm running to a meeting with Pompous, so this will have to be quick. The Bank of New Babylon has been financing the construction of a summer house for the Ross family on Lake Exclusive up in Remote County. We have a mortgage on record up there, and it secures the price of the land as well as any funds we advance for construction. It covers the land and any additions, fixtures or improvements. We have a problem with the cabinet supplier, Exotic Woods of New Babylon. Exotic Woods custom designed and built a set of mahogany kitchen cabinets for the summer place with a price of $50,000. Young Fletcher IV—you may remember his little trust fund problems—was supposed to take care of paying them. Instead, he signed a security agreement on behalf of the family with Exotic Woods giving them a security interest in the cabinets until he could pay in full in a few weeks. Apparently, Exotic knows who the Rosses are but is not familiar with young Fletch's reputation. Exotic also knew how to draft and file a fixture filing, which they did 7 days after the cabinets were permanently bolted to the floors and walls of the house. Construction is now nearly complete, and young Fletch is 3 months behind in paying Exotic. Exotic is threatening to "go up there and start yanking mahogany." Stop them.[55] Old Man Ross is a good friend of Pompous.*

*JR*

## Problem 5–35

*It seems your boss gave your phone number to your new friend, and he has found your voice mail.*

Carlson. This is John Morgan. I'm sorry we still have not met in person, but this will have to do. I've got another problem to add to your list. We at NB Mortgage are holding a first mortgage on the La Squinta Hotel out in Nouveau. We were granted the mortgage ten years ago. It's our standard form and properly recorded. There is a restaurant on the premises, and its commercial dishwasher had to be replaced in August. La Squinta acquired the replacement from Squeaky Clean, Inc., granting Squeaky Clean a security interest until the $10,000 price was paid in full. The security agreement was signed on August 10, and the dishwasher was delivered and bolted to the floor and the walls on August 11. I think it has become a fixture. Squeaky Clean apparently did not know how to draft a fixture filing, and they filed with the Secretary of State on August 12. Things are not going well at La Squinta these days, and by October 15, La Squinta had defaulted to Squeaky Clean. Squeaky Clean is threatening to repossess, although they will hold off if I can convince them our mortgage has priority. To make matters worse, an unpaid food supplier, Nouveau Cuisine, Inc., just got a judgment against La Squinta in the amount of $20,000 and recorded it as a judgment lien in the real estate records. Can you sort out the priority issues among the three of us?[56] Thanks.

## Problem 5–36

*And sometimes you hear from old friends as well. You have voice mail.*

Hey Carlson. Long time no see. It's Bubba from the Bovine State Bank. I've been talking to your buddy Morgan over at NB Mortgage about what he

**55.** [See Section 9–334.]

**56.** [See Section 9–334.]

calls "fixture filings." The reason I called him is that our local music store, The Sounds of Desolation, wants to buy a new fancy neon sign and wants us to finance it. We're happy to loan them the money ($5,000), and we know how to write a security agreement. Morgan says he can show us how to write a fixture filing, so you don't need to worry about that. But here's my problem. I really don't know if this sign is going to be a fixture or not. It will be bolted to the building, but you could remove it pretty quickly. I really don't understand this fixture filing business. If I make one of those, and the sign turns out not to be a fixture, what happens? Should I file a regular financing statement too?

Also, if the sign is a fixture and I make a fixture filing, I assume that will give us priority if Sounds of Desolation gives some other bank a mortgage on the building. But what if they grant a security interest in the sign to a lender who perfects by an ordinary filing? What if they go bankrupt and the trustee claims the avoiding power of a lien creditor? Are we protected? Should I even be worried about this stuff?[57] Call me.

## BANK OF NEW BABYLON
## LOAN OFFICER TRAINING AND
## OPERATIONS MANUAL

## CHAPTER 5: PRIORITIES

### VI.   Special Problems that Arise When the Debtor Files in Bankruptcy

In the scope of your duties as a loan officer, you will undoubtedly find that many of the debtors who default on loans made by the Bank will file for protection under the Bankruptcy Code. The commencement of a bankruptcy case has a number of important consequences, including the automatic imposition of a broad stay against creditor action without Bankruptcy Court permission under 11 U.S.C. 362. You are already familiar with this, and other, consequences of bankruptcy, and you are already aware that pursuit of claims against a debtor in bankruptcy requires close consultation with the Legal Department.

One of the most significant consequences of the commencement of a bankruptcy case is the fact that the trustee in bankruptcy is endowed by the Bankruptcy Code with certain "avoidance powers" that can adversely affect a creditor's pre-bankruptcy position. For example, you have already encountered the "strong arm clause" of Section 544(a), which gives the trustee the powers of a "perfect hypothetical lien creditor" as of the commencement of the case, even if there are, in fact, no real lien creditors. In effect, this enables the trustee to avoid any security interest that is not perfected at the commencement of the case, and that effectively relegates the (formerly) secured creditor to the status of an unsecured creditor.

The trustee has a variety of other avoidance powers, only one of which will be mentioned at present. Under Section 547 of the Bankruptcy Code, the trustee has the power to avoid transfers that can be characterized as "preferences." The policy basis for this avoidance power is the principle that, at least among unsecured creditors in

**57.** [See Section 9–317; Section 9–322; Section 9–334; 11 U.S.C. 544(a).]

bankruptcy, equality of treatment is equity. It is obvious that, absent a power on the part of the trustee to avoid some pre-bankruptcy transactions, the debtor could thwart this policy of equal treatment by treating selected creditors favorably in transactions on the eve of bankruptcy. For example, assume that a particular debtor owes three unsecured creditors—Creditors A, B, and C—$2,000 each. Assume that the debtor intends to file a bankruptcy petition at a time when the debtor's assets will leave only $3,000 for distribution to unsecured creditors. The Bankruptcy Code, and the policy of equal treatment it embodies, would dictate that A, B, and C each receive $1,000 in the bankruptcy distribution. But suppose that, shortly before bankruptcy, the debtor pays A her full $2,000 claim. That will leave only $1,000 for distribution to the only remaining unsecured creditors, B and C, and each will receive a distribution of $500. The potential for intentional (or perhaps unintentional or coerced) frustration of the principle that equality is equity is obvious. Section 547 permits the trustee to avoid the payment to A (i.e., to recover it from A) and ensure that A, B, and C each receive $1,000 in the bankruptcy distribution.

The elements of a preference are set out more systematically in Section 547(b) of the Bankruptcy Code. There must be a "transfer," a term defined in Section 101(54). In the simple case just discussed, the payment to Creditor A was the transfer. The transfer must be "to or for the benefit of a creditor," which is obviously satisfied by a direct payment to a creditor such as A. The transfer must be for or on account of an antecedent debt, i.e., a debt already in existence when the transfer is made. The transfer must be made while the debtor is insolvent, although there is a presumption of insolvency under Section 547(f) during the 90–day period immediately prior to the filing of the petition in bankruptcy. The transfer must have been made "on within 90 days before the filing of the petition" in bankruptcy, a period sometimes called "the slippery slope." If the transferee is an "insider," as defined in Section 101(30), the slippery slope extends out to a year before the filing of the petition. Finally, the transfer must enable the favored creditor to recover more than she would if the transfer had not been made and the creditor recovered whatever would be available to her in a bankruptcy liquidation of the debtor. In the simple case discussed above, A would receive payment in full ($2,000) if the transfer stands and $1,000 if it were erased and A had to share in a bankruptcy distribution with A and B. Accordingly, the payment to A is avoidable as a preference. Indeed, if a debtor is truly insolvent, any payment to a favored unsecured creditor on the slippery slope will be preferential. However, because of the very broad bankruptcy definition of "transfer," as well as certain other peculiarities of Section 547, the net of Section 547(b) captures a variety of other pre-bankruptcy transactions as well.

Indeed, Section 547(b), applied literally, would be broad enough to capture and invalidate some transactions that Congress did not consider inherently undesirable. Accordingly, Congress carved out a set of exceptions to the avoidance power that saves certain transactions that would otherwise be avoidable under Section 547(b). The exceptions in question are found in Section 547(c).

———————

## Problem 5–37

*Isn't it wonderful that old friends call you in time of trouble? But why so often? Here is the voice mail:*

Hello, Carlson. This is Bubba at the Bovine State Bank. I need you to call me back real quick, so I hope you get this. Heck, call me even if you don't. I've got three customers up here who have gone belly up and filed in bankruptcy. I need to know if our loans or security interests are in jeopardy.

The first debtor is our local plumber, Elwood Leake. He's a friend of my brother Buford's, so I let him talk me into an unsecured loan of $5,000 about a year ago. Elwood's back has been bothering him for the last couple of months, and he hasn't worked much. I got worried, so a month ago I had him sign a security agreement giving us a security interest in his van. I perfected by getting it noted on the certificate of title, just like you told me before. Anyway, Elwood filed a chapter 7 bankruptcy yesterday. I hope I didn't do something wrong here.[58]

Anyway, the second debtor is a new bar that opened up here in Desolation very recently. It's called the Desolate Keg, and its owner, Harold Plonk, kind of put one over on me. The Bank loaned Plonk $20,000 on October 15 and had him execute a security agreement giving the Bank a security interest in his present and after-acquired inventory. I mailed in a financing statement, which was actually filed on October 30. It turns out that Harold has been drinking up a lot of our collateral and mismanaging the business. He filed a petition in bankruptcy on November 15. Do you think our security interest will hold up?[59] I thought nothing was safer than a bar.

Just a second here. I may have misread the financing statement here—I don't have my bifocals on. Now it looks like the date stamp on the financing statement says October 20, not October 30. Would that help? Doggone it! I'm having trouble with the date on the security agreement, too. I know we loaned him the money on October 15, but I can't tell if the date on the security agreement is the 15th or the 17th. Does it matter?

One last debtor. You may remember our local construction contractor, Buddy Diggs.[60] Well, he paid off his debt to Bank of Amerigo, so he doesn't have another lender any more. So last July 1, I authorized a loan in the amount of $50,000, secured by all of Buddy's present and after acquired equipment. We made the loan on July 1 and signed the security agreement on July 2. We filed our financing statement on July 6. His equipment was worth about $75,000 at the time. Anyway, I knew Buddy wouldn't get paid in full on his current job until mid-October, so I set up a balloon payment for October 20. Apparently, the job did not go well, and the owner held back some of Buddy's money. On October 20, Buddy could only pay us $10,000. Then on November 15, Buddy filed for bankruptcy. I think the equipment is still worth $65,000, so I'm not too worried. But the trustee in Buddy's case is that Bobby Bellicose kid again. He says I have to cough up the $10,000 payment. Can that be right? Oh, he also says the equipment is only worth

**58.** [See 11 U.S.C. 547(b); 101(54).]     **60.** [See Problem 4–16, supra.]
**59.** [See 11 U.S.C. 547(b) and (e).]

$30,000. Does that make a difference?[61] Hey, I'm sorry about the long message. I'll get off the phone so you can call me back.

## Problem 5–38

*While that voice mail was playing, you received another.*

Hello, Carlson. This is Sal Vache from NB Commercial Finance. I have a bankruptcy problem, and I am told you are becoming our new expert. For three years, we have been financing the inventory and accounts of a local lawn mower and yard equipment dealer, Rip 'N Clip of New Babylon, Inc. Our security agreement (which we have appropriately perfected) contains formulae (based on eligible inventory and accounts) for determining the amount we will advance each month and the amount Rip 'N Clip must pay to stay out of default. The business has gone poorly since the summer was so dry. On June 1, Rip 'N Clip owed us $60,000, and its inventory and accounts were collectively valued at $30,000. Payments to us are due on the second of each month, and Rip 'N Clip made payments of $5,000 each on June 4, July 2, and July 31. In each case, that was the amount dictated by the payment formula in the security agreement, and it is not at all unusual for Rip 'N Clip to be a few days early or late with a payment. Under our security agreement formula, Rip 'N Clip was not entitled to any advances, and we made none. Rip 'N Clip filed a bankruptcy petition on August 15. Will we have to return any of these payments?[62]

## Problem 5–39

*A couple of days later, you receive an e-mail from the same loan officer.*

TO:        S. Carlson, Megabank Legal Dept.
FROM:     Sal Vache, NB Commercial Finance
RE:         Locust Lawn Equipment

This drought has really been tough on lawn mower dealers. I have another one that just filed for bankruptcy, specifically on December 1. This was a relatively new customer, with the following history. We signed a security agreement covering the present and after-acquired inventory and accounts of Locust Lawn Equipment (and containing the usual future advance feature) on February 1. We filed a financing statement and made our first advance on February 2. By the end of the summer, on September 1, our outstanding loan balance was $100,000, but the value of Locust's inventory and accounts was down to $80,000. On September 30, Locust somehow acquired new inventory—perhaps on open account—worth another $10,000. Here's where things get a little odd. My records do not reflect any advances by us after September 1. If that is accurate, I need to know if there are any problems if we try to repossess Locust's entire inventory. However, it may not be accurate. There is a handwritten note in the file that reads, "$5,000 advance—late Sept. or early Oct." It looks like it might be Cal Cavalier's handwriting. There is thus a possibility that we made a $5,000

---

**61.**   [See 11 U.S.C. 547(b) and (c)(2).]       **62.**   [See 11 U.S.C. 547 (b) and (c)(2).]

advance to Locust sometime in late September or early October that no one recorded. I'm going back to our bank records to double check. Anyway if we made such an advance in October, does that affect your analysis? How about if we made it in late September and Locust bought some of the new inventory with it? Please advise.[63] And a plague on Locust and Cavalier.

## Problem 5–40

*You have taken to bringing your lunch on Fridays so you can read in detail the "Weekend Journal" section of the* Wall Street Journal. *This week there is an article about a corporate executive who was laid off and is now making Lattés. He professes to like the job.*[64] *You wonder if you might like it, too. You quickly put down the paper and pick up the memorandum on your desk.*

### NB COMMERCIAL FINANCE
### INTEROFFICE MEMORANDUM

TO:        S. Carlson, Megabank Legal
FROM:      R. Comstock, NB Commercial Finance
RE:        Effete Organic Vegetables File

Thanks for helping Sal Vache out on the Rip 'N Clip and Locust files. I have another bankruptcy problem for you, and I hope it will be the last for a while. This has been a bad month for us. The customer here is Effete Organic Vegetables, a huge produce wholesaler catering to the health food market. Frankly, its inventory spoils so quickly we really did not think it prudent to finance inventory, but its accounts are very high quality. So, for the last two years, we have been making periodic advances to Effete secured by present and after acquired accounts. We have a future advance clause, and you may assume the security interest is properly perfected.

At the beginning of this year, our loan balance was $250,000, and Effete's accounts were worth $260,000. Things were looking good. I was somewhat surprised, therefore, when Effete filed a bankruptcy petition yesterday. So I looked back at our records, as well as Effete's, and pieced together the following picture. Ninety days ago, our loan balance had dropped to $200,000, but the value of the accounts on hand was down to $160,000. Now, one thing you have to understand about these accounts is that they turn over very quickly. Credit in the produce business is very short-term credit—Effete typically gives its credit customers only 5 days to pay. That's reasonable, since the produce that was sold on account is either resold or rotten within that time. But it means that, over the next ninety days, all of Effete's accounts turned over several times. As of yesterday, our loan balance was $150,000, and the accounts were worth $140,000. My question is the obvious one. Do we have any preference problems here?[65] Please advise. If I hear from the trustee, it will be soon.

---

**63.** [See 11 U.S.C. 547(b), (c)(3) and (4), and (e).]

**64.** Wall Street Journal, March 14, 2003, W13.

**65.** [See 11 U.S.C. 547(b), (c)(5), and (e)(3).]

# Chapter 6

# MULTI–JURISDICTIONAL TRANSACTIONS

## BANK OF NEW BABYLON
## LOAN OFFICER TRAINING AND
## OPERATIONS MANUAL

## I.   Introduction to Multi–Jurisdictional Transactions

It should come as no surprise to you that secured transactions, like the rest of commerce, are frequently interstate, and even international, transactions.[1] The inter-state character of such transactions poses two distinct problems that require statutory resolution. The first problem is an ordinary choice of law problem. If the debtor resides in one state, the lender is located in another, and the collateral is kept in yet another, which of the three states supplies the law governing the transaction? The answer the statutory draftsman provides to that question will determine, among other things, the proper place to file a financing statement in order to perfect a security interest.

The second question arises no matter how the first is resolved. Assuming, for example, that the debtor's location dictates the state whose law applies, what happens if the debtor moves to another state? Or, if collateral location is the choice of law criterion, what if the collateral is goods, and the goods are transported to another state? The answers to such questions determine whether the governing law changes and whether a security interest perfected in one state must be "re-perfected" in an additional jurisdiction when such a significant change occurs.

The Code attempts to streamline the multi-state transaction rules to eliminate, to the extent possible, the need to re-perfect in another state. The primary choice of law rules are found in Section 9–301 through Section 9–307. The type of collateral at issue is the initial determinant of the choice of law criterion. However, the location of the *debtor* assumes great importance as a choice of law criterion for selecting rules related to perfection. *Collateral* location plays a reduced role in selecting the rules governing perfection, although it does remain significant for specialized forms of

---

**1.** For a useful overview of this topic see Hans Kuhn, *Multi-State and International Secured Transactions Under Revised Article 9 of the Uniform Commercial Code*, 40 Va. J. Int'l L. 1009 (2000) and Neil Cohen and Edwin Smith, *International Secured Transactions and Revised UCC Article 9*, 74 Chi–Kent 1191 (1999).

collateral, for selecting the state rules governing perfection of *possessory* security interests, and for selecting state priority rules. See Section 9–316. Changes in the feature used as a criterion for choice of law (i.e., changes in collateral or debtor location) often trigger a requirement of "re-perfection," which must be accomplished within the earlier of four months after the critical change or the remaining period of perfection in the original jurisdiction, although it extends the re-perfection period to one year for one subset of such changes.

---

## II. Perfection in Multi–Jurisdictional Transactions

### A. Place of Initial Perfection

#### Problem 6–1

*Your good friends at the Bovine State Bank are becoming increasingly proficient at the use of e-mail.*

TO: S. Carlson, Megabank Legal Dept.
FROM: Bubba O'Reilly, Bovine State Bank
RE: Fragrant Fertilizer Start-up Loan

I think I told you about the fertilizer plant that closed down up here. Well, one of our local entrepreneurs, Einar Jetick, just bought it lock, stock and barrel. He thinks he can run it profitably, and, frankly, so do we. So we have approved a start-up loan in the amount of $500,000, to be secured by a mortgage on the land, as well as a security interest in the existing and after acquired equipment, inventory, and accounts receivable. As you know, we have a local attorney up here who can draft and record the mortgage, and I can handle the security agreement and the wording of the financing statement. But I need you to tell me where to file it. Einar is going to operate the company as a sole proprietorship, although he's using "Fragrant Fertilizer" as a trade name. The plant is here in Gilmoria, just outside Desolation, and that's where the equipment and some of the inventory will be kept. Desolation is sort of tucked up here in the northern corner of the state, very close to the borders of two other states, Confusion and Apoplexy. Einar actually lives across the border in the town of Mild in the state of Confusion. Some of the inventory will be sold out of a storefront Einar runs over in a small town called Total in the State of Apoplexy. If you need any other information, feel free to call. Oh, one last question. Like I said, Einar plans to run this operation as a sole proprietorship. However, he might set it up as a new corporation instead. Would that make any difference? Thanks for your attention to this matter.[2]

#### Problem 6–2

*Once again, the Ross family financial empire manages to make your day.*

---

**2.** [See Section 9–102(a)(70); Section 9–301; Section 9–307; Section 9–501.]

## BANK OF NEW BABYLON
## INTEROFFICE MEMORANDUM

TO:        S. Carlson, Megabank Legal
FROM:     P.L. Driver, V.P., BNB
RE:        Ross Family Business Ventures

I have good news. Apparently our accommodations to young Fletcher Ross have paid dividends. His father, Fletcher Worthington Ross, III, just brought us some new business. He wants us to take over operating capital financing for two of the Ross family companies, Ross Crude, Inc. and Clearcut Timber. Ross Crude is an oil drilling company. It is incorporated in Oklahoma, although the Ross family sold all its Oklahoma properties years ago. However, the company still has a large oil-producing tract in Fort Stinkindesert, Texas. We would like to make periodic advances to the company, secured by the crude oil it pumps out of the ground and the accounts generated when it is sold at the wellhead. I was told you would be able to help with the security agreement and financing statement including where we should file.[3]

Clearcut Timber is actually a partnership of which various Ross children and relatives are members. It's actually run by old man Ross (Fletcher, Jr.) out of a downtown office here in New Babylon. There is also another small office in Picayune, Mississippi, since all the timber acreage owned or leased by the partnership is in Mississippi. Clearcut either buys or leases timber acreage and then hires a crew to cut down and load the timber on trucks. It is then transported and sold to a variety of Mississippi lumber mills. In return for advances of operating capital, we would like to take a security interest in the standing timber, the cut timber, and the accounts generated by its sale. Again, I need your help with the security agreement and financing statement including where we should file.[4]

## II.  Perfection in Multi–Jurisdictional Transactions

## B.  Location Changes Affecting Perfection

### Problem 6–3

*Your voice mail light is on again.*

Hello, Sidney. This is Sal Vache at NB Commercial Finance. You remember our old friend Herman Hodad?[5] We filed a new financing statement to perfect our security interest in inventory and accounts when he incorporated his business as The Board Room, Inc. Well, anyway, Herman seems to think he's some kind of corporate magnate, and he's talking about merging the business with a similar operation (surfboard sales, etc.) owned

---

**3.** [See Section 9–102(a)(6); Section 9–301 and Comment 5.c; Section 9–501 and Comment 3; Section 9–502(b) and Comment 5.]

**4.** [See Section 1–201(28); Rev. Sections 1–201(b)(25) and (27); Section 9–102(a)(70);

Section 9–301 and Comment 5; Section 9–307; Section 9–501 and Comment 3; Section 9–502(b).]

**5.** [See Problems 4–16 and 4–19.]

by some friend of his named Murphy. Herman, as you recall, has his shop on the Gulf Coast here in Gilmoria, and he organized The Board Room, Inc. as a Gilmoria corporation. Murphy has a store in Destin, Florida, operating under the trade name, Murph the Surf's. However, the business is really a Florida corporation registered under the name, "Board Silly, Inc." All this is still in the planning stage, but I think this is what they are going to do. The Board Room, Inc., is going to merge into Board Silly, Inc., which will be the surviving corporation. Murphy and Herman will each own half the stock. As part of the deal, Board Silly, Inc. assumes both the assets and the liabilities of The Board Room, Inc. The surviving corporation then operates both the Gilmoria and the Florida stores. My question is, assuming these guys carry out their plans, do I need to do anything further to protect our position? If so, how soon? Thanks.[6]

## Problem 6–4

*Some business ventures succeed. Some do not. When they do, you are seldom thanked. When they do not, you hear about it. Bubba is about to ruin your day with the following:*

### THE BOVINE STATE BANK
### DESOLATION, GILMORIA
### "Serving Desolation for Fifty Years"

### MEMORANDUM

TO:      S. Carlson, Megabank Legal Dept.
FROM:    Bubba O'Reilly, Bovine State Bank
RE:      Einar Jetick Loan

You may remember that, last January, we made a start-up loan in the amount of $500,000 to this borrower. He used the money to re-open the fertilizer plant near Desolation, and we took a security interest in the existing and after-acquired equipment, accounts, and inventory of the business, as well as a mortgage on the land. Einar has been operating the business as a sole proprietorship, although he uses a trade name, "Fragrant Fertilizers" both here at the plant and at a retail outlet in the State of Apoplexy . However, you had us file in Confusion, because that's where Einar was living.

Well, apparently the business went down hill pretty quickly, although we were not aware of it at the time because Einar was submitting inaccurate financial statements to us. On May 1 of this year, Einar moved to a huge beach house on the Florida Panhandle. We think he saw the financial handwriting on the wall and starting pouring his assets into the house so he could take advantage of Florida's unlimited homestead exemption. Anyway, he did not tell us about the move, and he continued to spend enough time up here that he could often call us locally, from the plant. His payment record to us was spotty, but he made payments just often enough to keep us from

**6.** [See Section 9–102(a)(28)(A); Section 9–203; Section 9–301; Section 9–315; Section 9–316(a) and Comment 2; Section 9– 325; Section 9–326; Section 9–507; Comment 4 to Section 9–508.]

foreclosing. He also started taking fairly desperate measures to keep cash coming into the business, most of which we think he has diverted into his house. On July 1, he borrowed $50,000 from Saltwater Bank of Pensacola. He granted Saltwater a security interest in his equipment, and Saltwater filed a financing statement in Florida the same day.

The most valuable pieces of equipment, by the way, were three huge grinding machines at the plant just outside Desolation used for the purpose of grinding raw materials into finished fertilizer. On August 1, Einar sold one of them to Tyson's Chicken plant in Confusion, as they apparently have a lot of raw material for fertilizer. Tyson's paid $25,000 and picked up the machine that very day. On September 15, he sold another to Iowa Beef Processors (IBP) for $35,000, and they likewise hauled it away, bound for the home plant in Des Moines.

Meanwhile, on August 15, a fellow with a judgment against Einar arising out of a car accident got the local sheriff in Total to levy on the inventory at the Apoplexy store. We had not been monitoring that store closely, and so we were unaware of it. We finally learned about much of this when another judgment creditor had the local sheriff here in Desolation levy on the last remaining grinding machine on October 1. In the course of investigating the matter, I learned of Einar's move, as well as some of these transactions. On October 15, I filed a financing statement listing Einar as debtor in Florida, just in case it would help.

Obviously, this is a total mess. The cash Einar received from Saltwater, Tyson's and IBP appears to be gone. Most of the fertilizer inventory seems to have been sold out the back door to unknown buyers and the money used for the beach house. We could foreclose on the land. However, we are reluctant to do so, as it appears likely that it will become a Superfund cleanup site. Einar was not very careful about what he put into his fertilizer, according to some of the EPA folks that have been swarming around here lately. Our best hope to recover something would seem to be pursuing the grinding machines and the Apoplexy inventory seized by the lien creditor. Obviously, we will be fighting with Saltwater, Tyson's, IBP, and both lien creditors. Do we have any chance for success?[7] Please advise.

### Problem 6–5

*You are beginning to long for the day when you, too, will be able to delegate unpleasant tasks to others. Memoranda like the next one from your boss form the major reason for this newly-discovered urge.*

### BANK OF NEW BABYLON
### MEMORANDUM

TO:         S. Carlson
FROM:     J. Robinson
RE:         Hurrier Couriers

**7.** [See Sections 1–201(32) and (33); Rev. Sections 1–201(b)(29) and (30); Section 9–102(a)(28); Section 9–315(a)(1); Sections 9–316(a) and (b); Sections 9–317(a) and (b); Section 9–322(a); Section 9–325; Section 9–507(a) and Comment 3.]

You may already be familiar with this account. Hurrier Couriers is a delivery service that does extensive business in the States of Gilmoria, Confusion, and Apoplexy. They have numerous offices in all three states and some extremely high quality corporate accounts. We have provided operating capital for the company for years, secured by an interest in the company's accounts receivable. Our security agreement and financing statement actually date back five years, specifically to October 1 of that year. The loan has always performed well and continues to do so, but I need you to look at one issue while I am out of town.

Hurrier Couriers is actually a general partnership with half a dozen members. The chief executive office of the company has always been here in New Babylon, and our financing statement is on file in Gilmoria. Last September 15, the managing partner, Harry Furrier, moved the main office to Gilingham, Confusion. Fortunately, President Pompous was informed within a couple of weeks, and he saw to it that a financing statement was filed with the Secretary of State in Confusion on our behalf by October 15. Apparently, the Trust Company Bank of Gilingham made a loan to Hurrier's on September 26 and likewise took a security interest in the company's accounts. They filed in Confusion the same day. Normally, I might be concerned about that. However, since we refiled within four months of the move, I assume we still have priority. That's right, isn't it?[8] Assuming it is, call Pompous and reassure him, will you? Thanks.

## II. Perfection in Multiple–Jurisdiction Transactions

## C. Certificate of Title Issues

### Problem 6–6

*You have hitherto assumed that your friend Bubba could display his literary gifts only in missives not exceeding one page. He is, unfortunately, about to prove your wrong.*

**THE BOVINE STATE BANK**
**DESOLATION, GILMORIA**
**"Serving Desolation for Fifty Years"**

**MEMORANDUM**

TO:       S. Carlson, Megabank Legal
FROM:   Bubba O'Reilly, Bovine State Bank
RE:       Miscellaneous Car and Boat Loans
DATE:    June 15

You probably already know that we do a lot of lending to finance car and boat purchases up here, as well as some non-purchase money lending against the same types of collateral. As you know, Desolation is very close to the borders of two states, Confusion and Apoplexy. This creates some problems

---

**8.** [See Section 1–201(28); Rev. Sections 1–201(b)(25) and (27); Section 9–102(a)(70); Section 9–307; Section 9–316 (a) and (b) and Comment 2, Example 2; Section 9–515.]

for us because sometimes our borrowers move across one or the other border and take our collateral with them. I have several such cases at the moment, and I need your advice.

First of all, as you know, Gilmoria has a certificate of title statute for cars, but not for boats. So, when we take a security interest in a boat, we normally file. When we take a security interest in a car, we have it noted on the certificate of title, and, when no one makes a mistake, we actually retain the title certificate. Both Confusion and Apoplexy have certificate of title statutes for both cars and boats.

In December of last year, the last sugar refinery factory here in Desolation closed down. As a result, a number of our borrowers who had worked at the plant moved to Confusion and Apoplexy beginning in January of this year. One of them, Barry Bayliner, had a bass boat subject to a security interest in favor of the Bank. We took the security interest two years ago when we financed the acquisition of the boat. Your boss said we were probably automatically perfected but should file a financing statement here in Gilmoria anyway. I didn't really understand why, but we did what she said. Anyway, Barry moved to the town of Hopeless in the State of Confusion on January 5 of this year. He applied for a Confusion certificate of title for the bass boat the very next day. Apparently, either the application process does not require that the applicant disclose security interests or Barry just didn't do it. Anyway, Confusion issued a clean certificate of title for the boat on February 1. We, of course, didn't even know Barry had moved, let alone that he had obtained a Confusion title certificate for the boat. At that point, he was still making his payments on the boat, although I see in the file that he missed this month. Anyway, we knew nothing of the move or anything else until two days ago (June 13), when I got a call from the sheriff of Hopeless. It seems Barry had not had any success finding work up there, and he had written some bad checks. One of the payees had Barry sign a confession of judgment (no doubt in order to avoid a criminal prosecution). Once the judgment was entered, the payee had the sheriff levy on the bass boat (on the morning of June 13). Suddenly, Barry miraculously remembered our security interest in the boat and told the sheriff about it. The sheriff then called me, and I confirmed it. The sheriff had already taken the boat to the courthouse parking lot, but he says he'll hold off on the execution sale until he hears from you. I'd appreciate it if you could get back to him quickly.[9]

There is another borrower, Carla Catamaran, whose story is a lot like Barry's, with a little bit different twist in the end. Carla moved to the town of Roaring in the State of Apoplexy on January 10. She had a sailboat subject to a security interest in favor of the Bank, again dating back about 2 years. Whether we needed to or not, we filed a financing statement here in Gilmoria at that time. Carla applied for an Apoplexy certificate of title for the boat on January 15, and a clean title certificate was issued on February 15. Unlike Barry, I don't think Carla was really trying to fool anybody. However, she continued to use her Gilmoria checking account to make her

**9.** [See Sections 9–303; Section 9–309(1); Section 9–310; Section 9–311; 9–316.]

payments to us, so we thought she was still around. When she made her May 1 payment, however, one of our people noticed she did it with a check drawn on her account at the Bank of Roaring. This set off some bells in our collective heads, and we called her. (The phone number was on her check). We reached her on May 8, and she told us the whole story. It took her a while to find a job in Roaring, but she finally did. She asked for a little leeway on her June 1 payment, and I gave her an additional week. In the meantime, I called the Apoplexy Department of Motor Vehicles to find out what we needed to do to get our security interest noted on the title certificate for the Bass Boat. They faxed me the right forms, and I filled them out and drove them up there myself. Carla had to sign them, which she did quite willingly. Anyway, on May 25, the DMV issued a new title reflecting our security interest. I figured everything was fine. Well, Carla missed the June payment even with the extended deadline, so I went up there to discuss a possible surrender of the boat to us. Only when I got there, there was no boat in sight. Carla explained that she felt she could no longer afford a sailboat, and she had sold it to a used boat dealer, Roaring Surf and Yacht, Inc., on May 13. The dealer, of course, has no interest in talking to me. Can I do anything, or should I just write this one off?[10]

The next borrower, in my opinion, is the worst apple in this whole barrel. His name is Calvin DeCartage, and he's a trucker by trade. He used to haul cane to the sugar refinery, and, when it closed, he tried to find other work in Gilmoria for a while. Apparently, he gave up around May 1 and moved to the town of Dire up in Confusion. We have a security interest in his truck, appropriately noted on the Gilmoria certificate of title. Somehow, however, Cal has just obtained a clean Confusion certificate of title on the truck. That should not have happened, because I'm still holding the Gilmoria certificate of title, and I know the title application process for trucks in Confusion requires surrender of any out of state title. My suspicion is that Cal paid somebody off at the Department of Motor Vehicles. There were all sorts of stories about him and kickbacks back when he worked for the refinery. Anyway, the rumors are that Cal is flashing this clean Confusion title certificate around town and trying to sell the dump truck to other truckers. There are a bunch of independent owner/operators up there in Dire, so he might succeed. I only found out about this because he also tried to borrow money secured by the truck at the Dire Straight Bank, where my cousin Seamus works as a loan officer. (Seamus had heard me mention the stories about Cal over the occasional drop of whiskey, and he did not make the loan). I really don't know what to do about this one. I have contacted the Confusion DMV to try to get our security interest noted on Cal's title, but I need Cal's cooperation. He's not returning my calls. Even if he did, it would probably take 3 to 4 weeks to get the new title. Any suggestions?[11]

Finally, I have a question about a loan we have not made yet that's sort of the reverse of the last three. This is about a guy named Corey Matsu who's moving here to Desolation from Apoplexy. He's an excavation subcontractor by trade, and he owns his own bulldozer. Corey seems to be a pretty straight shooter. He wants to borrow $5,000 secured by the bulldozer. He

**10.** [See Sections 9–303, 9–316; Section 9–317(b).]

**11.** [See Section 9–313(b); Section 9–316; Section 9–337.]

readily admits that there is already a security interest in the bulldozer in favor of the Apoplectic Bank, which is located in Roaring. I checked with them, and they faxed me a copy of the Apoplexy certificate of title for the bulldozer, and it reflects their security interest. They don't mind if we make the loan, and I think there is plenty of value in the bulldozer to support the Apoplectic security interest and ours, as the Apoplectic Bank's balance is now nearly paid off. But here's my question. As you probably gathered, Apoplexy issues certificates of title for bulldozers. Gilmoria does not. So, assuming I make the loan, how would I perfect the security interest?[12] I appreciate your help.

## III.   Priorities in Multi–Jurisdictional Transactions

### Problem 6–7

*You are planning dinner with your friend, Randy Grossman at New Babylon's most posh restaurant. His firm just got a $4 Million fee in a class action case and everyone got bonuses. Guess who is paying. But you have to get the following off your desk before you can leave.*

**BANK OF NEW BABYLON**
**INTEROFFICE MEMORANDUM**

TO:         S. Carlson, Megabank Legal Dept.
FROM:     P.L. Driver, V.P., Bank of New Babylon
RE:         Max's Contract Harvesters

Max Amilion is a contract harvester. As the name implies, a contract harvester goes from farm to farm harvesting crops for the farmers who own them. He operates his business as a sole proprietorship. The Bank has been lending Max money to purchase his equipment for years and we have a purchase money security interest in all of his harvesting equipment. Max lives here in Gilmoria, but does contract harvesting in Gilmoria and Apoplexy. We have filed an appropriate financing statement here in Gilmoria to perfect our interest since our certificate of title law does not apply to this type of equipment. A problem has arisen regarding an expensive piece of harvesting equipment worth in excess of $50,000. It was being used extensively in Apoplexy when it broke down. Max took it to a local repair shop to be fixed but neglected to get an estimate first. When Max got the bill he went ballistic and refused to pay. The repair shop has refused to give the piece of equipment back to Max. Max says it is a matter of principle with him and that the equipment can just sit there. Gilmoria has a statute that deals with possessory garageman's liens. The Gilmoria statute expressly provides that the repair shop's lien is subordinate to a perfected security interest. Apoplexy also has a garagemen's lien statute that is silent in regard to priority. While unlikely, if Max were to default as to our loan, would the Bank have priority over the repair shop?[13]

---

**12.**   [See Section 9–303 and Comments 2 and 3; Section 9–307(b).]

**13.**   [See Section 9–9–301(3); Section 9–333.]

## IV.  Perfection and Priorities When a Foreign Jurisdiction Is Involved

### Problem 6–8

*Dinner was great last night and the wine was particularly good. That's why it was difficult to drag yourself into work today. When you turn on your computer, your are startled to find an e-mail from Mr. Houseman. You click on it with some trepidation.*

TO:        S. Carlson, Megabank Legal Dept.
FROM:    I. N. Houseman, General Counsel, Megabank, Inc.
RE:        Heidorf, A.G. Loan

Carlson:

I saw you at the restaurant last night. We must be paying our young lawyers too much money. However, I have been following your progress and I am pleased with what I have seen so far. I met with President Pompous yesterday to discuss the possibility of the Bank of New Babylon lending money to a German Corporation, Heidorf, A.G. As you may know, Heidorf has a plant here in New Babylon that makes automobile transmissions. Some of the transmissions are sold to automobile manufacturers here in the United States and some are exported to buyers in Germany. The Bank is contemplating providing a substantial line of credit to Heidorf and to take a security interest in the plant equipment, and the inventory and accounts generated by the New Babylon plant. Before we make a decision, I would like to know where we would perfect our security interest and if there were a priority battle, whether U.S. law or German law would apply? Please let me know the answers to these questions as soon as possible.[14]

### Problem 6–9

*As you return from making copies of your memorandum to Houseman (with a copy, of course, to Jane Robinson), you notice that your voice mail light is on.*

Carlson. This is Roy Comstock at NB Commercial Finance. You remember Bud's Studs?[15] I was concerned about Bud's but he seems to have turned things around. To further protect ourselves, we took a security interest in all of Bud's equipment, including any after acquired equipment. I was out visiting Bud's and when we were walking around I saw a large new piece of equipment. Bud told me that he had purchased it a week ago from a Japanese manufacturer, Sumimasen. I looked at the paperwork and it is a contract, whereby Suminasen retains title to the machine until Bud's pays the full price. The contract also says: "any disputes as to this contract are to be resolved by Japanese law." I have three questions: First, will any priority dispute be resolved under Japanese law or under the UCC?[16] Second, if the UCC applies, and if Suminasen has somehow perfected its security interest

---

**14.**  [See Sections 9–102(a)(70) and (76); Section 9–301; Section 9–307.]

**15.**  [See Problems 4–1 and 5–8, supra.]

**16.**  [See Section 1–105 and Rev. Section 1–301.]

in the machine in Japan, does the four-month rule apply?[17] Third, if the four-month rule does not apply, is there anything else I need to worry about, or does NB Commercial have priority?[18]

**17.**  [Section 9–307(c); Section 9–316(a).]     **18.**  [Section 9–324(a).]

# Chapter 7

# DEFAULT, REMEDIES, AND DEBTOR PROTECTIONS

### BANK OF NEW BABYLON
### LOAN OFFICER TRAINING AND
### OPERATIONS MANUAL

## I. Meaning of Default and Limitations on the Exercise of Remedies

Secured lending agreements may take a variety of forms, and the nature of the events that may trigger the exercise of the secured creditor's remedies under Article 9 vary, to some extent, depending on the form of the transaction at issue. Perhaps the simplest form of secured transaction is documented with a demand note accompanied by a form security agreement. As the name implies, the entire balance on a demand note may be rendered immediately due and payable at the secured creditor's discretion upon giving proper notice. Obviously, upon such a demand and the obligor's failure to pay, the secured creditor may resort to Article 9 remedies.[1]

Indeed, the debtor's failure to make payment when it is due is probably the most common form of default even under more complex lending arrangements. For example, the Bank often enters into loan agreements requiring the obligor to pay the loan balance in installments, rather than in a lump sum. The payment obligation may be embodied in a separate installment note, or it may be incorporated into a single loan and security agreement. In either case, since Article 9 does not define the term "default," it is necessary, under such an arrangement, to include in the note and/or security agreement a specification of the events or actions that will constitute an event of default and trigger the secured party's right to exercise Article 9 remedies.

---

**1.** The remedies for default and the various debtor protections are found in Part 6 of Article 9. There are two excellent articles by the same author analyzing and explaining these provisions on a section-by-section basis. See Timothy Zinnecker, *The Default Provisions of Revised Article 9 of the Uniform Commercial Code: Part 1*, 54 Bus. Law. 1113 (1999) and Timothy Zinnecker, *The Default Provisions of Revised Article 9 of the Uniform Commercial Code: Part 2*, 54 Bus. Law. 1737 (1999). For a more integrat-ed analysis see Donald Rapson, *Default and Enforcement of Security Interests Under Revised Article 9*, 74 Chi–Kent L. Rev. 893 (1999). In the alternative, the secured party may exercise non-Article 9 rights by reducing the claim to judgment and then sell the collateral based on a write of execution. See Section 9–601(a)(1). In such a case, the execution lien relates back to the earlier of the date of filing or perfection. See Section 9–601(e).

Nonpayment is the most obvious candidate for inclusion in the default provisions. However, such provisions must be drafted carefully and include other contingencies or actions that might impair the Bank's prospects for repayment, increase the Bank's risk, or even make it advantageous to require the debtor to renegotiate some aspect of the transaction.

Moreover, a lending arrangement requiring installment payments also makes it necessary to include an acceleration clause, i.e., a clause permitting the secured creditor to declare the entire obligation due and payable even in advance of dates specified for payment of installments. Acceleration clauses likewise require careful drafting. Moreover, a decision to exercise Article 9 remedies should only be made in consultation with the Legal Department, as there may be contractual or non-contractual restrictions on the determination that a debtor is in default, the right to accelerate a loan balance, or the resort to particular remedies.

---

### Problem 7–1

*The phone rings. As soon as you answer, you detect the familiar fragrance of country air.*

S.C.: Carlson.

B.O.: Hey, Carlson. Bubba here. Where you been so long? I haven't talked to you in a long time.

S.C.: Hello Bubba. How are things at the Bovine State Bank?

B.O.: Well, I have a little problem here. I'm having Ethylene send you a fax of the documents.

S.C.: Who's the borrower?

B.O.: Good question. Wish I knew the answer. We thought it was Robby Sanders.

S.C.: What do you mean, "you thought?" How hard is it to get the borrower right?

B.O.: Harder than you might think. See, here's the deal. Robby Sanders is a well-regarded local businessman. But Robby's got this lowlife son named Romie who doesn't do much else besides sittin' around the house all day smokin' cigarettes and suckin' down RC Colas.

S.C.: I think I can see this one coming.

B.O.: Yeah, you can probably guess it. Romie wanted a red pickup truck they had on the lot over at Remote Motors. Of course, Romie's credit is awful, so Robby went over there with him and made the down payment. Then somebody, I think it was Robby, but it could have been Romie, signed a loan and security agreement for the balance of the purchase price. And get this. The name printed on the contract is "R. Sanders," and the signature's pretty much illegible.

S.C.: Well, as you folks in Desolation say, it looks like Remote Motors really stepped in it this time. Please tell me this has nothing to do with the Bank.

B.O.: Wish I could, little buddy. But you may know we've been buying chattel paper from Remote Motors at a discount for years. So we are now the assignee of the security interest, and Robby says Romie is the one responsible for the payments. Obviously, we never would have done the deal if we'd known it was Romie. We thought "R. Sanders" was Robby.

S.C.: [Audible sigh.] I don't suppose either one of them is making payments, right?

B.O.: Well, now that's the funny thing. They are making the payments. We found out about the confusion over who's responsible when we were checking to make sure our interest was noted on the insurance policy. I really didn't want to have anything to do with Romie, so we sent them both a letter accelerating the loan. The loan and security agreement says we can do that. Here, I'll read it to you: "If the holder deems itself insecure, it may accelerate the payment of the installments not yet due.

S.C.: Okay. So what's the problem?

B.O.: Well, you remember the Bellicose kid.

S.C.: [Audible groan.]

B.O.: Yeah, that's the guy. The lawyer. He called me today and said that I could not accelerate the debt. I don't need this. What should I tell him?

S.C.: Let me call you back. I need to take some aspirin and think about this.[2]

## Problem 7–2

*While you are at the water cooler, your voice mail begins collecting messages. Here is the first:*

Hello, Carlson. This is Sal Vache at NB Commercial Finance with another little land mine from our friend, Cal Cavalier. Our borrower here is a truck stop located in the remote suburbs of New Babylon called Big Diesel Truck Stop, Inc. Oddly enough, we do not finance its inventory of petroleum products. Their primary lender for that purpose is one of our competitors, Crude Oil Commercial Finance. But about two years ago, when video poker was legalized in this state, Cavalier approved a loan of $50,000 to Big Diesel to enable Big Diesel to acquire 10 video poker machines. Cavalier documented the transaction as follows. The basic payment obligation is set out in a demand note with interest at a favorable rate until payment is made. There is a separate security agreement, however, and its default provisions list fourteen specific events of default, culminating with the usual language that it is an event of default if we, in good faith, believe the prospect of payment is impaired. In fact, Big Diesel has been paying us quite regularly in monthly installments of $500. But last week, when President Pompous visited here, he made it quite clear that neither video poker generally nor this customer in particular projected the sort of image with which we wish to be associated. So he wants me to pull the plug on Big Diesel and get us out of the deal. Between you, me and the trees, their money is as green as anyone else's, but hey, no skin off my nose. I assume, since we have a demand note,[3] we can

---

**2.** [See Section 1–208; Rev. Section 1–309; Section 9–102(a)(43).]

**3.** [See Section 1–208 and Comment; Rev. Section 1–309; Section 9–102(a)(43);

just make a formal demand for payment of the entire balance and, if Big Diesel can't pay, repossess and sell the machines. Do you see any problem with that?[4] Call me back.

## Problem 7–3

*And here is the next one:*

Hello, Carlson. This is Jimmy Drabb at Friendly Finance. I need to talk to you about a borrower named Delia Torrey. Two years ago, we loaned Ms. Torrey $8,000 to buy a new set of living room furniture. We set up the usual installment payment schedule and took a purchase money security interest in the furniture. Her record of payment has been spotty. On approximately ten occasions over the last two years, she has paid between seven and 14 days late. Each time, she enclosed the late charge imposed by our security agreement, so we accepted the payments without comment. But her payment is 15 days late this month, and my boss is sick of this. Our security agreement says that, "No waiver by the Secured Party of any default shall be effective unless in writing, nor operate as a waiver of any other default or of the same default on future occasions." Since we have that language, I'm protected if I repossess the furniture, right?[5] Please give me a call.

## Problem 7–4

*While you were in the library, your boss left you another note.*

Reid v. Key Bank of S. Me., Inc, 821 F.2d 9 (1st Cir.1987); KMC Co. v. Irving Trust Co., 757 F.2d 752 (6th Cir.1985); In re Martin Specialty Vehicles, Inc., 87 B.R. 752 (Bankr. D.Mass.1988), rev'd on other grounds, 97 B.R. 721 (D.Mass.1989), appeal dism. 892 F.2d 5 (1st Cir.1989).]

**4.** [See Section 1–203; Rev. Section 1–304; Section 1–205; Rev. Section 1–303; Section 1–208; Rev. Section 1–309; PEB Commentary No. 10; and Section 9–102(a)(43). Compare Kham & Nate's Shoes, No.2, Inc. v. First Bank of Whiting, 908 F.2d 1351 (7th Cir.1990) and In re Clark Pipe & Supply Co., 893 F.2d 693 (5th Cir.1990) with In re Martin Specialty Vehicles, Inc., 87 B.R. 752 (Bankr.D.Mass.1988), rev'd on other grounds, 97 B.R. 721 (D.Mass.1989), appeal dism. 892 F.2d 5 (1st Cir.1989), KMC Co. v. Irving Trust Co., 757 F.2d 752 (6th Cir. 1985), Lane v. John Deere Co., 767 S.W.2d 138 (Tenn.1989), and Security Pacific Housing Services, Inc. v. Cape Mobile Home Mart, Inc., No. CV191–866CC (Franklin County, Mo.1995).]

**5.** [See Section 1–103; Rev. Section 1–103(b); Section 1–205; Rev. Section 1–303; . Compare Westinghouse Credit Corp. v. Shelton, 645 F.2d 869 (10th Cir.1981), Moe v. John Deere Co., 516 N.W.2d 332 (S.D. 1994), Battista v. Savings Bank of Baltimore, 67 Md.App. 257, 507 A.2d 203 (1986), and Nevada Nat'l Bank v. Huff, 94 Nev. 506, 582 P.2d 364 (1978), with Wade v. Ford Motor Credit Co., 455 F.Supp. 147 (E.D.Mo.1978), Gaynor v. Union Trust Co., 216 Conn. 458, 582 A.2d 190 (1990), Kessel v. Western Sav. Credit Union, 463 N.W.2d 629 (N.D.1990), Hudak v. Central Bank of the South, 529 So.2d 936 (Ala.1988), and Riley State Bank of Riley v. Spillman, 242 Kan. 696, 750 P.2d 1024 (1988).]

*Sidney:*

    *Pompous and I are going up to Desolation to review the operations of the Bovine State Bank. I need you to review the default clauses in their standard form security agreements. As I recall, they identify as events of default failure to make any payment when due, failure to maintain, repair, or insure the collateral, failure to pay taxes on the collateral, any form of insolvency proceeding, and the Bank's good faith belief that it is insecure. Determine if we need to add anything and call me up there. Thanks*

*--JR*

## Problem 7–5

    *Perhaps the worst thing that can happen to you at work is to have a call forwarded to you by your boss's secretary because your boss is out of town and the caller says the matter is "urgent." For example:*

S.C.: Carlson

P.L.D.: Hello Carlson. Driver here. I was actually looking for Robinson. Where is she?

S.C.: In Desolation with Pompous looking at the Bovine State Bank. You want the number?

P.L.D.: No. Absolutely not. It would be, shall we say, awkward if the old man knew about this conversation. Look, Carlson. You and I have worked together a great deal lately, and you seem to be a discrete person. I need to speak to you about a rather delicate matter. I have a problem, but this conversation needs to remain confidential.

S.C.: I'll help you if I can, Driver, but if it's a D.U.I. or a domestic matter, I'm going to give you someone outside to call, so you don't have to tell me the details.

P.L.D.: Actually, I almost wish it were personal, but it's nothing like that. Do you know who Orville Duffield is?

S.C.: I've heard the name. Oil speculator, isn't he? Made a lot of money in the oil patch if I'm not mistaken.

P.L.D.: That's the one. He's been a customer of the Bank of New Babylon for years. He's from a tiny town not too far from Desolation. Not educated, but quite shrewd and one of the last of the self-made oil multi-millionaires. He struck me as a little rough around the edges at first, but I've grown to like old Orville over the years.

S.C.: Sounds like a happy ending.

P.L.D: Up until a few months ago, it was. I mean, the oil business is up and down, and all these guys are leveraged to the hilt, but Duffield is good at what he does, and you and I would both kill to have his balance sheet. Anyway, he borrowed a little over two million from the Bank three years ago. He owns some oil producing land, leases some more, and subcontracts out the actual production. Our loan is secured by mortgages on the land he owns, security assignments of his leases, and perfected security interests in the crude oil and gas he extracts and the accounts generated by selling them. His payments under our loan and security agreement are about $60,000 a month in principal and interest. He's always made enough money from his operations that we let him collect the proceeds of his oil and gas sales and just remit the monthly payment to us. In fact, while he can't sell any of our other security without our consent, oil and gas sales in the ordinary course of business are excepted.

S.C.: This sounds pretty plain vanilla to me.

P.L.D.: As I said, until four months ago, it was. Unfortunately, Orville's daughter died at that time. He took it very, very hard. I really can't convey to you the depth of his grief. In fact, since then, he has not been able to concentrate much on his business affairs. He missed the first monthly payment thereafter, although he did eventually pay it late. Then he missed two more, and those have not been made up. Then he neglected to send in an updated financial statement, as the loan documents require him to do periodically.

S.C.: Well, it sounds like he has a reason to fall apart. Has anyone from the Bank talked to him?

P.L.D.: Oh yes. I've talked to him once or twice, and I've spoken extensively with his office manager, Mr. Riggs. In fact, Riggs came up with a plan to bring the loan current. He wants to sell one of Orville's tracts of land for about half a million dollars, and he already has a buyer. Of course, that will reduce our security, so I told him we would need at least $350,000 out of the sale proceeds to reduce the loan balance so that the remaining collateral base was adequate. He had no problem with that. In fact, what he and Orville want to do is apply the remaining proceeds to eliminate all arrearages and even prepay a couple of loan installments so Orville can get his life in order without having to worry about us.

S.C.: Sounds like a reasonable workout.

P.L.D.: It is actually. And I think Orville has other, unencumbered property he could add to the collateral base if we asked him to. I told Riggs I would consider it, although I have not agreed to it yet. Although one problem is that I heard through the grapevine that Orville thinks I've already agreed to it. But I have extended this sort of accommodation to the Ross family oil businesses for far less emotionally wrenching reasons.

S.C.: Well, if you're going to agree to it, what does it matter that Orville is jumping the gun a little.

P.L.D.: The problem can be summed up in one word: Pompous.

S.C.: You would not be referring to the venerable President of Megabank, Inc., for whom we both ultimately work?

P.L.D.: That's what I like about you Carlson. You're a quick study. I presented the workout proposal through channels, along with my recommendation that it be approved. The word I received was that Pompous personally killed it.

S.C.: Why would he do that?

P.L.D.: He does not take me into his confidence. I do know that he has never liked Orville. Pompous prefers our more white shoe clients (like the Ross family). And it didn't help that Orville joined Pompous' country club over his objection. Anyway, here's what he wants me to do. I am not to commit to any specific application of the land sale proceeds. When we get the half million from the real estate sale, I am to apply it *all* to the reduction of current principal balance. That, of course, will leave the outstanding arrearages of principal and interest intact, and Orville squarely in default. Then, I am to exercise a power granted in the loan documents to collect the proceeds of oil and gas sales directly from Orville's operators. I am to tell Orville we are doing this only after the operators have been properly notified in writing to remit to us. Rest assured, they will comply.

S.C.: Hardball.

P.L.D.: Hardball indeed, my friend. Technically, of course, I think it's all permitted by our loan agreement. The agreement says we can apply payments in any fashion we choose, and, if Orville is in default, it allows us to begin direct collection at any time, without prior notice to Orville or any opportunity to cure defaults. Indeed, further extensions of credit are not required, and our insecurity clause would let us call the whole loan based on even less than what Orville has done. But I feel terrible, and I don't think Orville deserves this. How much do you know about the oil business?

S.C.: Mostly what you've told me.

P.L.D.: Well let me tell you what will happen next. Word gets around fast in that business. When his other lenders find out we have shifted to direct collection, they will pull the plug on Orville. Without his oil and gas revenues and without an alternative source of credit, Orville's operating capital will dry up. His business may be worth a lot as a going concern, but once it's known to be in distress, the vultures start circling and bargain basement prices go into effect. Orville will lose it all and still owe us money. My guess is he will be out of business in another two months, although he is probably too depressed to care.

S.C.: Yeah, but guys like him don't stay depressed forever.

P.L.D.: Agreed. And remember Orville started out poor. He won't like going back there. Anyway, I'm really in a bind, and I don't think Orville is the only one with something personally at stake here. So what should I do?[6]

---

## BANK OF NEW BABYLON
## LOAN OFFICER TRAINING AND
## OPERATIONS MANUAL

## CHAPTER 7: DEFAULT, REMEDIES AND DEBTOR PROTECTIONS

### II.  Alternative Remedies

#### A.  Collection Rights of Secured Parties

As you know, a significant number of the Bank's commercial loans are secured by collateral consisting of payment obligations to our borrower (the debtor) due from

**6.** [See Section 1–203; Rev. Section 1–304; Section 1–205; Rev. Section 1–303; PEB Commentary No. 10; Section 1–102(3); Rev. Section 1–302; Section 9–102(a)(43); *Duffield v. First Interstate Bank of Denver, N.A.*, 13 F.3d 1403 (10th Cir.1993).]

third parties. These payment obligations may take a variety of forms, including accounts, general intangibles, chattel paper, negotiable instruments, or deposit accounts. They may be obligations to pay in a lump sum on demand or on a date certain, or they may be installment obligations that generate an income stream. If our borrower defaults, direct collection of these payment obligations from the third party obligors may be one of the easiest, and most effective, means of liquidating the Bank's collateral and retiring the borrower's debt.[7]

Upon default by the borrower, Article 9 permits a secured party to notify the account debtor[8] or other third party obligor that the payment owed the debtor should be paid directly to the secured party. See Section 9–607(a)(1) and Sections 9–406(a)–(c). Under Article 9, there are procedures for direct collection of deposit accounts held as original collateral. See Sections 9–607(a)(4) and (5). If the Bank proceeds with direct collection on third party payment obligations, the Bank may deduct reasonable expenses of collection (including attorneys' fees) from the amounts collected. See Section 9–607(d). As a loan officer, however, you should bear in mind the following limitations on the foregoing rights of direct collection. First, if the Bank has recourse against the debtor for debt that remains unpaid, the Bank, as secured party, must proceed with its direct collection efforts in a commercially reasonable manner. See Section 9–607(c). Failure to fulfill the duty of commercial reasonableness may render the Bank liable for any loss suffered by the debtor as a result. See Section 9–625.

Second, direct collection from third party account debtors is not a foolproof method of realizing on collateral. If the account debtor has a defense against our borrower on the purported obligation, that defense may be asserted against the Bank as the assignee of the obligation. See Section 9–404(a)[9].

Third, while both security interests in, and outright sales of, accounts and chattel paper trigger the perfection obligations of Article 9, direct collection is one situation in which the distinction between a security interest in and a sale of such collateral is significant. If the underlying transaction is a loan coupled with a security interest in collateral consisting of payment obligations, the secured party making direct collections must account to the debtor for any surplus collections, and the borrower (the debtor/obligor) is liable for any deficiency in the amount collected. See Section 9–608(a)(4). On the other hand, if the underlying transaction is an outright sale of accounts, chattel paper, payment intangibles, or promissory notes, the Bank need not account to the debtor for any surplus, and the seller is not liable for any deficiency. See Section 9–608(b).

---

**7.** For a good overview of this area see Donald Rapson, *Default and Enforcement of Security Interests Under Revised Article 9,* 74 Chi–Kent L. Rev. 893, 897–907 (1999).

**8.** See Section 9–102(a)(3).

**9.** See Systran Financial Services Corp. v. Giant Cement Holding, Inc., 252 F.Supp.2d 500 (N.D.Ohio 2003).

## II. Alternative Remedies

## B. Obtaining Possession of the Collateral

### Problem 7–6

*Just when you thought it was safe to turn on your computer, your e-mail alert begins humming.*

| | |
|---|---|
| To: | S. Carlson, Megabank Legal Dept. |
| FROM: | B. O'Reilly, Bovine State Bank |
| RE: | Repo Stories |

Hello again, Carlson. As you know, President Pompous and your boss have been up here reviewing our little operation for a couple of days. I think they're on their way back now. But last night, we were relaxing over a couple of beers at the Desolate Keg, and we got to talking about some of the repossessions we've done up here. We have a fair number of them, since we buy chattel paper from Desolation Motors, and we handle the repos when the account debtor defaults. We also do our own repos on consumer loans, which occasionally requires repossession of furniture or other consumer goods. Usually, my brother Buford helps me out. Anyway, I'll tell you, we really had old man Pompous laughing. He's actually a pretty good guy, but that boss of yours is really a worrier. She wanted me to call you and tell you some of this stuff. I'm really not sure why. I told her it would be easier to write you a letter, but she didn't seem to want anything in writing. So I figure e-mail's ok. So here goes.

Cars and pickups are the easiest to repossess, since Desolation Motors will loan us their tow truck. Usually, Buford and I just tow the vehicle away while the debtor is not around, especially if it's parked on the street[10] or in a parking lot.[11] Once in a while, the vehicle is in the debtor's driveway,[12] but we'll take it anyway, as long as he's not home. We've picked up several right out of people's garages as long as the door was open.[13] One time, this really stubborn guy tried to keep us from getting a pickup by locking his garage day and night, but we got it anyway. Buford is still skinnier than I am, so he climbed through a garage window the guy left unlocked and popped open the door from the inside.[14] After we got it on the tow truck, Buford set the garage door to lock again. The guy comes home to a locked garage and—no truck.

---

**10.** [See King v. General Motors Acceptance Corp., 140 F.Supp. 259 (M.D.N.C. 1956).]

**11.** [See Thompson v. Ford Credit Co., 324 F.Supp. 108 (D.S.C.1971); Census Federal Credit Union v. Wann, 403 N.E.2d 348 (Ind.App.1980); Howell v. Ford Motor Credit Co., 16 U.C.C. Rep. 881 (Okla. App.1975).]

**12.** [See Oaklawn Bank v. Baldwin, 289 Ark. 79, 709 S.W.2d 91 (1986); Raffa v. Dania Bank, 321 So.2d 83 (Fla.App.1975); Dearman v. Williams, 235 Miss. 360, 109 So.2d 316 (1959); Rea v. Universal CIT Credit Corp., 257 N.C. 639, 127 S.E.2d 225 (1962); Gregory v. First Nat'l Bank of Oregon, 241 Or. 397, 406 P.2d 156 (1965); Pioneer Finance & Thrift Corp. v. Adams, 426 S.W.2d 317 (Tex.Civ.App.1968).]

**13.** [See Henderson v. Security Nat'l Bank, 72 Cal.App.3d 764, 140 Cal.Rptr. 388 (1977); Pierce v. Leasing Int'l, Inc., 142 Ga.App. 371, 235 S.E.2d 752 (1977); Kroeger v. Ogsden, 429 P.2d 781 (Okla.1967).]

**14.** [See Bloomquist v. First Nat'l Bank of Elk River, 378 N.W.2d 81 (Minn.App. 1985).]

Buford and I nearly split a gut laughing about that. Then there was this other guy who pulled his truck inside the chain link fence around his back yard and padlocked a chain around the gate. I guess he didn't know Buford had a chain cutter. Actually, Buford can usually force just about any padlock with a hammer and a big screwdriver.[15]

Some of this stuff gets really funny. Like when we were doing a repo over in Bullmousse County, where they don't know us very well, and we got the debtor to tell us where the car was by telling him we were inspectors from Ford Motor Company trying to determine if his car needed to be recalled for faulty brakes.[16] I heard the guy wrote an angry letter to Ford complaining about how their inspectors stole his car. Another time, Buford flashed a badge he bought at a flea market and told them he was a sheriff's deputy. In fact, another time we even brought along our cousin Harlan, who is a deputy over there.[17] The debtor was actually there on that one, but he got real quiet when Harlan got out of the car. It's always nice to bring a man with a gun. Oh—and then there was the time we had old man Tompkins pickup on the tow truck and he came out in his underwear with a Dixie longneck in one hand, yelling "Stop you #@% & * thieves!" We put pedal to the metal on that one.[18] But my absolute favorite did not actually involve Buford and me. We were busy and we hired Dale Pitman as an independent contractor to repossess Delores Purvis' Trans Am. When she saw Dale hooking her car to the tow truck, she locked herself in it to try and stop him. He just hauled it away with her in it and parked it in the Desolation Motors lot. Of course, the lot is locked and patrolled by Dobermans and Delores had to spend the night in the car.[19] Man, she was spitting' nails by the time they opened in the morning and let her out. I thought Buford and I would die laughing when we heard about it.

Cars are the most fun, but occasionally we have some good times with furniture. I usually stay out of people's houses, but some people up here still leave their doors unlocked. Or you can sometimes get in through a window. If they're not home and the collateral isn't too heavy, we occasionally make a quick grab and getaway.[20] A couple of times, we have waited until the debtor

---

**15.** [See Laurel Coal Co. v. Walter E. Heller & Co., 539 F.Supp. 1006 (W.D.Pa. 1982); Henderson v. Security Nat'l Bank, 72 Cal.App.3d 764, 140 Cal.Rptr. 388 (1977); Martin v. Dorn Equipment Co., 250 Mont. 422, 821 P.2d 1025 (1991); General Electric Credit Corp. v. Timbrook, 170 W.Va. 143, 291 S.E.2d 383 (1982).]

**16.** [See Thompson v. Ford Credit Co., 550 F.2d 256 (5th Cir.1977); Pleasant v. Warrick, 590 So.2d 214 (Ala.1991); Cox v. Galigher Motor Sales Co., 158 W.Va. 685, 213 S.E.2d 475 (1975); Benschoter v. First Nat'l Bank of Lawrence, 218 Kan. 144, 542 P.2d 1042 (1975).]

**17.** [See Walker v. Walthall, 121 Ariz. 121, 588 P.2d 863 (App.1978); First and Farmers Bank of Somerset v. Henderson, 763 S.W.2d 137, 7 UCC Rep.2d 1305 (Ky. App.1988); Stone Machinery Co. v. Kessler,

1 Wash.App. 750, 463 P.2d 651 (1970); Comment 3 to Section 9–609.]

**18.** [Manhattan Credit Co. v. Brewer, 232 Ark. 976, 341 S.W.2d 765 (1961); Deavers v. Standridge, 144 Ga.App. 673, 242 S.E.2d 331 (1978); Hester v. Bandy, 627 So.2d 833 (Miss.1993); Morris v. First Nat'l Bank & Trust Co. of Ravenna, 21 Ohio St.2d 25, 254 N.E.2d 683 (1970). But see Chrysler Credit Corp. v. Koontz, 277 Ill. App.3d 1078, 214 Ill.Dec. 726, 661 N.E.2d 1171 (1996).]

**19.** [See MBank El Paso v. Sanchez, 836 S.W.2d 151 (Tex.1992); Comment 3 to Section 9–609.]

**20.** [Compare Girard v. Anderson, 219 Iowa 142, 257 N.W. 400 (1934) and Gulf Oil Corp. v. Smithey, 426 S.W.2d 262 (Tex.Civ. App.1968) with Calderon v. United Furniture Co., 505 F.2d 950 (5th Cir.1974).]

and his or her spouse went out for the evening and gotten permission to go inside and repossess from a kid or a babysitter.[21] I'll tell you though. Pompous liked the car stories the best. I think your boss might have been more cheerful, but I think she may have been coming down with something. She looked a little pale. She muttered something about "breach of the peace,"[22] but I told her not to worry. Buford and I never laid a glove on anybody. By the way, your boss said to tell you she wanted to talk to you as soon as she got back.

—Bubba.

## Problem 7–7

*The phone rings. It's your boss!*

J.R. Sidney, did you hear from Bubba?

S.C. You won't believe this, but he sent me an email with all the details. I have deleted the email and I'm thinking of shredding the hard copy I made for the file.[23] In any event, I called him back and set him straight on what constitutes breach of the peace. I don't think he was very happy, but he said he would be more careful in the future and would call us if he was unsure of what is permitted.

J.R. Good, so long as he calls you and not me. In any event, I am also calling on another matter. The Bank lent a large sum to Dulce, Inc. They make ice cream. We took a security interest in their equipment and they are now in default. Some of the equipment is enormous. How do we take possession of it for purposes of a repossession sale?[24]

## BANK OF NEW BABYLON
## LOAN OFFICER TRAINING AND
## OPERATIONS MANUAL

## CHAPTER 7: DEFAULT AND REMEDIES

### II. Alternative Remedies

#### C. Alternative Ways of Obtaining Possession

There are two primary alternatives to self-help repossession. First, the secured party can simply ask the debtor to turn over the goods. The Code not only expressly validates contractual requirements that the debtor assemble and surrender collateral at a designated place, but gives the secured party the right to impose such a requirement after default regardless of the provisions of the security agreement.[25] Requests that the

---

**21.** [Compare Bing v. General Motors Acceptance Corp., 237 F.Supp. 911 (E.D.S.C.1965) and Benschoter v. First Nat'l Bank of Lawrence, 218 Kan. 144, 542 P.2d 1042 (1975) with Luthy v. Philip Werlein Co., 163 La. 752, 112 So. 709 (1927).]

**22.** [See Section 9–602(6); Section 9–603(b); Section 9–609.]

**23.** [See Rule 3.4(a) and Rule 8.4(d), Model Rules of Professional Conduct. They are available on the Web at http://www.abanet.org/cpr /mrpc/ mrpc_toc.html]

**24.** [See Section 9–609(a)(2).]

**25.** See Section 9–609(c).

debtor surrender the collateral are successful in a surprising number of cases, although it is our experience that voluntary surrender is less successful in consumer cases than commercial cases.

The second alternative is to have the sheriff seize the property under a judicial writ. There are some variations among the states in the requirements for issuance of such a writ. Normally, an affidavit that the debtor is in default and proof of the creditor's security interest are necessary. From 1969 through 1975, there was a series of cases that challenged the constitutionality of state repossession statutes. Essentially, those cases established that seizure by the sheriff of property subject to a security interest without notice to the debtor and an opportunity for a hearing prior to seizure violated the Due Process Clause of the Fourteenth Amendment. See *Sniadach v. Family Finance Corp.*, 395 U.S. 337, 89 S.Ct. 1820, 23 L.Ed.2d 349 (1969), *Fuentes v. Sheven*, 407 U.S. 67, 92 S.Ct. 1983, 32 L.Ed.2d 556 (1972), *Mitchell v. W.T. Grant Co.*, 416 U.S. 600, 94 S.Ct. 1895, 40 L.Ed.2d 406 (1974), and *North Georgia Finishing, Inc. v. Di–Chem, Inc.*, 419 U.S. 601, 95 S.Ct. 719, 42 L.Ed.2d 751 (1975).

As a result of these cases, a number of states amended their repossession statutes to comport with constitutional requirements by providing for routine pre-seizure notice and a right to a pre-seizure hearing. The issuance of writs *ex parte* or without a hearing is now confined to very limited classes of cases in which immediate action is demonstrably necessary, e.g., in cases in which the debtor is removing the collateral from the jurisdiction.

---

## II. Alternative Remedies

### D. Sale of Collateral

### Problem 7–8

*The good news is that both your computer system and the computer system at the Bovine State Bank is down. The bad news is that the fax machines are still working. This one's for you wherever your are [Sing it Barry].*

### THE BOVINE STATE BANK
### DESOLATION, GILMORIA
#### "Serving Desolation for Fifty Years"

#### MEMORANDUM

*VIA FAX*

TO:  S. Carlson, Megabank Legal Dept.
FROM: Bubba O'Reilly, Bovine State Bank
RE:  MacGregor Tractor Sale

Our computers are down, so I hope you don't mind a fax. I need some advice pretty quick. About two and a half years ago, we loaned old man MacGregor $100,000 to buy a top of the line John Deere tractor. At that time, MacGregor had one of the largest vegetable farms in the state, and we thought that if anyone was a good risk, he was. Naturally, we took and perfected a security interest in the tractor. Unfortunately, a plague of rabbits decimated MacGregor's crop this year, and the loan is now in default. The current balance is $65,000.

On October 1, we sent MacGregor a letter accelerating the loan and notifying him of our intent to repossess and sell the tractor. We conducted the repossession without incident on October 5 and left the tractor on the lot of the old Charm of the Farm Implement Company, which is not too far away. On October 12, I sent another letter to MacGregor informing him that the tractor would be sold at a public sale at the Charm of the Farm lot on October 20, at 1:00 P.M. I also told him in the letter that I would send him an accounting of either any surplus or deficiency. I put ads in all the local papers advertising the sale. Both the letter and my ads noted that we reserved the right to refuse all bids if they were too low.

We hired an auctioneer, and, on October 20, I accompanied him to the auction. MacGregor also attended. The highest bid we received was $25,000, which I thought was too low. MacGregor was griping that we hadn't touched up the paint job or pressure washed the tractor, but I doubt that was the problem. Anyway, wholesale book value on the thing is $45,000, so I instructed the auctioneer to refuse all the bids. I announced to the bidders who were there that I would be happy to negotiate with any of them privately, if any of them were willing to submit a higher bid. I am sure MacGregor heard this. I then went home, and that was the last time I spoke with MacGregor until yesterday. Over the next few days, I called some of our local farmers, as well as all the farm implement dealers in the neighboring four counties. Eventually, one of the guys who bid at the auction came up with $35,000, and I sold it to him on October 30. The next day, I sent a letter to MacGregor informing him that, after deducting expenses of sale, the tractor had brought $32,500, and that he owed us a deficiency of $32,500. My letter also gave him 30 days to come up with the money and warned him of our intent to pursue legal action if he did not.

Yesterday, I got a letter from MacGregor's lawyer. He claims we messed up. In particular, he claims that we failed to fix up the tractor and we did not give a timely notice of the public sale or notice of the private sale. What should I do? I assume we should go after MacGregor anyway, but I'd like to know if there are any problems with our case.[26] Please advise.

**26.** [See Section 9–610(a); Section 9–611; Section 9–612; *Van Brunt v. BancTex-* *as Quorum, N.A.*, 804 S.W.2d 117 (Tex.App. 1989).]

## BANK OF NEW BABYLON
## LOAN OFFICER TRAINING AND
## OPERATIONS MANUAL

## CHAPTER 7: DEFAULT, REMEDIES, AND DEBTOR PROTECTIONS

## II. Alternative Remedies

### D. Sale of Collateral

#### 1. Contents and Recipients of Notification

Article 9 requires that every aspect of a sale or other disposition of collateral be commercially reasonable (Section 9–610(b)), and that the secured creditor send the debtor notification of the time and place of a public disposition or the time after which a private disposition is to be made (Section 9–613(1)(E))[27]. The Code further prescribes the necessary contents of a notification and sets out certain safe harbors for the secured creditor. Section 9–613(1) provides that, in non-consumer cases, a notification is sufficient if it includes a description of the debtor and the secured party, a collateral description, a description of the method of intended disposition, a statement that the debtor is entitled to an accounting of the unpaid indebtedness and of the charge for an accounting, and the time and place of sale of collateral if the creditor has elected to conduct a public sale or reasonable notification of the time after which a private sale will be made if the creditor has elected not to sell publicly. A notification in a commercial case that contains this information is sufficient as a matter of law, unless the parties have agreed otherwise. (Section 9–613, Comment 2). If some of the information is omitted, whether the notification is reasonable is a question of fact. (Section 9–613(2)). A notification substantially providing the information specified in Section 9–613(1) is sufficient even if it contains additional information or has minor errors that are not seriously misleading. (Section 9–613(3)). Section 9–613(5) provides a safe harbor form for the secured creditor's use.

The Code also specifies the minimum content of the notification necessary in a consumer goods transaction. In addition to the information required by Section 9–613(1) in commercial cases, the notification of a disposition in a consumer goods case must include a description of any liability for a deficiency, a telephone number from which a redemption amount may be obtained, and a phone number or mailing address from which to obtain further information concerning the disposition and the secured obligation. See Section 9–614(1). Omission of any of the foregoing information is fatal, in the sense that the notification becomes unreasonable as a matter of law. In consumer goods transactions, there is no provision comparable to Section 9–613(2), applicable in commercial cases, permitting an incomplete notice to reach the trier of fact on the issue of reasonableness. Once again, the drafters provide, in Section 9–614(3), a safe harbor form for use by the secured creditor.

The *persons* to whom notification must be sent are specified in Section 9–611(c). The Code requires notification of the debtor, secondary obligors, and, except in consumer goods transactions, secured parties on file in the Article 9 records or

---

**27.** See In re Downing, 286 B.R. 900 (Bankr.W.D.Mo.2002).

perfected under alternate governing statutes,[28] and any other persons who have timely notified the secured party of an interest in the collateral by an authenticated record. The Code contains exceptions to the notice requirement if the collateral is perishable or threatens to decline speedily in value or if it is of a type customarily sold in a recognized market (e.g., the stock exchange). See Section 9–611(d) and Comment 7.

---

## Problem 7–9

*Your voice mail light is on almost continuously these days. Here's the latest.*

Hello, Carlson. This is Roy Comstock over at NB Commercial Finance. I've got a somewhat unique problem here, and I think I need a little research. Robinson said you had some time. Our customer is Mighty Fowl Industries, Inc., the largest chicken and turkey processor in the state of Gilmoria. We have been providing Mighty Fowl with operating capital for years, secured by a floating lien on all of Mighty Fowl's inventory and equipment. The company's business has declined for the past several years, and the loan went into default three months ago. We had to accelerate the loan, and we repossessed everything a week ago. The inventory of processed chicken and turkey, of course, had to be sold right away. However, it was pretty easy. I sold it at prevailing market prices to Mighty Fowl's usual grocery wholesaler.

I have two questions on the equipment, though. First, Mighty Fowl's whole operation was automated, so a lot of this stuff is very specialized machinery. Basically, only another chicken processor would have any use for it, and it would probably have to be a large outfit at that. Normally, when I sell more garden-variety equipment, I either advertise a public sale in the local papers or, if we have another customer who either uses or deals in the kind of equipment in question, I use a private sale. But Mighty Fowl is the only chicken processor left in Gilmoria. I could call Tyson's up in Confusion or Miss Goldy over in Apoplexy, but I don't know if that's enough. Do you have any suggestions as to how I should set up the sale?

The other problem involves a specific machine, an automatic chicken plucker. While we were doing the repossession, the President and majority shareholder, Rebecca Poulet, told me there was another loan secured by the machine. Apparently, Poulet borrowed the money to buy it from Buffalo Finance Company. I'm a little worried that they may have a priming lien on the darn thing. Do we have to tell them when we sell it? I'm worried they'll demand we surrender it to them or demand a share of the proceeds. So far, they seem not to be monitoring their collateral, and we might be able to get the whole thing done before they find out.[29]

Oh, one other thing. Poulet signed a guarantee of our loan to Mighty Fowl. Do we need to keep her posted on everything?[30] Call me back.

---

**28.** See also Section 9–611(e).

**29.** [See Comments 2 and 3 to Section 9–610; Section 9–611.]

**30.** [See Section 9–611(c)(2).]

### Problem 7–10

*Some days it is very clear that this is not a great way to make a living. Unfortunately, you have few alternatives, all of which pay substantially less.*

**BANK OF NEW BABYLON**
**INTEROFFICE MEMORANDUM**

TO:        S. Carlson, Megabank Legal
FROM:   P.L. Driver, V.P., Bank of New Babylon
RE:         King of Babylon Brewery

As you know, the King of Babylon Brewery, the last of New Babylon's local brewing operations, is rumored to be on its last legs. (I personally won't miss Nebuchadnezzar's Special Christmas Ale, but that's another story.) We provided financing to the brewery on a non-purchase money basis for years. The current loan balance is $95,000, and it is secured by a first priority security interest in all of King of Babylon's equipment. Most of the equipment is pretty dilapidated and nearly worthless—the vats all leak, for example. There are only two pieces of equipment worth enough to repossess. The first is a bottling machine worth about $100,000 by my best estimate. The other is a machine that packs bottles of beer into cardboard cases. That packing machine is worth about $50,000. King of Babylon has been in default for about six weeks, and it is clearly time to pull the plug and repossess the collateral.

Obviously, we have a collateral cushion, and I am not terribly worried. I can't see any way we will end up under water on this one. However, I was talking with Binky Worthington, an old friend of mine from Yale and now my counterpart at Bank of Amerigo. You may know Binky, he's a cousin of the Ross family. Anyway, Binky told me that Bank of Amerigo loaned King of Babylon the money to buy the packing machine and took a security interest in it. Bank of Amerigo's financing statement was filed after ours, although I'm sure they were trying to prime us. However, they filed too late for that, if my math is right, and I am fairly sure we have priority. Here's my question. Binky says that, even if Bank of Amerigo is second in priority as to the packing machine, they can compel us to realize on the bottling machine first. I've never heard of such a thing, although, frankly, I wouldn't be terribly averse to helping out old Binky. He's not the brightest of fellows, but quite pleasant. Anyway, let me know if there's any truth in what he says.[31]

## II.  Alternative Remedies

### D.  Sale of Collateral

#### 2.  Distribution of the Proceeds and Protections for the Transferees of the Collateral

### Problem 7–11

*You find the following letter on your desk when you return from lunch. It is marked "Personal and Confidential."*

---

**31.**  [See Section 1–103; Comment 5 to Section 9–610.]

Dear Sidney:

I think I have a real problem and I am hoping that you can figure a way out of this. Remember the Mighty Fowl Industries situation I spoke to you about a few months ago?[32] Well you told me to give notice to Buffalo Finance Company. I meant to do it, but I just forgot. In any event, we sold the automatic chicken plucker. I now have a phone message from Buffalo's president to call her. I am concerned about calling her back because of the notice issue. I checked into the matter further and I am almost positive that Buffalo did, in fact, have a senior lien on the machine. How bad is this? Could you let me know what affect my failure to give notice has?[33] In addition, do I have to worry about Pluck–A–Duck, the company that bought the machine.[34] It was a private sale.

Yours faithfully,

Roy Comstock

## II. Alternative Remedies

### E. Retention of Collateral in Satisfaction of Debt

#### Problem 7–12

*Once again, the voice mail light greets you.*

Hello, Sidney. This is Jimmy Drabb at Friendly Finance. I have a couple of questions for you. About a year ago, we loaned a guy named Mort Torque $10,000 to buy a Jet Ski. As always, we took a purchase money security interest in the thing. Now Mort, who is having a mid-life crisis, has decided he prefers his new red sports car and has defaulted on our loan. The principal balance is around $8,000 at this point. The guy is pretty overextended at the moment, so he's not resisting a repossession and foreclosure. Here's my first question. I'm not sure this guy is good for a deficiency, so we might just want to accept the Jet Ski in satisfaction of the whole debt. I assume we can do that any time we want to, can't we? I talked to my friend Sal Vache over at NB Commercial Finance, and he seems to think it's totally in our discretion, absent an objection from someone entitled to complain.[35] My second question is this. It may be that a deficiency against this guy might be worth pursuing some day, if not now. The Jet Ski is now worth only about $5,000 at wholesale book value. But you know how dicey it is selling these things at public auction. Could we accept the thing in partial satisfaction of the debt at a $5,000 designated value and then have Mort stipulate to a deficiency of $3,000?[36] It strikes me as better for all concerned than the outcome of a fire sale. I talked to Sal about this, and he says he's done it before. Call me back as soon as you can.

---

**32.** [See Problem 7–9 supra.]

**33.** [See Section 9–102(a)(64); Section 9–203(f); Section 9–315(a)(2); Comment 5 to Section 9–610; Section 9–615; Section 9–617; Section 9–625(b).]

**34.** [See Section 9–610 and Comment 11; Section 9–617 and Comment 2.]

**35.** [See Sections 9–620(e) and (f); Section 9–624(b).]

**36.** [See Section 9–620.]

## Problem 7–13

*Unfortunately, the computers at the Bovine State Bank are up and running again. Bubba's e-mail is unchained:*

TO:         S. Carlson, Megabank Legal Dept.
FROM:   B. O'Reilly, Bovine State Bank
RE:         Schmode's Inc./ M & R Trucking File

I have an old transaction here that I was afraid might come back to bite us, and it has. Three years ago, a local couple doing business as M & R Trucking bought a tractor truck and trailer from a local dealer, Schmode's, Inc. M & R signed a conditional sale contract obligating them to pay the purchase price over 60 months. Schmode's then sold the conditional sale contract to us at a discount under a longstanding chattel paper arrangement.

Within a year, M & R had defaulted and voluntarily returned the tractor and trailer to Schmode's. Under the terms of our agreement with Schmode's, they are obligated to repurchase the conditional sale contract, and we have charged it back to them. We have only been paid in part for this. Schmode's did some repair and paint work on the tractor and trailer in an effort to make them salable. This took several weeks, and the tractor and trailer were then displayed prominently for sale along with the rest of Schmode's inventory. However, Schmode's initial efforts to sell were unsuccessful. So Schmode's leased the trucks to a succession of lessees over the next two years. This added about 60,000 miles to the tractor and trailer. Between leases, the tractor and trailer were displayed on the Schmode's lot, and every effort was made to sell them.

Finally, last week, Schmode's found a buyer for the tractor and trailer. However, the price paid by the buyer did not retire the M & R debt. When Schmode's took the initial steps to pursue a deficiency, however, they ran into a snag. M & R's lawyer, Bobby Bellicose, you remember him, says Schmode's can't recover any deficiency. He says something about "implied elections" and "constructive strict foreclosure," which I can't make head or tail of. I know it's really Schmode's problem, but it's in our interest if Schmode's can collect from M & R. Schmode's is having some cash flow problems and really can't pay off our charge back right now. The principals of M & R, on the other hand, have gone on to a successful business as Amway distributors and have plenty of money. Our best shot at collecting from Schmode's is for Schmode's to collect a deficiency from M & R. Can you help us out?[37]

––––––––

**37.** [See *Schmode's, Inc. v. Wilkinson*, 219 Neb. 209, 361 N.W.2d 557 (1985). See Comment 3 to Section 9–610; Section 9– 620(b) and Comment 5; Section 9–625(b); Section 9–626.]

## BANK OF NEW BABYLON
## LOAN OFFICER TRAINING AND
## OPERATIONS MANUAL

## CHAPTER 7: DEFAULT, REMEDIES, AND DEBTOR PROTECTIONS

### II.  Alternative Remedies

#### E.  Retention of Collateral in Satisfaction of Debt

##### 1.  Procedures for Strict Foreclosure

The procedure for strict foreclosure requires the consent of the debtor if the secured party is to accept the collateral either in full or partial satisfaction of the underlying debt. See Section 9–620(a)(1). In the case of full satisfaction of the obligation, such consent may be manifested either by a post-default authenticated record or by a procedure in which the secured party sends the debtor a written proposal to retain the collateral in satisfaction of the debtor's obligation. If the secured party does not receive a written objection from the debtor within 20 days of the time the proposal is sent, the secured party may carry out his or her proposal. See Section 9–620(c)(2). Consent to retention in *partial* satisfaction of the debt requires the debtor's express consent in a post-default authenticated record and is unavailable entirely in consumer transactions. See Sections 9–620(c)(1) and (g).

The Code also makes it clear that the express consent of the secured party is required, either in the form of an authenticated record or by resort to the familiar proposal and objection procedure. See Section 9–620(b)(1). If a secured party wishes to use the proposal and (absence of) objection procedure for strict foreclosure, the Code expands the class of recipients of the proposal. See Section 9–620(c) and (d) and Section 9–621. The proposal must be sent not only to the debtor, but also to any person who has notified the secured party of a claim of interest in the collateral, any secured party or lien holder on file within specified time limits (either in the Article 9 records or perfected under an alternative governing statute), and any secondary obligor. See Section 9–621. Even if the holder of an interest in the collateral subordinate to the security interest of the foreclosing secured party does not receive a proposal but somehow hears of it, the holder may make an effective objection to it. See Section 9–620(a)(2)(B).

---

### III.  Debtor's Right of Redemption

#### Problem 7–14

*He's back! More Bubba e-mail.*

TO:          S. Carlson, Megabank Legal Dept.
FROM:     B. O'Reilly, Bovine State Bank
RE:          The Grandchildren's Shoppe

Emma Maya runs a small shop here in Desolation called the Grandchildren's Shoppe. It is a place where you can buy very expensive toys and clothing for small children. We lent Ms. Maya the money to purchase a sophisticated new cash register that allows her to keep track of inventory and purchasers. The price of the cash register was $3,600. We lent her the money on an installment loan over two years at a very good interest rate. Unfortunately, either there were fewer grandparents in Desolation or they became poorer and the Grandchildren's Shoppe fell on hard times. Ms. Maya missed payments seven and eight so we repossessed the cash register. It seems that Ms. Maya has found a new investor, Ella Max, who has put some substantial cash in the business and they both came to see me with a certified check in the sum of the two missed payments. They have demanded the cash register back. Are they entitled to it? This is important since I have entered into a contract to sell the cash register to another local business and they want me to deliver it to them tomorrow. What should I do?[38]

## BANK OF NEW BABYLON
## LOAN OFFICER TRAINING AND
## OPERATIONS MANUAL

## CHAPTER 7: DEFAULT, REMEDIES AND DEBTOR PROTECTIONS

### IV.  Remedies for Creditor Misbehavior

#### A.  Introduction

The Code imposes a variety of requirements on the secured party who exercises his or her rights against the collateral upon default by the debtor or obligor. What remedy does the debtor/obligor or a rival secured party have if the foreclosing secured party fails to meet these requirements? The Code's primary answers to that question appear straightforward at first glance. The Code authorizes a court to restrain or control an ongoing collateral disposition if the aggrieved party acts in time. See Section 9–625(a). If prevention of the offending behavior is not possible or effective, the Code permits an aggrieved party (typically the debtor/obligor or a rival secured party) to recover as damages "any loss caused by a failure to comply" with the requirements of Article 9. See Section 9–625(b).

Of course, the nature of the "loss caused by failure to comply" with Article 9 depends on exactly what the secured party does wrong. Repossession when the debtor is not in default or by means of self-help in breach of the peace is a taking of the debtor's property without justification. As such, it is a form of common law conversion,[39] and common law rights and remedies are preserved under the Code unless specifically displaced. See Section 1–103 and Comment 3 to Section 9–625. Presumably, the measure of such loss would be the value of the debtor/obligor's equity in the collateral, i.e., its value less the amount of outstanding debt.[40] Moreover, because conversion is a tort, punitive damages may be available in egregious cases. Similarly, repossession of collateral subject to a prior security interest held by a rival secured party might also subject the repossessing secured party to liability in conversion to the rival secured party. See Comment 5 to Section 9–609.

---

**38.**  [See Section 9–614(1)(C); Section 9–615(a)(1); Section 9–623.]

**39.**  See B. Clark, The Law of Secured Transactions Under the Uniform Commercial Code 4.05[2][a] (2000).

**40.**  See 4 J.J. White and R.S. Summers, Uniform Commercial Code (4th ed.) 34–18 (1995).

A different question of loss measurement is presented when a secured party conducts a collateral disposition and the proceeds received are insufficient to retire the secured debt. If the secured creditor has complied in all respects with Article 9, he or she is normally entitled to a deficiency judgment against the debtor/obligor. See Section 9–615(d)(2). If the secured party has not complied with Article 9, and, in particular, if the secured party has done something to make the disposition commercially unreasonable, it may be that the secured party's actions have depressed the resale price and thus increased the size of the deficiency for which the debtor/obligor is allegedly liable. This augmentation of the deficiency is quite clearly a loss caused by a failure to comply with Article 9 and should be remediable by the debtor/obligor in some fashion.

One possibility is to permit the debtor/obligor to assert the commercial unreasonableness of a collateral disposition defensively in the secured creditor's action on the deficiency. The debtor/obligor could be permitted a setoff against the deficiency to the extent he or she establishes that the resale price of the collateral has been depressed below its fair market value. This "setoff" approach is understandably unpopular with debtors, since it forces debtors to assume a burden of proving that the value of the collateral exceeds the resale proceeds. Debtors prefer a rule at the opposite end of the spectrum–an "absolute bar" rule, under which a secured creditor who conducts a commercially unreasonable collateral disposition is *per se* barred from any deficiency judgment. Between the foregoing two extremes is the possibility of a "rebuttable presumption" rule. A demonstration that the foreclosing secured party has conducted an unreasonable collateral disposition triggers a presumption that the true value of the collateral was equal to the outstanding debt, precluding any deficiency. However, the secured party is permitted an opportunity to prove that the fair market value of collateral is actually less than the debt, so that liability for a deficiency is proper.

The Code resolves the question of which approach is proper, in part. In nonconsumer cases, it adopts the rebuttable presumption rule. See Section 9–626(a). In the case of consumer transactions, the Code leaves it to the courts to select an appropriate rule and expressly makes the choice of the rebuttable presumption rule in commercial cases irrelevant to the choice of rules in consumer cases. See Section 9–626(b).

A secured party whose debtor succeeds in reducing his or her liability for a deficiency under 9–626(b) has one source of comfort. Section 9–625(d) provides that a debtor who has successfully invoked 9–626(b) to reduce or eliminate liability for a deficiency may not otherwise recover damages under 9–625(b) for failure to comply with Article 9. However, the scope of the secured creditors protection under 9–625(b) is rendered a bit murky by Comment 3 to 9–625, which expressly indicates that tort law continues to supplement Article 9 because of Section 1–103, subject only to the principle that double recovery for the same loss is not permitted.

While the foregoing remedies for secured creditor noncompliance with Article 9 are the most common and frequently litigated, they are not exhaustive. The Code provides a minimum statutory penalty for noncompliance in the disposition of consumer goods. See Section 9–625(c)(2). The Code also contains relatively minor statutory penalties for a variety of specific infractions of certain other Article 9 rules. See Sections 9–625(e) and (f).

However, perhaps most troublesome issue, from a secured party's point of view, is the lingering controversy over a secured creditor's potential liability for breach of the duty of good faith under Section 1–203 and Rev. Section 1–304. That section imposes a duty of good faith in both the performance and the **enforcement** of any contract under any Article of the Code, including Article 9. Prior to the revision of the Code in 1998, there was no special definition of "good faith" under Article 9, which meant that the definition of "good faith" contained in 1–201(19) governed. As the latter section defined good faith as "honesty in fact," a purely subjective standard, liability in connection with a collateral disposition appeared textually confined to instances of actual fraud or dishonesty. Doing what a security agreement actually permitted, even if stupidly or mistakenly, did not appear to be actionable. However, the courts occasionally went further and appeared to engraft some form of objective reasonableness requirement on a secured party's exercise of its remedies under Article 9. A few even appeared to regard the duty of good faith as an independent obligation, capable of overriding the express terms of an agreement. See *Duffield v. First Interstate Bank of Denver, N.A.*, 13 F.3d 1403 (10th Cir.1993); *KMC v. Irving Trust Co.*, 757 F.2d 752 (6th Cir.1985). To be sure, there were also contrary authorities that appeared to rein in the duty of good faith as a potential source of lender liability. See, e.g., *Kham & Nate's Shoes No. 2, Inc. v. First Bank of Whiting*, 908 F.2d 1351 (7th Cir.1990); PEB Commentary No. 10 (1994). Nevertheless, the expansive cases remain of interest for two reasons. First, they raise the specter of extremely large damage liability measured by the value of the entire business allegedly ruined by a wrongful exercise of Article 9 rights. Second, the 1998 version of Article 9 contains its own, objective definition of "good faith" in Section 9–102(a)(43). With the amendment of the Official Text of Article 1 by its sponsoring organizations in 2002, the objective definition of "good faith," which includes "reasonable commercial standards of fair dealing," became Rev. Section 1–201(b)(20). If revised Article 1 is broadly enacted, objective standards of good faith will apply under all articles of the Code. One of the more significant questions generated by the Code revision process is whether the new definition of "good faith," either under the Article 9 definition or the revised Article 1 definition, will generate a trend in favor of the expansion of lender liability presaged by the more liberal cases decided prior to the revision.

---

## Problem 7–15

*By now, you expect the voice mail light to bring bad news, and it does.*

Hello, Sidney. This is Jimmy Drabb at Friendly Finance. We loaned our customer, Chesterfield Davenport, the money to buy a new ski boat. He financed $15,243.65, and the total finance charges called for by the contract were $5,203.15. When he missed four payments, we felt we had no alternative but to repossess. The problem is that the two guys we sent to repossess the boat got a little over enthusiastic. Davenport wasn't home, and the boat was locked in his garage. Our guys broke the lock and towed the boat away. After that, everything was by the book. We gave Davenport proper notice of our sale of the boat. The sale itself was flawless, and we actually got book value for it. I don't think anyone could say our sale was unreasonable. But

Davenport is still hopping mad, and he wants $86.50 for the repair of his garage door lock. Do we have to pay him? Can he make a claim against us for anything else?[41]

# EPILOG

You cannot believe that 25 years have passed since you started working for MEGABANK, Inc. Pompous is dead and Houseman has retired. Jane Robinson has become the President of the Bank and she named you General Counsel three years ago. You have to admit that generally life has been pretty good, except, perhaps for the fact that while he is 76, Bubba O'Reilly is still President of Bovine State Bank and still either calls you or sends an e-mail almost every day. When you have time to reflect, which is rarely given the abilities of the recent law graduates you have hired, you realize that you owe it all to the secured transactions class you took in law school. Or maybe not!

**41.** [See Section 9–625; Section 9–626; *Davenport v. Chrysler Credit Corp.*, 818 S.W.2d 23 (Tenn.App.1991).

\*

# Index

References are to Pages

**ACCELERATION CLAUSES**
Generally, 152

**ACCESSIONS**
Priorities, 111

**ACCOUNTS RECEIVABLE**
See also Inventory and Inventory Financing, this index
Article 9 applicability, 36
Asset securitization, 37
Debtor, account, 15
Development of, 15
Direct collection remedy, 158
Factor's liens, 15
Inventory proceeds as, 106
Sales of intangibles vs secured interests in, 158

**ADVANCES**
See Future Advances, this index

**AFTER-ACQUIRED PROPERTY**
Generally, 57
See also Future Advances, this index
Bankruptcy priorities, 59
Farm products, 66
Federal tax liens, priorities, 120
Priorities, 95
Proceeds of collateral compared, 87
Purchase money priority vs, 104

**AGRICULTURAL LIENS**
Generally, 10
See also Farm Products, this index
Article 9 applicability, 29

**ASSET SECURITIZATION**
Generally, 37

**ATTACHMENT OF SECURITY INTERESTS**
Generally, 9, 43
Article 9 requirements, 20
Authentication, 55
Defined, 23
Possession, attachment by, 44
Priorities
Attachment timing and, 23
Compliance with rules, 93
Proceeds of collateral, 64
Rights in collateral, 58

**ATTACHMENT OF SECURITY INTERESTS**
—Cont'd
Timing of and priorities, 23

**AUTHENTICATION OF SECURITY AGREEMENTS**
Generally, 48
Retail installment sales, 48

**AUTOMATIC PERFECTION**
See Perfection of Security Interests, this index

**AUTOMOBILES**
Certificates of Title, this index

**BAILMENT LEASE**
Generally, 14

**BAILMENTS**
See also Leases, this index
Consignments as, 38
Definition, 38
Disguised sales and ostensible ownership, 33
Sale, bailment for, 38

**BANKRUPTCY LAW**
Generally, 17
Administrative expenses, 47
Asset securitization financing, 37
Automatic stay, 135
Avoidance powers of trustees, 19, 135
Discharge, effect of, 18
Organization, 18
Perfected security interests, priorities of, 25
Preemption of state laws, 18
Preferences, avoidance of, 135
Priorities
Generally, 19, 135
Administrative expenses, 47
After-acquired property, 59
Future advances, 62
Perfected security interests, 25
Tort claims, 77
Reorganization and liquidation under, 18
Strong arm powers of trustees, 135
Tort claims, 77
Trustees, 19

**BULK SALES LAWS**
Generally, 11

**BUSINESS INVENTORY**
See Inventory and Inventory Financing, this index

**BUYERS**
See Sales, this index

**CERTIFICATES OF TITLE**
Conflicts of laws, 91
Inventory financing of dealers, 91
Multi-jurisdictional transactions, 145
Notation of security interests on, 69
Notice of interests, 90
Perfection of security interests, 89
Priorities, 92
UCC applicability, 90

**CHATTEL PAPER**
Article 9 applicability, 36
Asset securitization, 37
Definition, 120
Electronic records, 69
Perfection of security interests in, 69
Priorities, 95
Sales of intangibles vs secured interests in, 158

**CHOICE OF LAW**
Generally, 140
See also Multi-Jurisdictional Transactions, this index
Certificates of title, 91
Exported goods, 140
Filing, 140
Transported goods, 140
UCC as solution to differing pre-code security interests, 15

**CLAIMANTS**
Priorities, 22

**COLLATERAL**
After-Acquired Property, this index
Control of Collateral, this index
Defined, 6
Descriptions of Collateral, this index
Embodiment by document of intangible right, 13
Future Advances, this index
Inventory and Inventory Financing, this index
Location of, 142
Possession of Collateral, this index
Proceeds of Collateral, this index
Protection of, 64
Real and personal property security interests in distinguished, 13
Repossession of Collateral, this index
Rights in, 58
Sales of. See Remedies, this index
Tangible and Intangible Assets, this index

**COLLATERAL**—Cont'd
Tracing, 65

**COMMINGLED GOODS**
Priorities, 111

**COMMON LAW LIENS**
Generally, 9
UCC exclusions, 39

**CONDITIONAL SALES**
Generally, 14

**CONFLICTS OF LAWS**
See Choice of Law, this index

**CONSENSUAL AND NONCONSENSUAL SECURITY INTERESTS**
Generally, 8
See also Liens, this index
Priorities, 29
Tort Claims, this index

**CONSIGNMENTS**
Generally, 37
Bailment for sale distinguished, 38
Disguised sales and ostensible ownership, 33
Inventory security interests as reaching, 105
Sales on approval distinguished, 38

**CONSTITUTIONAL PROTECTIONS**
Pre-judgment seizures, 9

**CONSUMER PROTECTION**
See also Debtor Protection, this index
Article 9 generally, 26
Financial statements, consumer goods, 127
Good faith duties of creditors, 172
Liens, statutory provisions, 10
Retail Installment Sales, this index
Self-help repossession
Generally, 161
Breach of peace, 170
Statutory repossession, 162

**CONTROL OF COLLATERAL**
Generally, 69, 74

**COPYRIGHTS**
Perfection of security interests in, 69

**CREATION OF SECURITY INTERESTS**
Generally, 43
Attachment of Security Interests, this index
Enforceability of Security Interests, this index

**CREDIT CARDS**
Secured and unsecured loans distinguished, 4

**CROPS**
See Farm Products, this index

**DEBTOR PROTECTION**
Generally, 170

**DEBTOR PROTECTION**—Cont'd
  See also Consumer Protection, this index
Breach of peace, self-help in, 170
Exemptions, this index
Fair market value, sale of collateral for, 171
Good faith duties of creditors, 172
Statutory penalties, 171
Tort remedies of debtor, 171

**DEFAULT**
  Generally, 151
Acceleration clauses, 152
Article 9 provisions generally, 20
Events of, 151
Payment defaults, 151
Risk impairments, 152

**DEFINITIONS**
Acceleration clause, 152
Accounts receivable, 15
Accounts receivable, UCC, 36
Agricultural lien, 10
Asset securitization, 37
Attachment, UCC, 23
Attachment lien, 9
Automatic perfection, 23
Bailment, 38
Bailment for sale, 38
Bailment lease, 14
Buyer, 121
Chattel mortgage, 14
Chattel paper, 120
Chattel paper, UCC, 36
Collateral, 6
Conditional sale, 14
Consignments, 37
Contract for deed, 42
Course of dealing, 126
Debtor, account, 15
Default, 151
Demand note, 151
Execution lien, 9
Factor's lien, 15
Field warehousing, 15
Fixture, 13
Fixture, UCC, 31
Foreign attachment, 9
Garageman's lien, 10
General creditors, 4
Goods, 21
Intangible assets, 9
Judicial lien, 8
Land sales contracts, 42
Levy, 9
Materialman's lien, 10
Mechanics' lien, 10
Ostensible ownership, 14
Partially secured claims, 8
Payment intangibles, 36
Personal property, 31
Pledge, 14
Proceeds, 87
Proceeds, UCC, 64
Promissory notes, 36

**DEFINITIONS**—Cont'd
Purchase money security interests, 70
Purchaser, 121
Sale on approval, 38
Sale or return, 39
Secured claims, 7
Securitization, asset, 37
Security interest, 31
Sellers' lien, 10
Set off right, 11
Special purpose vehicle, 37
Tangible assets, 9
Transaction costs, 7
True leases, 33
Trust receipts, 14
UCC definitional provisions, 21
Writ of execution, 9
Writ of garnishment, 9

**DEMAND NOTES**
Generally, 151

**DEPOSIT ACCOUNTS**
Direct collection remedy, 158
Perfection of security interests in, 69

**DEPOSITS**
Set off rights, 11

**DESCRIPTIONS OF COLLATERAL**
  Generally, 83
  See also Financing Statements, this index
Security agreement description, 48, 51
Subjective vs objective determination of sufficiency of description, 54
Timber, 52

**DISGUISED SALES**
Generally, 33

**DISGUISED SECURITY INTERESTS**
Generally, 32

**DISPOSITION OF COLLATERAL**
  Generally, 162
See also Remedies, this index

**DOCUMENTS OF TITLE**
See Certificates of Title, this index

**ELECTRONIC RECORDS**
Authentication of security agreement by debtor, 48
Authorization of unsigned financing statements, 79
Chattel paper, 69
Financing statements, 79

**ENFORCEABILITY OF SECURITY INTERESTS**
  Generally, 43
Attachment and perfection distinguished, 118
Authentication, 48, 55
Buyers of collateral, enforcement against, 121
Description of collateral, 48, 51

**ENFORCEABILITY OF SECURITY INTER-
ESTS**—Cont'd
Fixtures, 131
Interest in property secured, 43
Ordinary course, buyer in, 125
Perfection and attachment distinguished, 118
Power to transfer rights in collateral, 43
Purchasers of collateral, enforcement against, 121
Rights in collateral, 58
Value for security agreement, 43, 62, 63

**EVENTS OF DEFAULT**
See Default, this index

**EXECUTION LIENS**
Generally, 9

**EXEMPTIONS**
Generally, 5
See also Debtor Protection, this index
Homesteads, 5

**FACTOR'S LIENS**
Generally, 15

**FARM PRODUCTS**
See also Agricultural Liens, this index
After-acquired property, treatment as, 66
Buyers in ordinary course, 125
Buyers vs perfected secured creditors, 125
Food Security Act of 1985, 126
Priorities, 125

**FEDERAL PREEMPTION**
Generally, 39

**FEDERAL TAX LIENS**
Generally, 11
After-acquired property, priorities, 120
Future advances, priorities, 120
Notice of, 119
Priorities, 118
Requisites, 118

**FIELD WAREHOUSING**
Generally, 15

**FILING**
Generally, 69, 79
See also Financing Statements, this index; Perfection of Security Interests, this index
Automobile financing, 91
Choice of law, 140
Date of filing and of perfection distinguished, 95
Errors, 81
Fees, 82
Fixture filing, 131
Place of, 141
Priorities and time of, 94

**FINANCING STATEMENTS**
Generally, 49, 79
Article 9 requirements generally, 23

**FINANCING STATEMENTS**—Cont'd
Authorization, 79
Constructive notice by, 69
Consumer goods, 127
Continuation statements, 86
Descriptions of collateral
Generally, 83
See also Descriptions of Collateral, this index
Electronic records, 79
Errors, 81
Filing, this index
Fixture filing, 131
Lapse, 86
Name requirements, 79, 82
Place of filing, 85
Requirements, 79
Substantial compliance with UCC, 80
Transferees of collateral, effectiveness against, 122

**FIRST IN TIME, FIRST IN RIGHT**
Generally, 94
See also Priorities, this index

**FIXTURES**
Article 9 applicability, 31
Creation of security interests, 131
Definition, 13
Financing statements, 131
Priorities, 130
Real and personal property security interests in distinguished, 13

**FOOD SECURITY ACT OF 1985**
Priorities, 126

**FOREIGN ATTACHMENT**
Generally, 9

**FOREIGN TRANSACTIONS**
See Multi-Jurisdictional Transactions, this index

**FRAUDULENT CONVEYANCE STATUTES**
Generally, 14

**FUTURE ADVANCES**
Generally, 57
See also After-Acquired Property, this index
Bankruptcy priorities, 62
Federal tax liens, priorities, 120
Priorities, 95
Proceeds of collateral compared, 87
Purchase money priority vs, 104

**GARAGEMAN'S LIENS**
Generally, 10

**GARNISHMENT**
Writ of, 9

**GENERAL CREDITORS**
Definition, 4

**GOOD FAITH**
Duties of creditors, 172

**GOODS**
Affixation to real property, 130
Definition, 21

**GROWING CROPS**
See Farm Products, this index

**HOMESTEADS**
Generally, 5

**INSTALLMENT SALES**
See Retail Installment Sales, this index

**INTANGIBLES**
See Tangible and Intangible Assets, this
    index

**INTERSTATE TRANSACTIONS**
See Multi-Jurisdictional Transactions, this
    index

**INVENTORY AND INVENTORY FINANCING**
Bulk sales laws, 11
Certificates of title, dealers,' 91
Consignment goods, inclusion in, 105
Descriptions in financing statements, 51
Factor's liens, 15
Field warehousing, 15
Nature of collateral, 14
Ordinary course, buyer in, 125
Percentage calculations, 105
Priority rights of buyers vs secured credi-
    tors, 121
Proceeds of as accounts receivable, 106
Proceeds of sales, 88
Trust receipts, 14

**INVESTMENT SECURITIES**
Possession as evidence of security interest,
    74

**JUDICIAL LIENS**
Generally, 8

**LEASES**
    See also Bailments, this index
Installment sales distinguished, 33
Notices of ownership, 35
Security interests distinguished, 32
True leases, 33

**LENDER LIABILITY**
Consumer Protection, this index
Debtor Protection, this index

**LETTER OF CREDIT RIGHTS**
Perfection of security interests in, 69

**LEVY**
    Generally, 9
Lien by, 9

**LIENS**
    Generally, 8

**LIENS**—Cont'd
    See also Consensual and Nonconsensual
        Security Interests, this index
Agricultural liens, 10
Attachment, 9
Chattel mortgages, 14
Common law, 9
Consensual security interests distinguished,
    8
Execution, 9
Factor's, 15
Federal tax, 11
Foreign attachment, 9
Garageman's liens, 10
Judicial, 8
Levy, lien by, 9
Materialman's liens, 10
Mechanics' liens, 10
Possessory and Nonpossessory Liens, this
    index
Priorities between secured and lien credi-
    tors, 114
Secret liens, 119
Sellers' liens, 10
Statutory, 9
Tax, 11

**LIVESTOCK**
See Farm Products, this index

**LOCATION OF COLLATERAL**
Generally, 142

**MATERIALMAN'S LIENS**
Generally, 10

**MECHANICS' LIENS**
Generally, 10

**MOTOR VEHICLES**
Certificates of Title, this index

**MULTI-JURISDICTIONAL TRANSACTIONS**
    Generally, 140
    See also Choice of Law, this index
Attachment, foreign, 9
Certificates of title, 145
Location changes affecting perfection, 142
Perfection, 140, 149
Priorities, 148, 149

**NATIONAL CONFERENCE OF COMMIS-
SIONERS ON UNIFORM STATE LAWS
(NCCUSL)**
Generally, 15

**NONCONSENSUAL SECURITY INTER-
ESTS**
See Consensual and Nonconsensual Securi-
    ty Interests, this index

**NOTICE AND KNOWLEDGE**
    Generally, 68
    See also Perfection of Security Interests,
        this index
Actual knowledge of prior interest, 96
Buyers in ordinary course, 125

**NOTICE AND KNOWLEDGE**—Cont'd
Certificates of title as, 90
Disguised sales and ostensible ownership, 33
Federal tax liens, 119
Leases, ownership of lessor, 35
Perfection of Security Interests, 68
Secret liens, 119

**OSTENSIBLE OWNERSHIP**
Generally, 14, 33

**OUT-OF-STATE TRANSACTIONS**
See Multi-Jurisdictional Transactions, this index

**PARTIALLY SECURED CLAIMS**
Generally, 8

**PATENTS**
Federal preemption of UCC, 39
Perfection of security interests in, 69

**PAYMENT**
Default in, 151
Preferential transfers, 135

**PAYMENT INTANGIBLES**
Article 9 applicability, 36
Asset securitization, 37

**PERFECTION OF SECURITY INTERESTS**
Generally, 68
Accounts receivable, 37
Article 9 requirements, 20
Automatic perfection
Generally, 23, 72
Priorities, 94
Automobile financing, 91
Bankruptcy priorities of, 25
Buyers vs perfected secured creditors, 123, 125
Buyers vs unperfected secured creditors, 122
Chattel paper, 37
Constructive notice, 68
Constructive notice by filing, 69
Continuation statements, 86
Continuing as to proceeds, 88
Control as constructive notice, 69, 74
Copyrights, 69
Date of filing and of perfection distinguished, 95
Farm products, 125
Filing, this index
Financing Statements, this index
Fixture filing, 131
Intangibles, 76
Lapse of filing, 86
Location changes affecting, 142
Multi-jurisdictional transactions, 140, 149
Names of business entities, 85
Notice, 68
Patents, 69
Payment intangibles, 37
Pledge, 74

**PERFECTION OF SECURITY INTERESTS**
—Cont'd
Possession, perfection by
Generally, 23
Priorities, 94
Priorities
Automatic perfection, 94
Compliance with rules, 93
Importance to, 68
Perfection timing and, 23
Possession, perfection by, 94
Proceeds, 87, 88
Promissory notes, 37
Purchase money security interests, 70
Ship mortgages, 69
Timing of and priorities, 23
Title certificate notations, 69, 89
Unperfected interest, priority of, 24

**PERSONAL PROPERTY**
Definition, 31

**PLEDGE**
Generally, 14
Perfection of security interest in, 74

**POSSESSION OF COLLATERAL**
See also Possessory and Nonpossessory Liens, this index
Agent, possession by, 44
Agreement, possession pursuant to, 44
Attachment of security interest by possession, 44
Consensual, 44
Control as constructive notice, 69, 74
Investment securities, 69, 74
Ostensible ownership, 33
Overview, 6
Perfection by
Generally, 23
Priorities, 94
Physical possession, 44
Pledge, 14, 74
Risk of loss, 78

**POSSESSORY AND NON-POSSESSORY LIENS**
Chattel mortgages, 14
Fraudulent conveyance statutes, 14
Ostensible ownership, 14
Pledges, 14
Statutory possessory liens, 10

**PREFERENTIAL TRANSFERS**
Generally, 135

**PRIORITIES**
Generally, 93
Accessions, 111
Actual knowledge of prior interest, 96
After-acquired property
Generally, 95
Bankruptcy, 59
Purchase money priority vs, 104
Agricultural liens, 10
Article 9 determinants, 20, 22

PRIORITIES—Cont'd
Attachment requirements, 93
Attachment timing and, 23
Automatic perfection, 94
Bankruptcy
    Generally, 19, 135
  Administrative expenses, 47
  After-acquired property, 59
  Future advances, 62
  Perfection, 25
  Tort claims, 77
Buyers vs secured creditors, 121
Certificates of title, 92
Chattel paper, 95
Commingled goods, 111
Conflicts of law re, 40
Consensual and nonconsensual security interests distinguished, 8, 29
Farm products, 125
Favored classes of creditors, 95
Federal tax liens, 11, 118
Filing, time of, 94
First in time, first in right, 94
Fixtures, 130
Food Security Act of 1985, 126
Future advances
    Generally, 95
  Bankruptcy, 62
  Purchase money priority vs, 104
Knowledge of prior interest, 96
Lessors, 34
Lien creditors, 114
Liens, relating back of, 9
Multi-jurisdictional transactions, 148, 149
Nonconsensual possessory liens, 29
Ordinary course, buyer in, 125
Perfection
  Importance of, 68
  Requirements, 93
  Status and, 24
  Timing and, 23
Possession, perfection by, 94
Possessory liens, nonconsensual, 29
Proceeds of collateral, 106
Purchase money security interests, 70, 95, 101
Purchasers vs secured creditors, 121
Real property secured interests, 130
Relating back of liens, 9
Relative priorities of claimants, 22
Sale proceeds, distribution of, 166
Scope of Article 9, 20
Subordinate claims, 23
Subordination agreements, 101
Superpriorities, 95
Tax liens, 11
Tort claims
    Generally, 25
  Bankruptcy law, 77
Unperfected security interest, priority of, 24

PROCEEDS OF COLLATERAL
  Generally, 64

PROCEEDS OF COLLATERAL—Cont'd
Accounts receivable or inventory, 106
After-acquired interests compared, 87
Definition, 87
Future advances compared, 87
Identifiability, 87
Inventory or accounts receivable, 106
Inventory sales, 88
Perfection, 87, 88
Priorities
    Generally, 106
  Buyers vs secured creditors, 121
Sale proceeds on default
    Generally, 166
  See also Remedies, this index
Substituted assets, rights to, 7
Third party transferees, 7
Tracing, 65

PROMISSORY NOTES
Article 9 applicability, 36
Asset securitization, 37
Real property, notes secured by, 40
Sales of intangibles vs secured interests in, 158

PROTECTION OF COLLATERAL
Generally, 64

PURCHASE MONEY SECURITY INTERESTS
After-acquired property security interests vs, 104
Automobile financing, 91
Definition, 70
Future advancement security interests vs, 104
Perfection, 70
Policy considerations, 101
Priorities, 70, 95, 101
Requirements, status, 101, 102

REAL PROPERTY
Chattel mortgages, 14
Fixtures, this index
Goods affixed to, 130
Personal and real property security interests in distinguished, 13
Priorities, 130
UCC exclusions, 39

REDEMPTION, RIGHT OF
  Generally, 169
See also Remedies, this index

REMEDIES
  Generally, 151
Alternative, 157
Collection rights, 157
Commercial reasonability
    Generally, 158
  Deficiencies, 171
Creditor misbehavior, 170
Damages for creditor misbehavior, 170
Deficiency judgments, 171
Direct collection, 158

**REMEDIES**—Cont'd
Distribution of proceeds of sale, 166
Expenses of collection, 158
Fair market value, sale of collateral for, 171
Foreclosure, strict, 169
Good faith duties of creditors, 172
Misbehavior of creditor, 170
Notice of sale of collateral, 164
Perishables, sale of, 165
Possession of collateral, obtaining, 158
Priority rights in proceeds of sale, 166
Proceeds of sale, distribution of, 166
Public and private sales, 164
Redemption, right of, 169
Repossession of collateral, 158
Repossession of Collateral, this index
Retention of collateral in satisfaction of debt, 167
Sale of collateral, generally, 162
Satisfaction of debt, acceptance of collateral in, 169
Self-help repossession
    Generally, 161
    Breach of peace, 170
Sheriffs' and secured creditors' sales of repossessed collateral distinguished, 7
Statutory penalties, UCC, 171
Strict foreclosure, 169
Tort remedies of debtor, 171
Transferees' rights in sold collateral, 166
Wrongful collection, 158

**REPOSSESSION OF COLLATERAL**
    Generally, 158
Breach of peace, 170
Constitutional restrictions on pre-judgment seizures, 9
Foreclosure, strict, 169
Overview, 6
Perishables, 165
Redemption, right of, 169
Retention in satisfaction of debt, 167
Satisfaction of debt, acceptance of collateral in, 169
Seizure under writ, 162
Self-help
    Generally, 161
    Breach of peace, 170
Sheriffs' and secured creditors' sales of repossessed collateral distinguished, 7
Statutory requirements, 162
Strict foreclosure, 169
Third party transferees, 7
Writ, seizure under, 162

**RETAIL INSTALLMENT SALES**
Authentication of security agreements, 48
Automobile financing, 91
Credit agreements, 48
Purchase money security interests, 70
Title retention contract, 30
True leases and installment sales distinguished, 33

**RISK**
Default events, risk impairments as, 152
Possession of collateral, 78
Secured and unsecured loans, 7

**SALES**
Asset securitization financing, 37
Bailment for sale, 38
Buyers
    Definition, 121
    Ordinary course, 125
    Priority rights vs secured creditors, 121
    Repossession of collateral sold to, 7
    Sales of repossessed collateral to, 166
Collateral, repossessed
        Generally, 162
    See also Remedies, this index
    Sheriffs' and secured creditors' sales distinguished, 7
    Transferees' rights, 166
Consignments distinguished, 37
Disguised sales, 33
Farm products, collateralized, 125
Intangibles, sales outright vs secured interests in, 158
Liens, sellers', 10
On approval, 38
Ordinary course, buyer in, 125
Preferential transfers, 135
Priority rights of buyers vs secured creditors, 121
Prohibited sales of collateral, 121
Purchasers defined, 121
Retail Installment Sales, this index
Return, sale or, 39
Security interests distinguished, 32
Sheriffs' and secured creditors' sales of repossessed collateral distinguished, 7
Transferees. Buyers, above

**SECOND CONTRACT ANALYSIS**
Generally, 4

**SECRET LIENS**
Generally, 119

**SECRETION OF ASSETS**
Generally, 5

**SECURITIZATION, ASSET**
Generally, 37

**SEIZURE**
Pre-judgment, 9

**SELLERS' LIENS**
Generally, 10

**SET OFF**
Generally, 11

**SHIP MORTGAGES**
Perfection of security interests in, 69

**SIGNATURES**
Authentication of security agreement by debtor, 48

**SPECIAL PURPOSE VEHICLES (SPV)**
Definition, 37

**STATUTORY LIENS**
Generally, 9
Chattel mortgages, 14
Pledges, 14
UCC exclusions, 39

**SUBORDINATION**
See Priorities, this index

**SUBSTITUTED ASSETS**
See also Proceeds of Collateral, this index
Secured parties' rights to, 7

**TANGIBLE AND INTANGIBLE ASSETS**
Embodiment by document, 13
Levy on, 9
Perfection of security interests in intangibles, 76
Proceeds of collateral, 88
Sales of intangibles vs secured interests in, 158

**TAX LIENS**
Generally, 11
See also Federal Tax Liens, this index

**THIRD-PARTY TRANSFEREES**
See Sales, this index

**TIMBER**
Description of as collateral, 52

**TITLE CERTIFICATES**
See Certificates of Title, this index

**TITLE RETENTION CONTRACT**
Generally, 30

**TORT CLAIMS**
See also Consensual and Nonconsensual Security Interests, this index
After-acquired property, commercial tort claims as, 57
Bankruptcy law priorities, 77
Priorities
Generally, 25
Bankruptcy law, 77

**TRACING OF COLLATERAL**
Generally, 65

**TRANSACTION COSTS**
Generally, 7

**TRANSFEREES**
See Sales, this index

**TRUE LEASES**
Generally, 33

**TRUST RECEIPTS**
Generally, 14

**UNDERSECURED LOANS**
Generally, 7

**UNIFORM COMMERCIAL CODE (UCC)**
Adoption, 16
Article 1 revision, 16
Article 9 revision
Generally, 17
Consumer protections, 26
Debtor protection, statutory penalties, 171
Certificates of title, 90
Choice of law problems as to pre-code security interests, 15
Consumer protections, 26
Definitional provisions, 21
Development of, 15
Excluded transactions, 39
Federal preemption, 39
Interpretive aids, 17
Penalties for noncompliance, 171
Permanent Editorial Board, 17
Real and personal property security interests in distinguished, 13
Scope of Article 9, 28
Secured parties and secured creditors, 20

**UNSECURED LOANS**
Attachment liens to protect, 9
Distinguished, 4
Undersecured loans, 7

**VALIDITY OF SECURITY INTERESTS**
See Enforceability of Security Interests, this index

**WRITS**
Execution, 9
Garnishment, 9
Repossession, 162

†

0–314–26200–8

9 780314 262004

90000